DEC. 1 1985	DATE DUE	
DEC 1 5 89	MAR 2 9 1997	
MAY 3 0 1985	DEC 0 2 1997	
APR 2 0 1986	FEB 11 1999	
JUL 0 1 1988	SEP 3 0 2003	
JUL 1 1 1989	JUN 2 0 2005	
DEC 2 6 1990		
JUN 1 6 1991		
MAY 2 6 1992		
SEP 1 7 1992		
MAY 0 2 1994		

MANSIONS, MILLS,
and MAIN STREETS

MANSIONS, MILLS, and MAIN STREETS

Carole Rifkind and Carol Levine

SCHOCKEN BOOKS · NEW YORK

LIBRARY OF CONGRESS CATALOGING IN PUBLICATION DATA

Rifkind, Carole.
  Mansions, mills, and main streets.

    1.   Historic buildings—New York (City) region,
N.Y.   2.   New York (City) region, N.Y.,—Des-
cription and travel—Guidebooks.   I.   Levine,
Carol, joint author.   II.   Title.
F128.7.R53   917.47'1'044   74–26915

Maps by William Jaber

Contents

Introduction   vi

1. Hudson River Valley   1

2. The Valleys Between the Hudson
   River and Long Island Sound   35

3. Long Island Sound:
   New York and Connecticut   69

4. Long Island   97

5. Southern New Jersey   133

6. New Jersey:
   From Hope to Hoboken   167

7. Northern New Jersey and
   Southern New York   205

   Architectural Field Guide
   and Illustrated Glossary   237

   Index   244

Introduction

W ithin a fifty-mile radius of New York City—the imaginary circle that defines the area covered in this book—there are, waiting to be discovered, a wooden mill reflected in a quiet millpond, a brooding Gothic mansion high on a hill, a simple country church with a lofty tower, an intricate maze of nineteenth-century red-brick factories, the strong, clean forms of a modern university campus, and more. The communities in this area are ripe for exploring—river and canal towns, old mining centers, once-bustling seaports, prosperous county seats, rustic villages surrounded by a patchwork of farms and fences.

This is a guidebook to aid in discovering this exciting blend of architecture and history. We have traveled modern highways, historic roads, and twisting lanes in search of architecture that is truly expressive of American values and creativity. We have been delighted to find not only individual structures of significance, but also entire architectural configurations—streetscapes, village centers, modern complexes—that provide a pleasant ambience while respecting both human needs and the natural environment.

·The book is organized into seven sections, by geographical area. Within each section sites are arranged in a geographical progression, starting with the point nearest New York City. The order of sites is simply a suggestion of a possible route; we expect the reader to be guided by individual interests and inclinations, either following the order in the book or selecting certain sites and regions of special appeal. Of necessity, sites covered in different sections of the text may actually be very close to each other; we suggest checking the sectional maps before planning an itinerary.

The information provided about each open site is as up-to-date as possible. However, hours and days of opening change frequently; and it is always advisable to call ahead to confirm the times. Many sites are also open by special appointment. Those that charge an admission fee (usually nominal) are designated with an asterisk (*) next to the hours; other sites are free.

Drivers will find that any standard roadmap will lead them to the general vicinity, but detailed maps or atlases are extremely valuable.

Although the book is oriented toward reaching destinations by automobile, it is quite easy to visit many sites by public transportation. Most communities are accessible by rail or bus; many sites are a short walk or taxi ride from the station or bus stop.

The area covered in the book is so rich in architecture that, to our regret, we could not include all worthwhile sites and structures in the limited space of a guidebook. From the vast number, we have selected for inclusion those sites that have special aesthetic qualities or historic significance; but there are many more for the reader to find. All kinds of structures have been included: dwellings, schools, churches, factories, bridges, railroad stations, and others. No single type or style or period or building technology predominates. Local architectural types—such as the Hudson River Gothic mansions, salt-boxes in Connecticut and Long Island, and Dutch Colonial houses in New Jersey—have been emphasized, although, of course, there are many more examples that this book could not encompass. Public spaces—parks, village greens, cemeteries, landscaped highways—have also been viewed as part of the built environment.

Because an important criterion was that a structure should be easy to see, there are disproportionately few contemporary dwellings, most of which are nestled into some romantic and inaccessible landscape. Similarly, we have not been able to include a representative sample of the great period-revival houses of the early 1900's.

Throughout, we have been particularly concerned with building exteriors. We have included almost every open house and museum that came to our attention; these usually have guided tours or displays that interpret the architectural features of the interior and the furnishings. An illustrated glossary defines the major architectural styles and terminology.

We were guided in our research by many sources. The lists of buildings recorded in the Historic American Buildings Survey, begun in the 1930's, and the extraordinary volumes in the American Guide Series, published in the same period as a project of the Writers Program of the Works Progress Administration, were extremely valuable, even though much has changed since then. Inclusion in the National Register of Historic Places has given many structures just recognition, and a number of these places are described here. As an outgrowth of the National Historic Preservation Act of 1966, each state is compiling an inventory of historic or architecturally significant sites, and these lists have been useful. Periodicals, local histories, reminiscences, and scrapbooks have all been of value, although frequently the material is fragmentary and undocumented.

We have taken all the photographs in the book; they represent our own impressions and perceptions. Examples of the measured drawings of the Historic American Buildings Survey have been included both because they highlight certain architectural features more effectively than any photograph and because they represent significant historical documents in themselves. Similarly, examples of architectural renderings and historical depictions have been chosen to emphasize the social context.

A great many people have aided us in the preparation of this book. The librarians and historical societies in each community have been particularly helpful, as have individuals connected with the various sites. It would be impossible to mention each of them, but we would like to thank, for their special efforts: the staff of Avery Library, Columbia University; Richard Baehr; Virginia Daiker, Library of Congress; Elden Dustin, Stratford Historic Society; Cathleen Elgin; Helen Gearn, Newburgh City Historian; Donald Geyer; Barbara Hoskins, Morristown Library; Terry Karshner, Historic Sites Section, New Jersey State Department of Environmental Protection; Mary Ellen Kramer; George Levinson; Eva Lewis; Capt. Leon De Lorme, West Point Military Academy; Charles Lyle, Monmouth County Historical Society; Virginia Moskowitz, Mount Vernon Historic and Preservation Society; Laura B. MacKenzie, Fairfield Historical Society; Chris Muenchinger, Speedwell Village; Bert Prawl, New Jersey State Department of Environmental Protection; Dorothy Reinhart, Nassau County Museum; Maureen Singleton; and Ursula Theobald, Historic American Buildings Survey, Library of Congress.

In addition, we would like to thank the following people, all of whom read and commented on various portions of the manuscript: Mary Findlay; Professor James Marston Fitch, School of Architecture, Columbia University; Constance Grieff; Professor Jacob Judd, History Department, Herbert H. Lehman College of the City University of New York; Adolf Placzek, Avery Library, Columbia University; David Poinsett, Historic Sites Section, New Jersey State Department of Environmental Protection; Claire Tholl, Bergen County Historical Society; and Barbara Van Liew, Society for the Preservation of Long Island Antiquities. Needless to say, the responsibility for the final version is ours alone. In this regard, we echo Nathaniel Prime, who wrote in his *History of Long Island*, published in 1845, that he "assures his readers, that he made no statement, but upon his own personal knowledge, or on information which he had reason to believe was entitled to full credit."

We hope that this book proves to be, for both residents and visitors, a source of many stimulating trips and that our explorations inspire readers to embark on their own.

C.R.
C.L.

Hudson River Museum

1 | Hudson River Valley

The Hudson River valley has enjoyed a special significance for New Yorkers since the early Dutch settlers first explored its riches. In the nineteenth century the Hudson River—considered the Rhine of America—attracted visitors from all over the world.

The river and its adjacent valleys dominate the setting all the way from Yonkers to Beacon, the area covered in this section. And Broadway (Rte. 9)—the old Post Rd. that ran from New York City to Albany—winds through the river towns, affording travelers sudden views of the Hudson and easy access to nearby sites.

A few buildings date from Westchester's bucolic beginnings, and there are some striking modern structures as well, but the overwhelming influence felt today is that of the nineteenth century—the great Gothic mansions, the charming Victorian cottages, and the elegant commercial and public buildings erected by civic-minded citizens.

Some of the most famous homes in American history and some of the best restorations are here—but there is, in addition, a treasure trove of little-known buildings, perhaps the more captivating for their unfamiliarity.

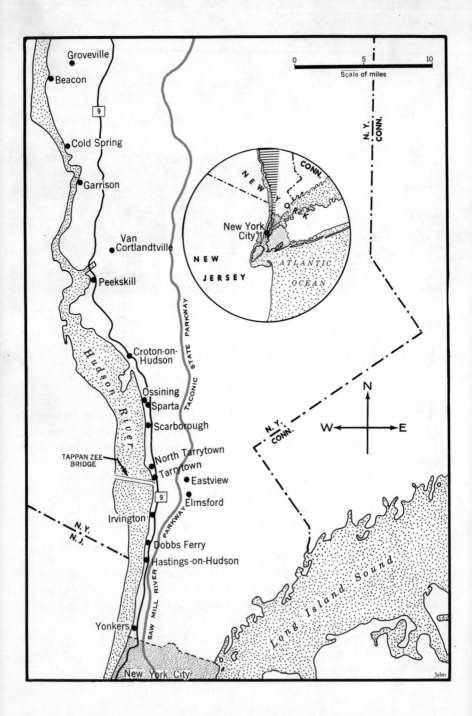

Groveville
Beacon
9
Cold Spring
Garrison
Van
Cortlandtville
Peekskill
Hudson River
Croton-on-Hudson
Ossining
Sparta
Scarborough
TACONIC STATE PARKWAY
North Tarrytown
Tarrytown
TAPPAN ZEE
BRIDGE
Eastview
9
Elmsford
Irvington
PARKWAY
Dobbs Ferry
Hastings-on-Hudson
SAW MILL RIVER
Yonkers
New York City

N. Y.
CONN.

0   5   10
Scale of miles

NEW
YORK
CONN.

New York
City

NEW
JERSEY
ATLANTIC
OCEAN

N. Y.
CONN.

N
W   E

N. Y.
N. J.

Long Island Sound

Jaber

Philipse Manor Hall

Warburton Ave. and Dock St., north of
Getty Sq., Yonkers
OPEN: By appointment
PHONE: (914) 965–4027

Milling was one of the most profitable industries along the Hudson River in the seventeenth and eighteenth centuries. The existence of a good mill on the Neperhan River, where it flowed into the Hudson, must have seemed very attractive in 1674 to Frederick Philipse, a Dutch carpenter with a gift for making money. He called this part of his vast holdings the Lower Mills; the Upper Mills are in North Tarrytown.

In spite of his wealth, the first house he built on the land, in 1681, was probably a simple, square stone structure with a steeply sloping roof. When he died in 1701, this "Yoncker's Plantation" (so called after the "Yoncker," or "Gentleman," Van der Donck from whom Philipse had purchased the land) went to his grandson Frederick. Frederick added a stone section to the west of the original house; in 1745, he built a brick north wing. This changed the orientation from south to east, and completed the transformation of the house from a simple Dutch cottage to a Georgian country seat.

That Frederick's son, another Frederick, was the third and last lord of the Manor, whose lands extended for 22 miles and who was one of the leading citizens of Colonial society. A Loyalist to the end, his holdings were confiscated and sold in 1785.

The Manor Hall went through various private hands until 1868, when it became the Yonkers Village Hall, and later the City Hall. An otherwise orderly sequence of rooms is breached by a vast Gothic space created in 1872 for a Council Chamber on the second and third floors.

A remarkable feature of Philipse Manor is the decorative plaster ceiling in the southeast parlor on the first floor. These ceilings were rare, although not unknown in the Colonies, because of the scarcity of skilled stucco-workers. The ceiling at Philipse Manor Hall is the only one of its type in the area. It was probably executed after 1745 by a European artisan who had access to contemporary English designs for ornate plaster ceilings. Each decorative element was probably modeled and cast separately and attached to its specially prepared spot on the ceiling.

The Georgian woodwork in this room is also distinguished. Fluted columns flank an elaborately detailed overmantle; the paneling and cornice details are virtuoso displays of fine craftsmanship. The Manor Hall will be reopened to visitors in 1975. Administered by the New York State Division for Historic Preservation.

Detail of ceiling, Philipse Manor Hall

Herald Statesman Building

Herald Statesman Building (Larkin Plaza, just west of Philipse Manor Hall, Yonkers). This newspaper office was built in 1933 by Frank Chase, a Chicago architect who also specialized in railroad stations. The sleek glass and polished metal wall surfaces still seem modern. The Otis Elevator factory buildings that surround the newspaper office trace the progression of factory design from the 1880's through the 1920's to the present.

Yonkers Railroad Station (Larkin Plaza). Built in the first decade of the twentieth century, the station reflects the contemporary taste for Baroque forms. The interior spaces are particularly pleasant.

Riverview I and II (just south of Getty Sq. on Riverdale Ave., between Vark and Prospect sts., Yonkers). Providing residential and commercial facilities, this concrete slab-and-block complex consists of a dynamic grouping of structures varying in height and mass. It is the design of Sert, Jackson & Associates.

City Hall (S. Broadway [Rte. 9], near Getty Sq., Yonkers). The soaring clock tower is a symbol of Yonkers' determination to join the "City Beautiful" movement in the early 1900's by employing elegant and formal French and Italian Baroque and Renaissance forms. Edwin A. Quick & Sons designed the building in 1908.

St. John's Episcopal Church (Getty Sq., Yonkers). The south wall, dating from the mid-eighteenth century, was retained for sentimental reasons in the 1870 and 1890 reconstructions by architect Edward T. Potter, which gave the church its Gothic Romanesque flavor. The tracery supporting the clerestory window is, rather surprisingly, cast iron.

The Woman's Institute (38 Palisade Ave., off Getty Sq., Yonkers). Home to a late-nineteenth-century ladies' society which, like many others of the time, tried to deal with problems of urbanization and industrialization, the Woman's Institute building itself may have seemed as radical to some as its social purposes. Its creamy-yellow bricks, molded and impressed with a foliated design, make a

City Hall, Yonkers

striking contrast to the prevailing darkness of neighboring structures.

Yonkers Water Works (Tuckahoe Rd., east of New York State Thruway interchange). The brick pumping station was part of the water-supply system established after a disastrous fire. Built in 1876, the high-style arched and gabled structure testifies to the importance placed on civic buildings by citizens of that era.

Sherwood House

340 Tuckahoe Rd., Yonkers
*OPEN: Thurs., Sun., holidays, 2–5 p.m., May–Oct.
PHONE: (914) DE7–8349

Few traces of southern Westchester's pastoral beginnings exist today, and wooden farmhouses from the eighteenth century are rare. Sherwood House is one, and a sturdy one at that, for it has withstood not only the ravages of the Revolutionary War but also more modern encroachments, such as the construction of the Sprain Brook Pkwy. nearby and the commercialization of Tuckahoe Rd.

Thomas Sherwood—tenant farmer, constable, and assessor—built the house in 1740 on land leased from Frederick Philipse, third and last lord of the Manor. The Philipse family chose the wrong side in the Revolutionary War and was forced to flee. Stephen Sherwood bought his father's house and land in 1785 from the Commissioners of Forfeiture, who confiscated and sold the Loyalists' land.

The house is built into the hillside, with its basement of native stone and the upper stories of clapboard. To visualize the house as it appeared in the eighteenth

century, imagine it without the wing on the south. That was added in stages, the first floor probably by Dr. John Ingersoll, who owned the house in the early 1800's, the upper story probably in the mid-1800's.

The interior has been restored and partly reconstructed. The 12-over-8 windows in the formal parlor on the second floor are typical of the pre-Revolutionary period. The wide center hall, with Dutch

Sherwood House

doors front and rear, appears to have been characteristic of the region. The Yonkers Historical Society acquired the house in 1955 and opened it to the public.

Alexander Smith and Sons Carpet Mills (Saw Mill River Rd. [Rte. 9A], Yonkers). When nineteenth-century America began to industrialize, not only efficiency but elegance was often deemed appropriate for an industrial building. The Alexander Smith and Sons Carpet Mills, begun in 1871, are a good example. The flared mansard roof of the towers, the brick quoins marking the corners, and the arch-headed windows reflect an affinity for the French Second Empire style then in vogue.

Along with the Otis Elevator Company in Yonkers, the mill was one of the few large-scale industrial sites in Westchester at the time. Its vastness impressed John Masefield, the late poet laureate of England who worked in the mill for a few years as a youth in the 1890's. The "great red brick building, three storeys high and of immense length and breadth," as he described it in his book *In The Mill*, "loomed up above the road, like a gigantic ship taking in passengers at a dockside."

Alexander Smith, along with a young man named Halcyon Skinner, revolutionized the carpet-manufacturing process with the first Axminster power loom. Alexander Smith and Sons have left the mills, and much of the space is leased to a variety of smaller manufacturers.

Alexander Smith Carpet Mills

Hudson River Museum

511 Warburton Ave., Yonkers
OPEN: Tues.–Sat., 10 a.m.–5 p.m.;
      Sun., 1–5 p.m.; Wed. eve.,
      7–10 p.m. Planetarium shows
      regularly scheduled
PHONE: (914) 963–4550

In August 1877, describing Glenview, the 23-acre estate and Victorian Gothic mansion recently built by John B. Trevor, the Yonkers *Statesman* commented: "The land is gracefully undulating, and from various points presents superb views up and down the Hudson, and of the stately Palisades."

Much has changed in Yonkers since then, but the Palisades are still stately, and the views of the Hudson from this spot are still superb. Better yet, Glenview was joined in 1968 by a striking modern building designed by Sherwood Mills Smith Partnership, and together they make up the Hudson River Museum. The museum complex is set in Trevor Park, where the terrain, dotted with copper beech and red oak trees, slopes steeply down to the Hudson. When Glenview was landscaped, new trees were artfully placed among those already growing there to create a parklike effect, the benefits of which are still being appreciated a century later.

The museum complex is a skillful blend of old and new. The spiky tower, steeply slanting roof, dormer windows, and angled bays of the Trevor mansion contrast with the low, clean sweep of the new buildings and the roundness of the planetarium dome. The two buildings are completely different in purpose and design, yet they live together in perfect harmony.

The award-winning concrete museum building is built into the slope on three levels. The entrance level is a single story, but inside the museum the exhibition space is on two levels, with a central two-story well. A third, lower level contains an auditorium, which opens on to a terrace, from which you can see sculptures on the lawn below and, of course, the river.

An open sculpture court (with another view of the river) links the modern museum to the Victorian house. In addition to the period rooms of Glenview, there are changing exhibitions. Fine original tiles, woodwork, and other decorative elements in the hall and period rooms are examples of the Eastlake spirit of interior design that guided Glenview's decoration. Recent restoration has reproduced elaborate original wall stenciling. The ebony and bird's-eye maple woodwork seems even richer when one has just come from the spare interiors of the new building.

Untermeyer Park (N. Broadway [Rte. 9], south of Odell Ave., Yonkers). From 1899 until his death in 1940, Samuel Untermeyer, millionaire lawyer and passionate gardener, lived in Greystone, an estate originally built for the hat manufacturer John Waring, and then lived in by New York governor and presidential candidate Samuel J. Tilden. During his lifetime and again in his will, Untermeyer offered the 200-acre estate to, in turn, his children, the State of New York, Westchester County, and the City of Yonkers. Each refused the offer, not once but twice, because of the enormous cost of maintaining the fabulous landscaping and greenhouses.

Eventually the city was persuaded to take over the estate (greatly reduced in size) as parkland, but the grounds were sadly neglected. Now, however, funds have been made available for at least a partial restoration. The house had been razed, but the stables remain, and among

Sculpture by Jacques Lipchitz,
Hastings-on-Hudson

the lavish trappings still to be seen are a formal Greek garden and an amphitheater for outdoor concerts, which Untermeyer built for his wife in 1924. The theater is ornamented by two tall columns topped with sphinxes by the Art Deco sculptor Paul Manship.

Lipchitz Sculpture

Maple Ave., foot of Spring St., west of Warburton Ave., Hastings-on-Hudson

For over twenty years, until shortly before his death in 1973, the sculptor Jacques Lipchitz lived and worked in Hastings-on-Hudson. To show his affection for this village, he decided a few years ago to give its residents a gift. What could be more appropriate, he thought, than one of his own sculptures?

And so today, in front of the Hastings Library and flanked by the Municipal Building, the site chosen by Lipchitz him-

self, stands "Between Heaven and Earth," an 11-foot bronze. It has a curving, central, heart-shaped mass, supported by lighter, intertwined figures, the whole striving upward to be crowned by an inverted dove.

Lipchitz's former studio is on Aqueduct Lane, off Washington Ave. It was built in the early 1950's after Lipchitz's Washington Sq. studio and most of his works were destroyed by fire. Although the studio commands a superb view of the river and the Palisades, the wall facing the Hudson has no windows. Lipchitz made this specification to the architect because, as he put it, "If I could see this magnificent scenery, I would probably never work."

Mount Hope Cemetery (Saw Mill River Rd. [Rte. 9A], at Jackson Ave., eastern part of Hastings-on-Hudson). Adorning the mausoleums in this fashionable burying place of the 1930's and 1940's is a particularly fine collection of sophisticated Art Deco sculptures. Mount Hope has the crypts of the Barricinis (topped with a stone box of candy), Bela Bartok (buried in a triple coffin), John Garfield, and George Gershwin.

Ciba-Geigy

Ciba-Geigy Corporation Headquarters (Saw Mill River Rd., just north of Mount Hope Cemetery, Hastings-on-Hudson). Designed by Skidmore, Owings & Merrill in the 1950's and 1960's, this corporate complex consists of sleek steel and glass curtain-wall structures, sensitively placed on the sloping site. The only piece of Ciga-Geigy's extensive collection of contemporary art on view to the general public is the black metal sculpture, called "Sentinel," by Bernhard Luginbühl that stands in front of the main building.

St. Christopher's School (71 Broadway [Rte. 9], Dobbs Ferry, just north of Hastings-on-Hudson). One of a number of Gothic Revival mansions Alexander Jackson Davis designed in Westchester, this house was built for E. B. Strange, a commuting silk merchant from New York. Sadly, many of the original details—moldings, finials, parapets—have been lost. The Gothic cottage near Broadway on the grounds of the school is a nineteenth-century updating of an earlier structure.

Mausoleum, Mount Hope Cemetery

Dobbs Ferry Railroad Station (waterfront, across railroad bridge). Echoing H. H. Richardson's great station in North Easton, Massachusetts, this station recalls the days when train travel was entirely civilized. The void of the arch in this rough-hewn masonry structure sharply contrasts with the heaviness of the main mass.

Summerfield Gallery (303 Broadway, south of Clinton Ave., Dobbs Ferry). Built in 1894 as the Summerfield Methodist Church, this structure later became a Greek Orthodox church. It does in fact convey a Byzantine feeling with its orange brick trimmed in dark stone, rounded windows, and central tower. It is now an art gallery.

Hudson River Valley Day Care Center (Wilde House) (Broadway and Oak St., Dobbs Ferry). The sophistication of the post–Civil War years is revealed in the stylish curve of the mansard roof and the pleasing red-brick trim bordering the bays and windows. The paired-bracket cornice at the eaves adds a crisp touch. Next door is the South Presbyterian Church and its parish house, both built in 1868 in a local vernacular expression of the Victorian Gothic style.

Wilde House

Estherwood, The Masters School

Clinton Ave., off Broadway, Dobbs Ferry

In an earlier day, when architecture by whim was more feasible than it is today, men of wealth built houses for idiosyncratic reasons and moved them just as lightly. James Jennings McComb, a wealthy New York businessman, purchased land in Dobbs Ferry in the 1860's and built a comfortable clapboard house.

On a trip to Europe, he acquired a stunning octagonal desk. Nothing would do but to build a new octagonal library to show it off. But, once the library was built, it so dwarfed the proportions of the original structure that he did the only sensible thing—he moved the house, left the library, and built a new, more palatial mansion around it.

The new building, erected in the 1890's, he called Estherwood, after his wife's maiden name. It is a ponderous structure, relieved by turrets, carved balconies, and a glass conservatory. A wide

Architect's rendering of St. Christopher's School

9

Estherwood

veranda of granite with vaulted ceilings and mosaic floors extends almost completely around the house.

The McCombs had lived in the house only a few years when they gave the property to the Misses Master, Sarah and Eliza, for the School for Young Ladies they had established in 1877. Estherwood is now home to senior girls and staff of the school, known informally as "Dobbs."

The original Masters School, now the Dobbs Ferry Women's Club, nearby at 54 Clinton Ave., is one of the fine late-nineteenth-century homes that line the street. Number 29, Park Cottage, is the McCombs' original house.

Zion Episcopal Church (55 Cedar St., west of Broadway, Dobbs Ferry).

The original small, square stone church, an early example of the Gothic Revival, retains its charm in spite of later additions. Adjacent to it is the more sophisticated memorial chapel, a later version of the same style. Washington Irving served as vestryman here from 1837 to 1843.

Dobbs Ferry Public Library (153 Main St.).

Although quaint, and seemingly antique, the village library was actually remodeled in 1923, the sophisticated design of architect Bertram Goodhue.

Croton Aqueduct (Irvington).

About 30 miles to the south of Croton-on-Hudson is New York City, and in the 1830's a new way was sought to provide a plentiful water supply for that burgeoning metropolis. The bold technological answer was the construction of the Croton Aqueduct, laid between 1836 and 1842 at a cost of $12 million. When the waters of the Croton River first reached the Manhattan reservoir at Fifth Ave. and 42nd St. in July 1842, the whole city rejoiced. A monumental parade was staged on October 14, 1842, the day water was distributed for the first time through pipes to houses.

Westchester residents were not as thrilled about the aqueduct. Landowners along the route complained that their land was being taken without fair compensation, that the construction costs were too high, and that the Irish workers who built the aqueduct were, to say the least, high-spirited. One landowner testified at a hearing in 1837 that "a residence near said aqueduct . . . is extremely unpleasant, by reason of the noises, riots, and drunken revels of the said laborers." Washington Irving, a resident of Irvington near the aqueduct route, shared the popular view of the Irishmen, but expressed it in his typically engaging way. In a letter dated March 17, 1840, to the editor of *Knickerbocker* magazine, he advised that groups of "Patlanders" on their way home "from certain whisky establishments" had been beset by "foul fiends," "misshapen monsters whisking about their paths, sometimes resembling men, sometimes hogs, sometimes horses, but invariably *without heads*; which shews that they must be lineal descendants from the old goblin of the [Sleepy] Hollow."

In recent years, the aqueduct has

proved more than functional; a grassy path along the top, called the Old Croton Aqueduct Trailway, accessible from many points along the route, is an ideal site for walking. It is particularly attractive in Irvington and affords an excellent way to savor the special charm of that village.

The fine masonry craftsmanship of the aqueduct is visible where Station Rd. passes under it. In addition, all along the route are ventilators, 14-foot circular, hollow stone structures placed at one-mile intervals. The aqueduct no longer carries water; its tunnels were relaid with telephone and electric cables in 1971.

Octagon House

W. Clinton Ave., off Broadway (Rte. 9), Irvington. Good view from aqueduct

What is the best shape for a house? Orson Fowler, a phrenologist of the mid-nineteenth century, asked himself that question; and the answer was as clear to him as the bumps on his head. The spherical form is the most beautiful, and the nearest practical shape to a sphere is an octagon. Octagonal houses, he reasoned, receive twice as much sunlight as ordinary four-walled houses; they are cooler in summer and warmer in winter; and they make housework easier by eliminating all those dark and useless corners.

Fowler published his ideas in 1849 in an immensely popular book called *A Home for All or the Gravel Wall and Octagon Mode of Building*. Soon hundreds of octagonal houses were built in the Hudson and Mohawk valleys. According to popular belief, the devil could not corner the residents of an octagon house.

Many of these houses are gone now;

but Octagon House in Irvington, owned since the 1940's by author and historian Carl Carmer, remains an excellent example of the style. The house was originally built by Philip Armour of the meat-packing family in 1860 as a two-story octagonal frame house with a flat roof. Ten years later Joseph Stiner, a prosperous tea importer, purchased the house and added a dome, cupola, and encircling porch. Because the octagonal form reminded him of the summerhouses he had seen in China, he decorated the house with many Oriental touches and built a pagoda-shaped well house nearby.

Octagon House

The most striking feature is the two-storied, eight-sided dome, crowned with an octagonal cupola, which towers even above the tallest trees. The house is painted in two shades of gray, with white trim, and the cornice is supported by paired brackets that emphasize the surface richness. The wide veranda ("a delightful place in which to spend twilight and moonlight evenings, with promenading or conversation," according to Fowler) circles the first floor.

The house has unmistakable charm and a sense of mystery. It also, very possibly, has not one but two resident ghosts. According to Carmer, they are the shades of a mother and daughter who lived in the house. The daughter ran away with a young man of whom her mother disapproved and was drowned in a steamboat accident. The two have reconciled, Carmer believes, for only happy vibrations are felt in the house.

Nevis (136 S. Broadway [Rte. 9], Irvington; good view from aqueduct). James Hamilton, a son of Alexander Hamilton, bought an estate in Irvington in 1836 and named it Nevis, after the West Indian island where his father had been born. Originally a simple Greek Revival building, it was substantially remodeled in the 1890's by Stanford White. It now houses the Columbia University Nevis Laboratories for physics research.

Ardsley-on-Hudson Railroad Station (Ardsley Ave. and Hudson Rd., Irvington). In the 1890's the rich worked hard at playing, and one of their favorite playgrounds was the nation's first golf and country club—the Ardsley Casino. Its membership roster included the elite of the day—John D. Rockefeller, J. Pierpont Morgan, and Cornelius Vanderbilt. As the ultimate in convenience, a railroad station was built adjacent to the club.

In architectural style the station harmonized with Stanford White's eclectic casino, with its Tudor timbering. Many members preferred an alternate means of

Ardsley-on-Hudson Railroad Station

transportation from the city, though: they came up the river in their yachts and docked at the casino. The casino was demolished in the 1930's to make way for an apartment-house complex, Hudson House, itself a rare combination of elegance and functionalism.

Sleepy Hollow Pottery (12 S. Broadway, south of Main St., Irvington). This must have been the ideal site for the imposing home of John Burnham, the proprietor of the biggest business in town.

12   *Lord & Burnham factory in 1886*

He was co-owner of the firm of Lord & Burnham, one of the first manufacturers of greenhouses and other horticultural equipment, whose red-brick factory is still located at the foot of Main St. near the river. Burnham's house, a large brick structure which is now the pottery, was built in the early 1880's; its gables are decorated with applied Gothic motifs.

Main Street, Irvington

Irvington typifies the changes that industrialization and urbanization brought to the villages of the Hudson River valley. Originally part of the vast manorial estates of the Philipse family, its bucolic pasturelands attracted Romantics of the 1830's and 1840's, such as Washington Irving, who built his home, Sunnyside, here.

Then came the railroad and, with it, the wealthy escaping from the city to the "country." Extravagant mansions on huge acreages replaced snug farmhouses tucked into the landscape. Irvington became the most fashionable village on the river, and some of the large estates are only now being broken up for housing developments.

Irvington had its beginnings in 1850, when the farmlands originally belonging to Justus Dearman were surveyed, laid into streets, and sold at auction in New York. The village was originally called Dearman and not renamed Irvington until 1854. A grid pattern included 266 building lots; the exceptional vista of the river from Broadway is a result of this plan. Later a New York reporter described the resulting changes: "In so short a time the germ of a beautiful village is producing new neighbors for Sunnyside. A main

street has been laid out, and side streets run north and south, much like the arms of telegraph poles." Main St. and the intersecting streets today retain much of their nineteenth-century character.

Ironically, Irving's home is no longer in Irvington. The northern part of Irvington—including Sunnyside and Lyndhurst, another great nineteenth-century home—was pulled in by Tarrytown in 1870, two years before Irvington got around to incorporating as a village.

Through the years Irvington has been the home of many artists and writers, as well as the wealthy and notable. Albert Bierstadt, the nineteenth-century landscape painter, lived here. So did Louis Comfort Tiffany, who designed the stained-glass windows of the Presbyterian Church on Broadway. Clarence Day summered here as a child with his family and recorded their adventures in *Life with Father*. Charles Sheeler, an artist who found beauty in industrial forms, lived here until his death. Carl Carmer, the chronicler of the Hudson, still lives in Octagon House. Cyrus Field, who laid the first Atlantic cable, built a complex called Ardsley for himself, and another extravaganza called Ardsley Towers for his son. Jay Gould at Lyndhurst was a neighbor of Field's, and a friend too, until Gould wiped him out in a business transaction.

St. Barnabas Episcopal Church (Broadway, north of Main St., Irvington). Built in 1853, this church is dominated by a square, crenellated stone tower, made more picturesque by the addition of a small turret at its base. The founder was Rev. John McVickar, who believed honesty in church architecture was basic to worship. St. Barnabas was built according

13

Presbyterian Church, Irvington

Villa Lewaro

to his eight principles, which included this one: "To decorate construction, only, and never to construct decoration."

Presbyterian Church (Broadway, north of Main St., Irvington). James Renwick, the architect of St. Patrick's Cathedral in New York City, built this church in 1869. Unlike that Gothic structure, this church is Romanesque in style. Its imposing single tower is surmounted by a rather French-looking dome. A porte cochere stands in front of the main entrance. The two-toned stone trim is a refined note.

Villa Lewaro (Broadway, north of Main St., south of Fargo Lane, Irvington). Madame C. J. Walker, a black woman who amassed a fortune by her astute handling of her own invention, an "anti-kink" hair lotion, built a high-style mansion in Irvington (over considerable protest from her upper-crust neighbors) in 1917. The house was designed by Vertner Tandy, the first black admitted to the American Institute of Architects; its ele-

gant forms recall Anglo-Palladian villas of the eighteenth century. Madame Walker called her home Villa Lewaro, a name coined from her daughter's (A'Lelia Walker Robinson) by her friend Enrico Caruso. It is now the Anna E. Poth Home for Convalescent and Aged Members of the Companions of the Forest of America.

Sunnyside

Broadway (Rte. 9), Tarrytown
*OPEN: Daily, 10 a.m.–5 p.m. Closed
      Thanksgiving, Christmas, and
      New Year's Day
PHONE: (914) 631–8200

At the beginning of the nineteenth century, America looked to Europe for its models in art, literature, and fashion. However, during the course of the century a distinctive national consciousness began to emerge, and one of its chief literary exponents was Washington Irving. Although he lived for long periods in England and Spain, and remained a dedicated

14

Anglophile all his life, he used local legends and the foibles of his fellow New Yorkers as the basis for his extraordinarily popular writings.

Washington Irving's home, Sunnyside, bears the imprint of a highly individualistic man. The house was originally the tenant farmhouse of the Van Tassel family (of "Legend of Sleepy Hollow" fame) on the lands of Philipse Manor. Its original tenant was Wolfert Ecker; hence its name "Wolfert's Roost." Irving had visited the Hudson River valley in his youth and returned to it in 1832 after seventeen years in Europe. A bachelor, he was anxious to provide not only a retreat for himself but a home where he could entertain his nieces and nephews.

Irving turned to his friend, the artist George Harvey, for help in turning the small Dutch cottage into a larger and more elaborate dwelling, one of the first in America in the picturesque mode. Irving followed anxiously every detail of the remodeling of what he called his "elegant little snuggery." He designed arched alcoves and ceilings to disguise the sharp angles under his gabled roof. He also built closets, and had the ceiling of one of the bedrooms papered "so as to resemble the curtain of a tent," copying an effect he had seen in France.

Irving lived at Sunnyside for twenty-five years, until his death in 1859. Sunnyside became a landmark in its own time. Nearly every American writer of note, and many foreign authors as well, made a pilgrimage to the literary shrine, spoke with the master, and then, of course, went home and wrote about the visit.

The landscaping pleased A. J. Downing very much. In his *Treatise on the Theory and Practice of Landscape Gardening* (1841), the country's first landscape architect described "the gently swelling slope reaching down to the water's edge, bordered by prettily wooded ravines through which a brook meanders pleas-

Sunnyside in 1841

antly; and threaded by footpaths ingeniously contrived, so as sometimes to afford secluded walks, and at others to allow
fine vistas of the broad expanse of river scenery. The cottage itself is now charmingly
covered with ivy and climbing roses, and
embosomed in thickets of shrubbery."
The grounds are pleasant for strolling
now, too, and the house has been restored
to its mid-nineteenth-century peak by
Sleepy Hollow Restorations, which acquired the property in 1947.

Sunnyside is unique—a house noted
not only for the accomplishments of its
owner but one that carries, in its architectural eccentricities, a sense of his style.
Irving relished his "little old-fashioned
stone mansion, all made up of gable ends,
and as full of angles and corners as an old
cocked hat."

At the corner of Broadway and Sunnyside Lane, as you enter the driveway, is
the Washington Irving Memorial. The
work of Daniel Chester French, this
bronze-and-marble panel has reliefs of
Rip Van Winkle and Boabdil, the last King
of Granada, facing a marble shaft topped
by a bust of Irving.

Lyndhurst

Lyndhurst

635 S. Broadway, Tarrytown
*OPEN: Daily, 10 a.m.–5 p.m., May–
        Oct.; 10 a.m.–4 p.m., Nov.–
        April. Closed Christmas and
        New Year's Day
PHONE: (914) ME1–0046

One of the great Hudson River houses,
Lyndhurst chronicles the changing tastes
of the wealthy in the nineteenth century.
Designing the house in 1838 as a "Country Mansion in Pointed Style" for Gen.
William Paulding, architect Alexander
Jackson Davis worked closely with his
friend Andrew Jackson Downing, a hor-
ticulturalist who popularized the nineteenth-century taste for "Romantick"
villas with sweeping gardens, to produce a
prime example of the style for which
Davis became famous—Hudson River
Gothic.

In 1864 the house was purchased by
George Merritt, a merchant, who commissioned Davis to enlarge his original plan,
maintaining its architectural integrity. The
existing southern portion was almost dou-
bled in size with a new wing to the north,
a new porte cochere to the east, and a

Greenhouses, Lyndhurst

tower to the west. Merritt also gave the house a new name—Lyndhurst.

To complete the changes that transformed a simple country house into an elegant estate, in 1870 Merritt constructed a huge greenhouse, the most grandiose of its kind in a day when the wealthy vied with each other for visible opulence. The greenhouse was about 380 feet long and 37 feet wide, with two 60-foot wings extending to the south. Soaring 100 feet above it all was a Moorish-style observation tower, whose onion-shaped dome served as a landmark for Hudson River vessels. In 1873 Merritt spent $5,000 on "sundry plants" to furnish the greenhouse.

Merritt died in 1873, and seven years later Lyndhurst was purchased by Jay Gould, the railroad tycoon. Soon after he took over the property, the greenhouse burned. Gould asked the original builders, Lord & Burnham of Irvington, to reconstruct the greenhouse to about the same size but without the cupola. The Gould greenhouse became renowned not only for its exotic plants, particularly orchids, but also for its innovative structure utilizing an iron frame. Greenhouses for private homes and municipal parks became fashionable throughout the United States in the late 1800's and early 1900's, and the Lyndhurst conservatory was a model to be emulated.

In the house Gould retained much of the earlier furnishings but added many objects of his own. Gothic-style woodworking was used throughout the house, and the dining-room furniture was designed by A. J. Davis.

Gould's daughter Helen inherited the house, and it later passed to another daughter, Anna, Duchess of Talleyrand Perigord. She left Lyndhurst to the National Trust in 1964. It has been restored to the early Gould period, with contributions of the earlier owners preserved. The greenhouse is presently being stabilized so that it can be opened to the public. Around the 67-acre estate are many trees planted in the nineteenth century, including larch, linden, weeping beech, gingko, star magnolia, and cut-leaf Japanese maples.

Olivetti Education Center (155 White Plains Rd. [Rte. 119], Tarrytown). Rusting

steel beams frame the discreet forms of this building designed by architect Richard Meier. Only two stories high, the well-sited structure encloses a small sculpture garden.

Elmsford Reformed Church (Rte. 9A, south of Rte. 119). Organized in 1788 as a Congregational church, this building then became Presbyterian and finally Dutch Reformed. In the cemetery nearby is a monument to Isaac Van Wart, erected in 1829; Van Wart was one of the three Westchester farmers who apprehended Maj. John André at Tarrytown (see André Captors Monument, Tarrytown).

Tappan Zee Bridge. This three-mile bridge, opened in 1955, spans the Hudson River, connecting Westchester and Rockland counties. Its eight concrete caissons, anchored to steel piles driven deep into bedrock, serve as buoyant underwater foundations.

Christ Church (Broadway and Elizabeth St., Tarrytown). This small brick church was built in 1838; gargoyles and angels' heads that project from the top of the tower add a fanciful note. Washington Irving transferred his church affiliation here in 1843, following the lead of his minister, Dr. William Creighton of Zion Church in Dobbs Ferry. Irving became a warden of the church, and his funeral was held here in 1859.

The Historical Society of the Tarrytowns (1 Grove St., at Neperan Rd., east of Broadway, Tarrytown). A Victorian house on a street of similar dwellings, this building is admirably suited to its purpose of housing historical materials about the Hudson River valley. It has a good re-

Fence, Historical Society of the Tarrytowns

search library and an art collection. The wrought-iron fence in front of the house was formerly atop the Fifth Avenue Bank in New York City. The building is open Tues.–Sat., 2–4 p.m., and by appointment. Phone: (914) 631–8374.

Music Hall (Main St., Tarrytown). Embellishments that give this building a jaunty air are scalloped shingles, decoratively inlaid brick, and pinnacled turrets—a fine example of the Queen Anne commercial style of architecture.

Music Hall, Tarrytown

Pierson School (18 N. Broadway, at Main St., Tarrytown). Brick is decorously trimmed with brownstone on this imposing school, built in 1897, while gables and molded terra cotta are lively touches.

Second Congregational Church (42 N. Broadway, Tarrytown). At the time of its construction in 1837, this red-brick Greek Revival church was a chapel of the Old Dutch Church of Sleepy Hollow. After the congregation became independent in 1851, the rectory was built next door. Arch-headed windows were added in the gable, and a few other "modernizations" were made. The portico, with its four well-proportioned Ionic columns, is still impressive.

Coffey Funeral Home (91 N. Broadway, Tarrytown). This is one of many reminders of Broadway's past elegance. The spirited flare of the mansard roof distinguishes the 1860's clapboard structure. The porte cochere has a great arched opening, and the wooden keystone is a humorous note.

Warner Library (N. Broadway, at Wildey St., Tarrytown). This library brings an urbane touch to the rusticity of much of the area. Built in 1928 in a severely restrained style, it has a frieze, decorated cornice, formal portico, and arched windows set in recessed panels.

André Captors Monument (Patriots Park, Tarrytown). Just north of the library is a monument to the captors of Maj. John André, the British officer who was apprehended here in September 1780 with information about the defenses of West Point, given him by Benedict Arnold. The young officer, whose fate inspired pity

even in his own time, was something of a poet. Prophetically, he concluded a long poem written a few months before his execution:

When the epic strain was sung
The poet by his neck was hung—
And to his cost he finds too late
The dung-born tribe decides his fate.

Coffey Funeral Home

Philipsburg Manor

Broadway (Rte. 9), North Tarrytown
*OPEN: Daily, 10 a.m.–5 p.m. Closed Thanksgiving, Christmas, and New Year's Day
PHONE: (914) 631–8200

In the early eighteenth century sturdy little sloops sailed up the Hudson River to a harbor in a deep cove (called "die Slapering Haven" by the Dutch settlers and later translated freely as "Sleepy Hollow" by Washington Irving). At that time the Pocantico River emptied into the cove and provided the water power for a busy gristmill. The boats, loaded with their cargo of barrels of flour and biscuits, then sailed back to New York. There the cargo was transferred to ships that sailed around the world.

The mill and the nearby Manor House—as well as the surrounding 200 square miles of beautiful land—were only part of the holdings of Frederick Philipse. Today only 20 acres remain, and these belong to Sleepy Hollow Restorations, which operates Philipsburg Manor as one of its three properties (the others are Sunnyside and Van Cortlandt Manor). Philipsburg Manor has been reconstructed to the period of about 1720–50, the height of its commercial power, when Adolph Philipse, the first Frederick's son, owned it.

An oak-timbered bridge spans the dammed millpond and leads to the gristmill, sheltered by a cedar-shingled millhouse on a stone foundation. The miller explains how the water turns the wheel that drives the shaft, an oak tree trunk 22½ feet long and 22 inches in diameter. A face gear on the shaft multiplies the action of the waterwheel and transfers the horizontal revolution of the shaft to the vertical rotation of the spindle. Each time the waterwheel turns once, the millstone on top turns about 4⅔ times. Milling is hard and continuous work; the millstones that do the actual grinding have to be resharpened or "dressed" by hand, a job that takes fourteen hours or so.

Outside on a small landing you can see the waterwheel in operation, and down a flight of stairs are the granary and the wharf, where the sloops would have moored. Behind the mill is the simple rubblestone structure known as the Manor House. When the reconstruction was begun, layer after layer of remodeling was removed until all that remained was three outer stone walls and an interior masonry partition. The house had to be almost totally rebuilt. The original structure built by Frederick Philipse had two stories, with two rooms to a floor, but Adolph added a duplicate wing. The reconstruction follows this design, so that there are now four rooms to a floor. The house is rather sparsely furnished in a utilitarian style, with solid furniture and little decoration.

Behind the Manor House lie a kitchen garden, an orchard, and a barn that contains farm implements of the period. Other

Mill, Philipsburg Manor

buildings existed on the property, but not enough is known about them to even attempt a reconstruction.

Philipsburg Manor is a carefully reconstructed early-eighteenth-century Dutch trading center. But it *is* a reconstruction and certain concessions had to be made to the ravages of time. Because the land has settled so much and the Pocantico has silted over, the original overshot wheel, if used today, would cause extensive flooding upriver. Therefore a modified breast-wheel has had to be used (the water is ejected with force below the axis of the wheel and the combination of this jet action and the water in the buckets turns the wheel).

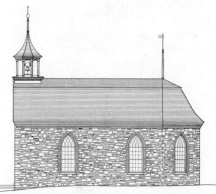

Old Dutch Church of Sleepy Hollow

Old Dutch Church of Sleepy Hollow

(Broadway, North Tarrytown). Hard by Philipsburg Manor is the small stone church that Frederick Philipse and his second wife, Catherine Van Cortlandt, built in 1699. Washington Irving was involved in alterations to it in 1837, and it was during his time that the original Dutch-style round-arched windows were changed to the present pointed arches in a concession to Gothic taste. The church has its original bell, cast in 1685 in the Netherlands, bearing the inscription *Si Deus Pro Nobis Quis Contra Nos* ("If God be for us, who can be against us?").

In his "Legend of Sleepy Hollow" Irving described the church: "It stands on a knoll, surrounded by locust-trees and lofty elms, from among which its decent whitewashed walls shine modestly forth, like Christian purity beaming through the shades of retirement."

Hammond House

Rte. 100C, off Rte. 9A, Eastview,
between North Tarrytown and Valhalla
*OPEN: Fri.–Sun., 2–5 p.m.,
May 1–Nov. 1
PHONE: (914) 592–3175

A dramatic illustration of the contrast between Westchester's past, its present, and its future exists on one short stretch of Rte. 100C.

To start with the old: Hammond House was built in 1719 by Capt. William Hammond; it is a typical pre-Revolutionary farmhouse which sits close to the road, still surrounded by rolling farmlands. The house has three sections today; the large central section was the earliest on the site. Although it is almost as old as the central section, the small section on the left was originally a little cottage built some distance away and added on here in 1835. The larger section on the right was added in the 1860's and is now the caretaker's cottage.

The roof of the central portion has an unusually long slope, continuing right over the porch in a graceful sweep. Six posts support the overhanging roof, and stone slabs pave the porch. Inside, the

Hammond House

rooms are furnished in the style of the period. The pine paneling in the parlor is notable, as is the tavern, or refectory, table, dating from 1760, in the cottage kitchen.

Around the grounds are lovely small gardens, including an aromatic herb garden common in Colonial times. A split-rail fence, of a type frequently found in the country in the early eighteenth century, borders the road.

Union Carbide Corporation, Tarrytown Technical Center

Rte. 100C, west of Hammond House

After one leaves the humble dwelling of early American farmer–patriots and travels west, the pastoral vistas are suddenly broken by a stunning modern building that literally straddles the quiet, tree-lined country road.

This structure was designed by Vincent Kling Associates in 1968 as an expansion to already-existing Union Carbide facilities on the site. A 1,200-foot-long spine connects wings on either side of the

road, which passes under a glass-enclosed walkway. Gleaming metal, shining glass, and solid concrete accentuate the horizontal lines of the spine. The building unifies the site both physically and visually.

Philipse Manor Railroad Station (foot of Palmer Ave., off Broadway, North Tarrytown). A one-ton cast-iron eagle with a 12-foot wingspread stands guard over the commuters of Philipse Manor. In the nineteenth century the bird, one of a set of sixteen, was part of the architectural sculpture atop Grand Central Terminal in New York City. It was moved here by a wealthy railroad man when the surrounding area was developed.

Tarrytown Lighthouse (Hudson River; can be seen from Kingsland Point Park; entrance near Philipse Manor Railroad Station, North Tarrytown). The last to be built of the great Hudson River lighthouses has a cast-iron tower and was the very latest in modern technology when it was erected in 1883, but transportation on the river was already declining. Someday it will serve as a museum, which is Westchester County's eventual plan for its preservation.

Pocantico Hills (Rte. 117, east of North Tarrytown). Here, hidden from public view, is the Rockefeller compound—the estate built by John D. Rockefeller in 1903 and the mansions, each in a different style, added as the sons of John D. Rockefeller, Jr., married. The village itself is a ''company town,'' inhabited mostly by people who work on the estates.

The original development was a romantically conceived suburban community planned in 1871 by Olmsted, Vaux &

Company for the Tarrytown Heights Land Company. Rockefeller purchased much of the land in 1893 and later arranged to have the railroad station and tracks moved, leaving behind part of the original hamlet and some street names—Bedford, Rafenberg, Coppock, and Requa rds.

Union Church in the center of Pocantico Hills has a stained-glass window by Matisse and several by Chagall, gifts from the Rockefellers.

Sleepy Hollow Country Club (Broadway [Rte. 9], Scarborough). One of the last of the grand country houses built on the banks of the Hudson was the proud brick-and-limestone mansion designed by McKim, Mead & White for Elliott Shepard in 1895. Gone was the picturesque asymmetry of previous decades; the studied proportions and formal language of the Renaissance now appeared in its place.

St. Mary's Episcopal Church (Broadway, Scarborough). John Bolton of Pelham, who popularized the craft of making stained-glass windows in America in the mid-nineteenth century, created the windows in this church. The present structure, modeled after the fourteenth-century Gothic parish church of St. Mary's of Scarborough in Yorkshire, was built in 1851. The west window, with five narrow vertical panels delicately drawn, is surmounted by a bell gable. Washington Irving planted the ivy on the church.

Scarborough Presbyterian Church (Broadway and Station Rd.). Rubble fieldstone and smooth sandstone are combined in an original way in this impressive neo-Baroque structure built in 1893. The high tower is surmounted by a belfry and cupola.

Sparta (just south of Ossining, between Revolutionary Rd. and Rockledge Ave., west of Broadway [Rte. 9]). The twentieth century crowds Broadway with apartment buildings and shopping centers at this point, but tucked away, just out of sight, is Sparta, a fragment of the eighteenth century that progress has overlooked—thus far.

Sparta was settled in 1759 but was later dwarfed in importance by the growth of Ossining, its bustling neighbor to the north. A cluster of pre-Revolutionary houses have hung on tenaciously. The Washington Inn, built in 1786 and now a private home, is particularly striking be-

Union Carbide

cause of its bowed façade. The Jug Tavern, at 88 Revolutionary Rd., is a two-story clapboard building built in 1770. Other houses in Sparta date from the early and mid-nineteenth century. The scale of the houses and their relationship to each other are vivid reminders of the earlier period. Nearby is the two-acre Sparta Burying Ground with many pre-Revolutionary gravestones.

Union Baptist Church (N. Highland Ave. [Rte. 9], Ossining). Built in 1874, this elegant version of the Stick Style, in combination with brick, has fine carved motifs at the eaves. The original spire has been replaced.

Main Street, Ossining

A reminder of the civic pride exhibited by the prosperous middle-class merchants of the late nineteenth century can be seen in the substantial rows of brick buildings on Main St. and nearby streets in Ossining. Unlike many of their counterparts, these Victorian commercial buildings have not been "modernized" beyond recognition, but retain their distinctive window moldings, brackets, and other rich decorative elements.

Main St. as it stands today was built in the 1870's and 1880's, a tribute not only to mercantile acumen but also to the wisdom of good insurance. Earlier buildings on Main St., which slopes down to the waterfront and dock area, were destroyed by a series of fires. But all the owners were heavily insured, and bad luck was quickly changed into good, as they rebuilt bigger and better stores.

Main Street, Ossining

Havahart Trap Company (Dr. Brandreth's)

N. Water St., foot of Main St., Ossining

Benjamin Brandreth's pill factory, now the home of the Havahart Trap Company, was one of many industrial sites on Ossining's waterfront. Brandreth, an Englishman, came to America in the early 1800's to promote his family's medicinal cures. In his original attic factory in Lower Manhattan, he prepared the pills, his wife pasted on the labels, and his son counted out the right number of doses for each box. In 1837, as business improved, he moved to Ossining to take advantage of the fresh-water springs for the manufacturing process and the river transportation for the finished product. Allcock's Porous Plasters, added to the line in 1848, contained frankincense and myrrh. Brandreth pioneered in the use of advertising, spend-

THE MAIN BUILDING of the PORUS PLASTER COMPANY VILLAGE OF SING SING NY

quarried here in the mid-nineteenth century. In 1825 the state built a prison at Sing Sing and transferred convict labor to work the quarries. Anyone sent "up the river" was assigned to Sing Sing. (The prison sits on the bank of the Hudson; the best view is from the train.)

The prison became so closely associated with the village that in 1901 the residents decided to change the name —from Sing Sing (which means "stone on stone" in Indian dialect) to a variant, Ossining.

ing over $3 million in his lifetime to persuade people to buy his medicinal products.

The faded letters of Brandreth's products can still be seen on one red-brick, mansarded factory building in the complex, which survived a fire because Brandreth's wise building plans called for widely spaced structures.

Double-arch Bridge (Broadway, off N. Highland Ave., Ossining). This remarkable bridge within a bridge was part of the Croton Aqueduct system; the upper bridge was built in 1838–40 to carry the aqueduct over the Kil Brook. The timber bridge that carried Broadway through the aqueduct arch was reconstructed in masonry in 1861.

Printex Corporation

34 State St., at Broad St., south of Main St., Ossining

Museum of the Ossining Historical Society (196 Croton Ave. [Rte. 133]). In this museum—a small gable-fronted

Another industrial site near the river, this time combining the Classical tradition with the Bauhaus mode, is the Printex factory, which manufactures silk-screened fabrics and accessories. The older part of the complex is a masculine Greek Revival structure built in 1840 as a residence by James W. Robinson, a steamship-company magnate. Printex took over this building in 1950, and in 1967 added the well-designed modern wing.

The Robinson home, like many others in the area, was made of Sing Sing marble,

The Croton Aqueduct at Sing Sing in 1850

25

1850's cottage—are paintings by the artist Robert Havell, Jr., who engraved most of the plates for Audubon's *Birds of America* and who lived for a time in Ossining. There are also changing exhibits and a good collection of local artifacts. Open Mon. and Wed., 2–4 p.m., and by appointment. Phone: (914) 762–4851.

Van Cortlandt Manor

Rte. 9, Croton-on-Hudson
*OPEN: Daily, 10 a.m.–5 p.m. Closed
Thanksgiving, Christmas, and
New Year's Day
PHONE: (914) 631–8200

For over 250 years members of the Van Cortlandt family lived in this gracious Manor House at the mouth of the Croton River. It has been restored by Sleepy Hollow Restorations to the period of its greatest historical significance, the mid-eighteenth century, when Pierre Van Cortlandt and his son Philip lived here. Both Van Cortlandts were prominent figures in New York politics before, during, and after the Revolutionary War. Pierre was lieutenant governor of New York for 18 years, and Philip was a brigadier general

Van Cortlandt Manor

in the Continental Army and later served in Congress for 16 years.

The property was bought by Stephanus Van Cortlandt in 1683, partly from previous Dutch owners and partly from the Indians. He was granted a patent for the Manor of Cortlandt, one of six quasi-feudal estates created by the English governors in Westchester County. Stephanus owned some 200 square miles of land, extending from the Hudson all the way to Connecticut.

The rubblestone walls and flare of the eaves recall that the Manor House is basically a Dutch farmhouse, but an extremely elegant one. It is not a formal building like Philipse Manor Hall in Yonkers but a country house. Notable features are the double stairs that climb to a veranda, and the broad, paneled Dutch door. The original one-story structure was subsequently enlarged by the addition of a second story and the porch.

The evolution of furniture design in America can be seen in the Manor House, because the superb family collections covered nearly three centuries. There are also fine collections of ceramics, pewter, and textiles.

Also on the property are a restoration of Ferry House—where intrepid travelers who crossed the Croton by ferry on the New York–Albany route used to stay—the Ferry House kitchen, a smokehouse, and the Necessary House, that is, a privy. A red-brick Long Walk between the Manor House and the Ferry House is bordered with a Colonial garden of herbs, flowers, and fruit trees.

Bethel Chapel (Old Post Rd., off Rte. 129, Croton-on-Hudson). Next to the concrete Croton Public Library, designed by Oscar S. Wiggens in 1965, is the tiny

Bethel Chapel, which commands a broad view from a high knoll in the cemetery. It was built in 1780 on land donated by the Van Cortlandt family and served as a center for Methodist camp meetings, at which revivalist preachers transfixed residents of the surrounding area. The chapel was used for funerals after the new Asbury Methodist Church was built, and was extensively restored in the 1930's.

Stone Houses, Croton-on-Hudson (N. Old Post Rd.). Croton was a favored place for artists in the 1920's and boasted many famous residents, such as Max Eastman, Edna St. Vincent Millay, Isadora Duncan, John Reed, and Stuart Chase. (The locals, to be sure, were not as impressed with the newcomers' styles as was the outside world.) Several lived in these houses, built at intervals into the stone wall that lines the sidewalk and forming a striking complex of highly individualistic dwellings.

New Croton Dam

Rte. 129, off Rte. 9A,
Croton-on-Hudson

The New Croton Dam, which replaced the original dam built to hold the waters of the Croton Reservoir as part of the Croton Aqueduct system, was begun in 1892 and completed in 1907. At the time of its construction it was the tallest masonry dam in the world—184 feet high.

An impressive staggered-stone spillway breaks the water flowing over the dam; a road leads across it, and you can also drive around to the bottom and see the dam from below. In its secluded setting it seems more a natural wonder than a man-made engineering feat.

New Croton Dam

Lindroos Hotel

636 Main St., off Rte. 9, Peekskill

In the 1840's the landscape architect A. J. Downing noted with some relief that "the Greek temple disease has passed the crisis." At its fever pitch in the 1830's and 1840's, the Greek Revival style had dominated American civic building and much private construction as well.

The style was in harmony with the Romantic yearning for remoteness of time and place. No doubt, too, it was encour-

Lindroos Hotel

27

aged by American sympathy for the Greeks who were then fighting their own war of independence from Turkey. To be *au courant*, every city had to have its own Greek temple, complete with Classical columns and porticos. Though the style was often diluted by modifications, at its best it had a direct simplicity that well suited the young Republic.

Remarkably, several handsome examples of this style surivive today in Peekskill. The Lindroos Hotel, originally built by Frederick Irving, Washington Irving's nephew, is one. Almost next door is a house built for Chauncy Depew, the railroad magnate and senator, whose family lived in Peekskill. Another example is the Presbyterian Church at 705 South St.

St. Peter's Episcopal School (E. Main St., across from Beach Shopping Center, Peekskill). Rev. Henry Ward Beecher used this building as his country residence in the 1870's. He was a gentleman farmer as well as a cleric, selling cabbages at a dollar a head and appearing on the streets of the village "nearly every day, driving the fine span of bays recently purchased." The expansive house itself has great porches on three sides, and intersecting gables.

St. Peter's Episcopal Church (Oregon Rd. [Rte. 130], Van Cortlandtville, east of Peekskill). This beautifully restored Colonial church has a brown-shingled exterior, typical of its pre-Revolutionary date of 1767. The entrance and two triple-hung, arch-headed windows are the only break in the simple façade. More than fifty soldiers of the Revolutionary War are buried in the graveyard nearby.

First Presbyterian Church of Yorktown (2880 Crompond Rd. [Rte. 202], Yorktown Heights). This impressive Greek Revival church was built in 1840, the third on the site. Rev. Samuel Sackett, minister during the Revolution, was an outspoken patriot; the parsonage was used as a meeting place for the Committee of Safety. The British marched to Crompond especially to burn the parsonage. Sackett escaped to Connecticut, but returned to the church after the war and is buried in the adjoining cemetery.

Garrison Landing

Railroad Station, Garrison

Because of its resemblance to Yonkers in the Gay Nineties, Garrison was chosen as the site for filming some scenes of *Hello Dolly!* Ferry gates were built as part of the set and were never removed. Nor should they be, for just as ferry boats shuttled back and forth between Yonkers and Alpine, the depot at Garrison at one time served boats crossing the river to West Point.

St. Peter's Episcopal Church,
Van Cortlandtville

Garrison Landing

The feed and grain store is now a boutique, and the former railroad station is a real-estate office. The elaborate "new" railroad station, built in the early twentieth century, now serves as a community theater. Gothic cottages and the general store round out this picturesque enclave.

Dominating the little street is the spectacular view of the Hudson and across to West Point. The aqueduct is accessible for walking and more scenic views.

St. Philip's Church in the Highlands

(Rte. 9D, Garrison). When it was founded in 1770, St. Philip's was a simple wooden chapel, probably much like St. Peter's in nearby Van Cortlandtville, with which it was united until 1840. Then, in 1860, Richard Upjohn, who was a vestryman in the church as well as the architect of Trinity Church in New York, designed a new building. The low, simple, stone mass and the steeply pitched roof are reminiscent of English parish churches. It has a low buttressed tower and retains its multicolored slate roof. The church is well sited in relation to the road and to the graveyard, where Upjohn and Hamilton Fish, once governor of New York, are buried.

Boscobel

Rte. 9D, Garrison
*OPEN: Daily, except Tues., 9:30 a.m.–
    5 p.m., April–Oct.; 9:30 a.m.–
    4 p.m., Nov., Dec., March.
    Closed Thanksgiving, Christmas, Jan., Feb.
PHONE: (914) 265–3638 or
    (212) 562–7444

Boscobel has had two lives. In its first incarnation, it was located in Crugers in Westchester County, 15 miles south of its present site. It was the home planned by States Morris Dyckman for his young wife in 1806. Although of Dutch descent, Dyckman was an Anglophile, a Loyalist who served 12 years in the British Army but who returned to America after the war.

He planned his residence to rival the best then being built in London. Boscobel was accordingly designed in the style of Robert Adam, the Scottish designer noted for his graceful neo-Classical forms. Dyckman died before the house was completed, but his widow and son and four succeeding generations of the family did live in it.

In 1955, when the then-abandoned house was about to be destroyed, it was given a new life—but in a different location. Through the efforts of a citizens' group, and the benefactions of Mrs. DeWitt Wallace of *Reader's Digest*, the house was moved piece by piece to Putnam County on a hilltop across from West Point, and more attention and money were lavished on its rebuilding than it ever received in its own day.

The result is neither a genuine reconstruction nor a restoration—for the house never existed in this form—but an idealized completion of an unfinished plan. One commentator has called it, ac-

Chestnut Street, Cold Spring

curately, "modern elegance historically inspired." The superbly refined design of the house (particularly the delicate carving of the festoons that adorn the pediments), its fine furnishings, and the landscaped grounds have made Boscobel a popular tourist attraction.

Bird and Bottle Inn (Rte. 9, Garrison). A tavern in pre-Revolutionary days, this extensively restored inn is still serving the traveling public.

St. Mary's Church in the Highlands (corner of Chestnut and Main sts., Cold Spring). The interior space of this Victorian Gothic church, defined by open wooden trusses resting on carved wooden brackets, is particularly pleasant. George Harney was the architect for this fieldstone building, erected in 1868.

Cold Spring

The railroad tracks divide Cold Spring's center of town into two parts—old and older. Down by the river, on the west side of the tracks, a tiny cluster of diminutively scaled eighteenth- and nineteenth-century dwellings, some with raised parapets on the gable ends, surround an early-nineteenth-century gazebo. Dominating all is a breathtaking view of the river.

An extraordinary group of commercial structures from various periods, including the U.S. Post Office building, have been preserved in extremely good condition on the main street. The charming details of these buildings—iron cresting on one roof, carved lintels on another—are best absorbed slowly.

Just north on Rte. 9D are four nineteenth-century dwellings. A fine Italianate one, adjacent to the library, has particularly imaginative forms. Such a house might have been the inspiration for Edith Wharton (who spent some time as a child in her aunt's home in the Hudson River valley) when she described the style known as "Hudson River Bracketed" in her 1929 novel of that name: "Everything about the front was irregular, but with an irregularity unfamiliar to him. The shuttered windows were very tall and narrow, and narrow too the balconies, which projected at odd angles, supported by ornate wooden brackets."

The Foundry School Museum

63 Chestnut St., Cold Spring
OPEN: Wed., 9:30 a.m.–4 p.m.; Sun., 2–5 p.m.; and by appointment
PHONE: (914) 265–2781

This museum, formerly a schoolhouse, was built in the 1830's. It has displays connected with Cold Spring's past, especially the role of the West Point Foundry, which was chartered by Congress in 1818 to produce cannon for the army and navy. In 1851, R. P. Parrott took it over and manufactured the Parrott-rifled field pieces used extensively in the Civil War. In addition to weaponry and heavy machinery, the foundry produced an occasional decorative piece—the Gothic iron benches at Sunnyside, for example. Maintained by the Putnam County Historical Society.

Chapel of Our Lady (Hudson River waterfront, Cold Spring). Most of the thousand workers at the West Point Foundry were Irish Catholics. Gouverneur Kemble, supervisor of the foundry, and an Episcopalian, donated property, funds, and a plan for a church for the workers. The Chapel of Our Lady, a diminutive Greek Revival structure, was dedicated in 1834, in a scene reported by the *New York Mirror* as "full of lofty inspiration, accompanied by association of religion, of charity and of philanthropy."

Railroad construction in the 1840's isolated the chapel on its river-edge site, and it ceased to be used in 1906 when a new church was built in the center of Cold Spring. A fire in 1931 caused extensive damage. Nevertheless, the framework survived; and the chapel is being restored as a nondenominational house of worship.

Pollopel Island (Hudson River, south of Beacon; view from Rte. 9D). During the Revolutionary War, a *cheval de frise*, or series of iron-tipped spikes held in submerged wooden frames, stretched from Pollopel Island to Plum Point on the west bank of the Hudson. The obstruction was intended to prevent British vessels from invading the upper Hudson, but in 1777 the British sailed up the river anyway.

In 1900 the island was purchased by a munitions supplier, Francis Bannerman, who built a Scottish-style castle, complete with a stocked arsenal, which is now in ruins.

According to legend, the island was named for one Polly Pell, whose two ardent suitors, a minister and a farmer, vied for her affections. She and the minister went sleighing one day, but the ice broke and they fell into the frigid waters. The farmer saved them both and brought them to the island, whereupon the minister, so overcome by Polly's obvious love for the farmer, gave up his suit and married the couple straightaway.

Craig House (Tioranda)

Rte. 9D, Beacon

Craig House, called Tioranda when it was built in 1859 for shipping magnate and philanthropist Joseph Howland, was an early work of Richard Morris Hunt, recently returned from his apprenticeship in

Craig House (Tioranda)

Madam Brett Homestead

Paris. Contrasting black and white glazed bricks, incised motifs, fanciful woodwork, and clearly articulated structural members express the contemporary Victorian taste. Craig House is now a sanitarium.

The architect married the owner's daughter and moved into the circles of the very rich. Hunt's designs for this group expressed with consummate skill their vast financial resources. Later in the nineteenth century Hunt produced a series of lavish French Renaissance mansions, such as the Fifth Avenue townhouse and Biltmore, in Asheville, North Carolina, for William K. Vanderbilt.

Madam Brett Homestead (Teller House)

50 Van Nydeck Ave., Beacon
*OPEN: Wed.–Sun., 1–4 p.m., April
      15–Nov. 15 (approximately)
PHONE: (914) 831–9827

Catharyna Rombout Brett and her husband, Roger, built this ample house about 1714; and when he died young, Madam Brett became an active businesswoman, dealing in real estate, milling, and other enterprises. She was, in fact, one of the area's most powerful economic forces, and distances were measured in the number of miles to her mill. She sold off outright much of the lands she had inherited from her father, instead of following the more common practice of leaseholds—thus she encouraged the development of independent businessmen in the area.

Madam Brett's house, typical of its time, has few windows, and those are small. The sloping shed dormers are distinctive, and the round-butt shingles unusual for Dutchess County.

The house remained in the family until 1955, when it became a museum.

Main Street, Beacon. Large areas of Beacon have been razed for renewal, but the charm of the nineteenth century has not been completely obliterated. Typically, the closer to the river, the older the structures—and the more dilapidated.

Howland Library (477 Main St., Beacon). The first story of this small-scale library is brick with set-in glazed black and white brick bands. The attic, imaginatively detailed with dormers, is covered by red and gray slate; the central gable has exposed timbers. The library was designed in 1872 by Richard Morris Hunt, who also designed the benefactor's residence, Tioranda.

Reformed Church (Ferry St., Beacon).
The simplicity of this gable-fronted, redbrick church, built in 1860, is disarming; contrasting bands of brick decorate the façade and a tall spire crowns the tower.

St. Luke's Episcopal Church (Wolcott Ave., Beacon).
Frederick C. Withers, who later collaborated with Calvert Vaux on the plans for the Museum of Natural History in New York City, designed this stone church in 1868. A low spire and a gabled portico highlight the picturesque massing. The nearby gabled rectory, of brick and fieldstone, is particularly pleasing and makes a fine addition to the other attractive homes that line Wolcott Ave. Mount Beacon looms in the background, and large trees form a canopy over this distinguished street.

Beacon Piece and Dye Works (Rte. 52, Groveville, west of Beacon).
Originally the Groveville Mills, operated by New York merchant A. T. Stewart, this mill complex is a remarkable survival. It consists of brick workers' dwellings standing on either side of a much more impressive residence, probably originally the plant manager's, and continuing along a short approach to the mills. The complex, built about 1872 to produce carpets, was sited along a railroad siding.

The brick homes are gabled over each half; brackets support overhanging eaves. Window openings, following the Italianate trend, are arch-headed. There have been few changes over the years, although the workers' homes no longer belong to the mills.

Workers' homes, Groveville

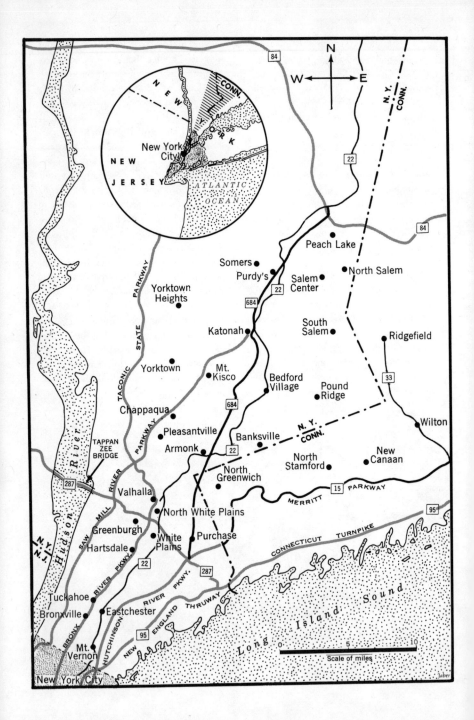

2 | The Valleys Between the Hudson River and Long Island Sound

In the eighteenth century the valleys of the Saw Mill and Bronx rivers and the gentle hills of northern Westchester and western Connecticut were mainly farmland. By 1850 the railroads linked the southern portion inexorably with New York City. This area—from Mount Vernon to White Plains—is today densely populated and urban as well as suburban. Fine architectural reminders of the nineteenth and early twentieth centuries remain among the more numerous structures built after World War I.

North of White Plains, however, the pastoral quality is vivid still. There remain many small towns, amiably linked by country roads lined with rustic farmsteads which seem to have ignored the bustle to the south. But the landscape may yet change immeasurably as corporate empires command large parcels of land beside new housing developments and shopping centers.

Because no single historic road joined this large and sprawling area, the towns and villages included here follow no orderly geographic progression. Sites tend to be clustered along Rtes. 22 and 684 in New York and Rte. 33 in Connecticut, and are generally arranged on a circular route from Mount Vernon to Ridgefield, Connecticut, and back to Purchase in New York State. However, this order is only a reference point; sample the area's rich and varied menu as you please.

John Stevens House

29 W. 4th St., corner of 6th Ave.,
Mount Vernon

Even in the mid-nineteenth century, it was hard to find a decent, inexpensive place to live in New York City. John Stevens, a successful tailor, thought that one solution would be for a group of workingmen to establish a small village not too far from the city, say, about forty minutes by train.

In 1850, with some like-minded associates, including Horace Greeley, then editor of the *New York Tribune*, he founded the New York Industrial Home Association No. 1. The qualifications for membership were good moral character, industrious habits, and a desire to promote the common purpose, which was "protection against the unjust power and influence of capitalists and against land monopoly as the main cause of poverty." Within six months he had enrolled a thousand members; and with their dues he bought five farms in East Chester, a total of about 370 acres.

The land was divided up into quarter-acre plots and sold to the Association members. The name the Association orig-inally chose for the village was Monticello, but the post office complained that there was already another village of that name in the state. Mount Vernon was substituted, and the village was so incorporated in 1853. The area built up by the Association is now part of downtown Mount Vernon.

John Stevens' own house, purchased from Sylvanus Purdy as part of the land deal, is basically the home of a well-to-do farmer rather than of a real-estate entrepreneur. A conservatively styled clapboard farmhouse, it is oriented to the south, blissfully ignoring the axis of the grid plan that was superimposed on the farmland. The house, which belongs to the City of Mount Vernon, will be restored if funds become available.

East Lincoln Avenue, Mount Vernon

205 E. Lincoln Avenue, Mount Vernon. Here is one of the most extraordinary Shingle-style homes in an area that is rich with them. The gables, dormers, and a corner turret of this house punctuate the active massing. Scalloped shingles, wreaths, festoons, sunbursts, and other fanciful details abound.

John Stevens House

Old Marble School (California and New Rochelle rds., Town of Eastchester). From 1835 until 1884, the school bell on top of this one-room schoolhouse, built of local Tuckahoe marble, summoned the children of Eastchester's School District No. 2 to classes.

A pupil in the 1870's reminisced fifty years later: "Two rows of desks stood on each side of the room, the initials of former generations of pupils rudely carved on their tops. One side of the room was for boys, the other side for girls. Woe betide the pupil who ventured on the other's territory, except when a boy was punished by being forced to sit with a girl—such a disgrace was not quickly forgotten."

The school was moved in 1869 from its original location on White Plains Rd. to its present site. After it was closed as a school, it was used as a farm building and was donated to the Eastchester Historical Society in 1959, which has restored it to its mid-nineteenth-century appearance. Open by appointment. Phone: (914) 793-1900.

Thomas Paine Cottage and Memorial Building

Paine Ave., off North Ave.,
New Rochelle
OPEN: Daily, except Mon., 2-5 p.m.
PHONE: (914) NE2-5376

"Without the pen of Paine," wrote John Adams, "the sword of Washington would have been wielded in vain." But the nation rewarded Thomas Paine—whose "Common Sense" had embodied the Revolutionary spirit and whose "Crisis" papers had bolstered the patriot soldiers —with scorn and criticism.

Thomas Paine Cottage

To be sure, Paine was not exactly the soul of propriety. A prodigious drinker, he favored neither cleanliness nor godliness. It was in fact his antireligious outlook, proclaimed in *The Age of Reason*, that outraged his contemporaries. Then, too, they were shocked by Paine's criticism of George Washington.

Nevertheless, the State of New York gave Paine a 400-acre farm in New Rochelle on land confiscated from the Loyalist De Veaus, for "services he had rendered the country during the Revolutionary struggle for independence." There Paine settled in 1802. The house on the property, which had burned in 1793, was later replaced by a simple three-bay salt-box dwelling with side ell. Although Paine found New Rochelle "always green and agreeable," it was no haven from the insults and attacks heaped on him by his countrymen. In 1805 an unfriendly local fired a shot through the window of Paine's cottage and almost killed him. Not long after, Paine was denied his voting rights in a local election because he had taken a seat in the French National Convention in the 1790's.

Paine decided to do his drinking in New York City after that; he moved to Greenwich Village, where he died in 1809 at the age of seventy-two. Since no church in New Rochelle would permit him to be buried in consecrated ground, he was buried on his farm.

The British journalist William Cobbett, author of *Rural Rides*, decided that Paine would be more honored in England than in America. In 1819 he and a few associates dug up the coffin, and Paine's bones were shipped to England. The bones were shifted from owner to owner, until they finally disappeared.

For all its shabby treatment of Paine while he was alive, modern New Rochelle has done rather well by him. His cottage, restored and moved from its original hilltop site, sits on a pleasant, rolling piece of land with a brook and bridge nearby. It contains many objects connected with Paine's life, including a stove presented to him by Benjamin Franklin and a wax figure of Paine himself.

Also on the property are the Brewster Schoolhouse, a small wooden building dating from the 1830's; a large ceremonial image stone used by the Siwanoy Indians; and the nineteenth milestone from the toll road constructed in the early 1800's.

The Thomas Paine Memorial Building (983 North Ave.) houses the Thomas Paine National Historical Collection. A monument to Paine, enclosed by an iron fence, faces North Ave.

Jacob Leisler sculpture (corner of North and Broadview aves., New Rochelle). Close by the Paine Cottage is the heroic sculpture of the striding figure of Jacob Leisler, the German immigrant who became mayor of New York in 1689 after leading an uprising against the English. Leisler was later tried for treason and hanged, and is not much remembered.

But he is important to New Rochelle, for it was he who arranged for the transfer of 6,000 acres of land owned by John and Rachel Pell to French Huguenots seeking refuge in this country. The sculptor Solon Borglum created the memorial to Leisler in 1913.

New Rochelle High School (265 Clove Rd., off North Ave.). In 1926, when New Rochelle High School was built, school construction was a source of civic pride rather than taxpayers' outrage. This handsome three-story, red-brick building was designed by the architects Guilbert & Betelle but has been modified several times since.

Masterson House

90 White Plains Rd. [Rte. 22], south of Dusenbury Rd., Bronxville

Alexander Masterson, a Scottish immigrant and partner in the construction firm of Masterson & Smith, obtained a contract in 1832 to repair the buildings in Washington, D.C., that had been damaged in the War of 1812. He knew that there was a dependable supply of marble in Tuckahoe, and his contract opened a new era of expansion for the town. Quarries soon were in operation from Main St. in Tuckahoe all the way to Scarsdale. Tuckahoe marble has been used in the Washington Monument, the rebuilding of the Capitol, and St. Patrick's Cathedral in New York.

Masterson himself decided to settle in Tuckahoe, and built a house—of wood, though with marble foundations and marble chips for insulation in the walls—on White Plains Rd. The house still stands, although most of its original acreage and outbuildings are gone.

Bronxville Public Library (205 Pond-field Rd.). This red-brick structure (facing the Village Hall) has a central pavilion and massive chimneys. Harry Leslie Walker, who designed it in 1942, took his inspiration from the Georgian style. The library has a fine collection of landscape and genre paintings by the artists of the "Bronxville School," who flourished nearby in the early twentieth century.

Bolton Gardens (Pondfield Rd., across from Bronxville High School, Bronxville). Although the predominant building pattern in Bronxville in the early 1900's was the lavish single-family dwelling, garden-apartment complexes were built as early as 1914, influenced to some degree by forward-thinking German and English planning schemes.

Bolton Gardens, well adapted to its quiet cul-de-sac, is one of these developments. It is a sympathetic grouping of four- and six-unit dwellings, surfaced in stucco, with exposed wood framing. Among the period details are flaring eaves and a slate roof.

Bronxville Railroad Station. The nearby Hotel Gramatan (demolished) set the tone for this railroad station built in the pre–World War I period. Both were built in Mission style. The window grille is fine metalwork. The caduceus-and-helmet motif above the window symbolizes the swiftness of Mercury.

Lawrence Park, Bronxville

Behind Bronxville Railroad Station; streets include Valley Rd., Wellington Circle, Prescott, Sunset, and Tanglewylde aves., and Paradise Rd.

"Exhibition catalogues now bear Bronxville addresses so frequently that it may not be long before the cities sit up, take notice and gravely note the existence of a 'Bronxville school,' in much the same manner as the 'Barbizon school' is referred to," wrote Will H. Low, a noted muralist, in 1912. The artists and writers of the "Bronxville School," including Low himself, lived mostly in Lawrence Park, a remarkable architectural achievement as well as an art colony.

William Van Duzer Lawrence bought some 80 acres of farmland for development here in 1890; and many future residents boarded in the Italianate manor house (8 Prescott Ave.) while their homes were being built. William Bates, a prominent architect of the Shingle Style, designed many of the homes built in the first decade of the development, and his romantically massed wood-and-stone dwellings were a decisive influence on later building. One of the surviving Bates houses is the former home of Will H. Low at 25 Prescott Ave.

The dramatic siting of many Lawrence Park homes is remarkable. Narrow streets, some still paved with cobblestones or brick, wind among the rocky eminences. Dwellings seem to grow out of the rock they are built on. Rough-cut stones, used in foundations, appear again in rounded towers, in great chimney stacks, and on parapets.

Dark shingled surfaces define the flowing masses of these ample homes, breached by ribbon windows, loggias, or arched openings. Scattered through Lawrence Park are later period-revival and modern homes; their crisp elegance enhances the romantic moodiness of the earlier dwellings.

Bronx River Parkway

At the turn of the century, the Bronx River from White Plains to the Bronx was an open sewer. Westchester residents were joined in agitating for pollution control by the New York Zoological and Botanical societies, which foresaw the danger to the wildlife and plants in their Bronx Park headquarters. After considerable effort, enough property was acquired (by purchase and condemnation) to protect the river. A sewer system was completed in 1911; the Bronx River Pkwy. system in 1924. New York City paid three-quarters of the cost.

In creating the scenic parkway, considerable care was taken to follow natural contours; five miles of river channel were relocated and deepened where curves were too dangerous. Elaborate landscaping created shady dells and beautified natural ponds.

Architecturally, no effort was spared. The undercrossing at Tuckahoe Rd. and the bridge over Scarsdale Lake were designed by the prestigious New York firm of Delano & Aldrich. Among the thirty-seven stone-faced bridges of the parkway system, designed by a number of architects, were the first ones to be built of reinforced-concrete arches.

In a salute to the tastes of the motoring public, four service stations were designed by Penrose V. Stout, a "society" architect of the 1920's.

Sarah Lawrence College

Kimball Ave., Bronxville; main entrance at Glen Washington

William Van Duzer Lawrence and his wife Sarah were strong advocates of liberal education for women; and when in 1928 Lawrence founded a women's college in memory of his wife, their home, Westlands, became its nucleus. Westlands, an expansive Jacobean Revival mansion which had been designed by Bates & How in 1915, is now the Administration Building.

Among the other period mansions acquired by the college, the most extraordinary is the President's House (935 Kimball Ave.), designed in 1921 by Lewis Bowman. Details are Tudor in inspiration, but the conception is fresh. Impeccable workmanship is evident throughout.

A new library, designed by Warner Burns Toan Lunde, and dormitories following a "townhouse" scheme are sensitively integrated into the surrounding campus and residential structures.

President's House,
Sarah Lawrence College

Asbury Methodist Episcopal Church

(Underhill St. and Scarsdale Rd., Yonkers). Built in 1834, this charming, small-scaled rectangular structure is constructed of Tuckahoe marble. A stepped parapet embellishes the gable end, surmounted by a wooden belfry.

Westchester Historical Society (43

Read Ave., Tuckahoe; across Bronx River Pkwy. from Asbury Methodist Church). A fine collection of historical materials is housed in this Tudor Revival dwelling. Open Tues. and Sat., 2–5 p.m. Phone: (914) DE7–1753.

U.S. Vitamin Factory and Old Mill

(Main St., Tuckahoe). Around 1800 a three-story stone mill was built on the east bank of the Bronx River, one of the first cotton mills in the area. It still stands, tucked away almost out of sight behind U.S. Vitamin's Parking Area B, in the midst of a later industrial development.

The complex was considerably enlarged in 1906 by the creation of a striking group of six-story concrete-and-glass block structures, whose simple geometric forms still appear remarkably modern.

Scarsdale Railroad Station and shopping area (Popham and Crane rds.). The

Scarsdale station was designed in 1904 by the experienced firm of Reed & Stem. The style reflects the inspiration of the cottages of rural England. Although the garb is rustic, the building material—reinforced concrete—was decidedly modern in its day. The Tudor theme was extended to the adjacent shopping center and to the service station on Popham Rd., architect-designed in 1935.

Wayside Cottage

1039 White Plains Post Rd. (Rte. 22), Scarsdale
OPEN: By appointment
PHONE: (914) SC3–6130

A milestone just south of Wayside Lane reads "XXI miles to N. York 1771." Wayside Cottage had probably been built fifty years earlier (the name dates from the 1860's), when Eastchester Rd. was cleared.

James and Michael Varian, descendants of Huguenot settlers, lived in the cottage during the Revolution. They were plagued by the marauding "cowboys" who stole cattle to supply British troops and so they moved to the safety of Connecticut for the duration of the war.

James Varian's son Jonathan became a cattle drover and offered hospitality at the house to his colleagues heading south to market with their herds of cattle. But it was his brother, James, Jr., who obtained a license to keep an inn or tavern in 1828. The house remained in the Varian family until 1853.

Wayside Cottage

The historical and architectural value of Wayside Cottage was recognized early. In 1919 a member of the Butler family, the last owners, donated it to the Village of Scarsdale "for the purpose of creating an historical park . . . and for the purpose of fostering a general public and democratic spirit in the community." It was used by the Scarsdale Suffrage League (later the Scarsdale Women's Club), was the first home of the Scarsdale Public Library, and is now a community center, with fine period furnishings, maintained by the Junior League.

During its three centuries many changes have been made on the simple one-and-a-half-story cottage. Restorations have been undertaken on the interior.

Old Army Road , Scarsdale (east of Central Park Ave. [Rte. 100]). Away from the hectic shopping pace of Central Park Ave. (developed in 1867 by Boss Tweed as a new route to Albany and a new source of patronage) is a quiet street with several homes from the eighteenth and early nineteenth centuries. Its modern name, Old Army Rd., was chosen to commemorate its Revolutionary past.

The Hunt–Morris–Smith House (221 Old Army Rd.) dates from the mid-eighteenth century, when Israel Hunt, a tenant of Col. Frederick Philipse of Philipsburg Manor, built the earliest section. His son Joshua joined the British Army as a guide; and after the war, the tenant's property, like the landlord's, was confiscated. Richard Morris, brother of a signer of the Declaration of Independence and second chief justice of New York State, bought the Hunt house and later gave it to his son Robert. A small fieldstone building on the property is similar to known slave quarters and was probably used for that purpose.

Cotswold section, Scarsdale (Cotswold Way, off Ardsley Rd., east of Central Park Ave.). The charm of rural England was the model for the developers of this suburban area in 1925. They chose English street names, and used *Old English Cottages and Farmhouses in the Cotswold District* by W. Galsworthy Davie and E. Guy Dawher as their building manual for the Tudor-style dwellings. And as a final flourish, they named the entire section Cotswold—"Cots" meaning "buildings," and "wold" a "high meadow surrounded by woods." Forty-five houses were built in this manner, but, in line with the latest practice, all with attached garages.

Cotswold section, Scarsdale

Hartsdale Railroad Station (E. Hartsdale Ave.). Warren & Wetmore, who also collaborated on Grand Central Terminal in New York City, designed the Hartsdale station in 1915. Skillful handling of details—a spirited flare at the eaves, decorative scrolls marking the ridge of the roof, and a pleasant variety of materials—creates a fine effect.

Odell House

425 Ridge Rd. (Rte. 100A), Hartsdale

Odell House is a relic of the rustic past, but it is no stranger to elegance. In the summer of 1781 it was the center of the camp of the smartly attired French expeditionary forces and their aristocratic leaders.

In this house two great military leaders—Washington and Rochambeau—consulted during the summer months on the defeat of their joint enemy, Cornwallis, at Yorktown. This collaborative effort—in which the French committed not only their forces but also funds to help the virtually bankrupt Continental Army—was a turning point in the Revolution.

The house in which they met was at the time a simple one-story, cedar-shingled farmhouse, without even a basement, originally built in 1732 as a tenant farmhouse on Philipsburg Manor.

After the Revolution, the farmhouse and surrounding lands were acquired by John Odell, who had reached the rank of lieutenant in the Westchester Guides. He had served as the principal guide to George Washington and the Continental Army during their advance through the Saw Mill River valley in July 1781.

Subsequent generations of the Odell family enlarged the house, leaving a clear and honest record of change. Another wing joined the original east section, which was raised up over a new lower story in 1785; in the mid-nineteenth century a stone ell was added on the west. The Odells were the only family to inhabit the house; in 1965 a surviving member bequeathed it to the Sons of the American Revolution.

The dwelling exemplifies early American building technology. The walls are clay-and-hair daub, in almost original condition. The plank-and-beam construction over a dry-wall foundation is ingeniously secured by pegs.

Plans are under way for restoration of the house.

Greenburgh Housing Authority Low-Income Housing Project

Maple, Oak, and Beech sts., off Hillside Ave. (Rte. 100), north of Rte. 119

The awareness that abject slums exist in affluent suburban areas came to Greenburgh in the late 1950's when a compassionate teacher found that the reason for a pupil's poor performance was the lack of decent housing. The publicity that followed resulted in a remarkably rapid and rare instance of cooperation across racial and economic lines.

This distinguished low-income housing project proves that, in this case at least, clichés can be effective. Split-level and salt-box in profile, the grouped townhouses are reassuringly "homey" to the 131 families and elderly people who live

Greenburgh Housing Authority townhouses

there. Ten residential structures, each containing from six to fifteen units, are sensibly sited to provide urbanistic order. Courts, paths, and sitting areas are well scaled for the inhabitants' use—only the fences are a jarring note. The project, built with state funds, was the design of architect Louis Gardner, and was completed in 1961.

Westchester County Center (Rte. 119, at Central Park Ave., Exit 22 of Bronx River Pkwy., White Plains). Massive forms, starkly simplified, link the design of this reinforced-concrete sports and cultural center to the aesthetic of its period—1930. Gillette & Walker were the architects.

Berkeley School (W. Red Oak Lane, off Cross Westchester Expressway, adjacent

to Hitachi Headquarters, White Plains). The sprightly forms of the Berkeley School are a pleasant relief from the corporate behemoths that squat along both sides of the Cross Westchester Expressway. The two- and three-story complex, built of brick and concrete, welcomes the visitor by a driveway that passes under an enclosed bridge linking structures on both sides. Window bays, angled at the corner, gaily press forward to break the continuity of the wall. The complex was designed by Tasso Katzeles in 1969.

Saks Fifth Avenue (Maple Ave., Exit 8E of Cross Westchester Expressway, White Plains). Among the earliest of the postwar suburban branches of Fifth Avenue stores, Saks was designed by Kahn & Jacobs in 1952. As originally built, the structure was distinguished by judicious handling of mass and careful attention to detail. There have been several additions.

Jacob Purdy House

Park Ave. and Kirby Terrace,
off Ferris Ave., White Plains

For generations local historians have debated the location of Washington's headquarters in the Battle of White Plains in 1776, and later in 1778. In the 1920's the Elijah Miller House in North White Plains had been "saved" and declared to be the true and only headquarters; but old maps seemed to point to the Jacob Purdy House.

The debate has finally been settled. The clinching testimony was found in the Library of Congress by a White Plains lawyer, Stephen Holden, Jr., and concerns a report written by Ann Bates, a spy, in 1778 to her British superiors. She wrote:

"Washingtons Quarters are in Mrs. Purdies house to the left of the lines," verifying the previous report of her male partner. She placed Gen. Gates's troops "about 3 miles in the rear of Washington, upon a Hill that looks like a Hat," a location later pinned down by another British agent as "at Widow Millars at the head of White Plains."

The Purdy House had been built in 1721 on a farm of 132 acres on what then was known as Dobbs Ferry Rd. By the 1950's it had become a slum dwelling in the middle of an area slated for urban renewal. The Battle of White Plains Committee mounted a campaign to save it, and bought the house in 1960. It was moved by the White Plains urban-renewal agency in 1973 to a hilltop, part of the original Purdy lands, where it is now being restored.

Alumnae House, College of White Plains

Alumnae House, College of White Plains (78 N. Broadway [Rte. 22]).

Mapleton—a fine Italianate dwelling in an excellent state of preservation—was built in 1867 by William Dusenbury, a carriage manufacturer, and was taken over in 1884 by Nathan Hand, who made his fortune in Georgia gold. Ten years later it was sold to a religious order for use as a convent, and later it became a college building.

Also on the spacious campus is a gabled chapel built of cobblestone in 1895. Another example of this mode, popular at the time, is found nearby in the Chatterton Hill Congregational Church on Chatterton Ave.

Westchester Courthouse (Main St. [Rte. 119], White Plains).

The old courthouse is actually a complex built through the span of several generations. The oldest section, an Italianate granite courtroom of the 1850's, is visible only from the rear. Compare the rich complexity of these structures to the new twenty-story courthouse tower which looms over them.

New York Telephone Company (Main St., White Plains).

Dominating "renewed" White Plains, this dark gray aluminum-and-concrete building was designed by Haines Lundburg & Waehler. A previous structure was ingested by the new one.

Grace Church (33 Church St., off Main St., White Plains).

To the sober Gothic Revival church, built in 1864 of locally quarried fieldstone, architect Edgar Tafel has added a dignified modern Parish Hall. The addition, of the same local stone, was designed in 1967.

White Plains Rural Cemetery Office (N. Broadway).

Buildings, no less than species, survive by adapting. This one, for example, was originally built in 1795 as the First Methodist Church of White Plains. The congregation moved in 1882 to a new church in the center of White Plains, but the cemetery was permanent. The old church—a gabled and shingled

White Plains Rural Cemetery Office

structure without a tower—became the cemetery caretaker's residence in 1902.

Elijah Miller House ("Washington's Headquarters")

Virginia Rd., off Rte. 22,
North White Plains
OPEN: Wed., Thurs., Fri., 10 a.m.–
        4 p.m.; Sat., Sun., 1–4 p.m.
        Closed Dec. 15–mid-Feb.
PHONE: (914) 949–1236

"George Washington did not sleep in this bed," a sign on a fourposter warns. Neither, as it turns out, was this house his headquarters in the Battle of White Plains in 1776 and in 1778, as has been advertised for many years. That honor belongs to the Jacob Purdy House in White Plains. However, Gen. Gates, also a stalwart patriot, did stay here during that crucial period, so the historical interest is little diminished.

Mrs. Anne Miller, whose husband, Elijah, had been killed in the recent fighting, was Gen. Gates's hostess. The house had been built by the Miller family in 1738,

with an addition in 1770. With its wide front porch and steeply slanting roof, it would look like a typical Dutch Colonial farmhouse were it surrounded by 600 acres of farmland rather than by its present-day industrial and commercial neighbors.

The house, which is maintained by the Westchester County Department of Parks, Recreation and Conservation, is furnished with exhibits, mannequins attired in period clothing, and other memorabilia of the Revolution.

Kensico Dam and Plaza

Bronx River Pkwy., Exit 27, Valhalla

A large part of the landscape of upper Westchester and Putnam counties has been shaped by New York City's seemingly insatiable thirst for water. The Kensico Dam and Reservoir, built between 1910 and 1917 at a total cost of $158 million, was one of the most monumental construction projects of the water-supply system.

In 1905 the New York Board of Water Supply chose Kensico, where a low earth-and-masonry dam had already been built in 1885, as the site for a large storage reservoir. Kensico was well suited topographically for a new dam; it was near enough to the city to lay pipes economically, and the expense of relocating highways and buildings in this still sparsely settled area was minimal. Some of the residents resisted the condemnation of their land to the bitter end; others accepted their fate with resignation; a canny few diligently repaired and maintained their property, disregarding the impending flood, and were rewarded by higher appraisal values.

To build the 1,825-foot-long dam, the engineers blasted down to bedrock for the foundations. The visible part of the structure is only a third of its actual height. Large slabs of undressed stone were used as the basic building material, the structure is faced with smooth masonry quarried about a mile from the dam. An imposing entablature, including a carved frieze, tops the whole length of the dam.

Kensico Dam Plaza, a parklike area at the base, was part of the original landscaping program that created a public recreation area. The plaza is now maintained by the Westchester County Department of Parks, Recreation and Conservation, and is used in the summer for outdoor concerts.

Valhalla Station Restaurant (Rte. 100 and Bronx River Pkwy.). Old railroad stations make good antiques shops and—as in this case—pleasant restaurants.

Kensico Cemetery (Grasslands Rd. [Rte. 100], opposite Westchester Community College, Valhalla). Cemeteries are among the few places where the 1930's modernism can be viewed without the distractions of later modifications. The aggressively huge tower, commanding entrance gates, and simplified planes of gravestones and mausoleums are parts of a total conceptual scheme.

American Can Company Corporate Headquarters (American Lane, between Rtes. 120 and 684, North Greenwich). A triangular piece of land straddling the New York–Connecticut border is the site chosen by American Can Company for its corporate headquarters. The award-

winning building designed by Skidmore, Owings & Merrill for the 183-acre site was completed in 1970. The long, sweeping, three-story building bridges a deep ravine, above a two-acre man-made lake. The ravine provides room for six additional levels, five of them used for underground parking.

Bedford Road, Armonk (off Rte. 128, east of Rte. 22). Parking is not permitted on this short street, so its charm can be absorbed with ease. The Methodist Church at the western end adds a fresh Stick-style touch, but the north side of the street is best—a charming assemblage of early-nineteenth-century homes. On the eastern corner is St. Stephen's Church, a Greek Revival structure dating from 1842, perfectly in scale with its neighbors.

Bedford Road, Armonk

Octagon House (Round House Rd., off Banksville Rd., Banksville). One of two in Westchester, this clapboard octagonal house dates from 1849. A central chimney rises through a cupola atop the three-and-a-half-story structure. A porch wraps itself around the main floor.

Usonia

Usonia Rd. and nearby streets, off
Nanny Hagen Rd., west of Rte. 120,
Pleasantville. Just north of Kensico
Reservoir

"In the organic city of tomorrow ground
space will be reckoned by the acre,"
prophesied Frank Lloyd Wright. "On the
basis of an acre to each man, woman, and
child, architecture would come into the
service of man himself as a natural feature
of his life."

Usonia is one of the few places where
Wright's eloquent but uneconomical
dream was actually attempted. He drew
the site plan of this extraordinary development for what he called the "Uso-
nian" (U.S.-onian, or average American)
family in 1948, and David Henken, his
apprentice, carried out the rest of the work
in sympathy with his master's precepts.

Most of the houses follow the spirit of
Wright's architecture by using natural
stone, unpainted wood, and free-flowing
spaces. Wright designed three houses
himself, including one on Laurel Hill Rd. It

House at Usonia

consists of two intersecting circles, one for
service, the other for living. The brilliance
and spirit of the design are matched by the
finesse of its execution and—Wright's
special genius—the successful integration
of the dwelling into its environment.

King Street, Chappaqua (Rte. 120).
Fine old buildings have found new uses
on King St.—as flower shop, boutique,
real-estate office—proving that preservation can make good business sense.
Among these, the gift shop at 100 King St.
was Horace Greeley's "House by the
Main Road."

Quaker Meeting House

Quaker Rd., west of Saw Mill River
Pkwy., Exit 32, Chappaqua

New York was, from Colonial times, more
hospitable to religious diversity than many
of its neighbors. Groups of Quakers
moved from Long Island to the Sound area
of Westchester in the 1700's; in 1730 a
group moved inland to Chappaqua. At
first they held meetings in a home; then a
settler gave them land for a meeting house
and burial ground.

The meeting house, built in 1753 and
still in use, served a humanitarian purpose
in the Revolution when Gen. Washington
quartered some of the wounded of the
Battle of White Plains there.

Recently restored, the unadorned forms
of the building are a natural expression of
the simplicity of Quaker religious practice. The wood frame structure, with a
steeply pitched roof, is almost domestic in
scale.

Dwellings all along Quaker Rd. recall
the ambiance of the early Quaker settle-

Quaker Meeting House, Chappaqua

ment. In spite of much alteration, they reflect, in their site, scale, and proportion, Quaker values and life style.

The Thomas Dodge House (428 Quaker Rd.) was built in the eighteenth century and belonged to a prominent Quaker who was a farmer, cabinetmaker, caretaker of the burial ground, and the original author of the *Book of Deaths*, which listed the birth and death dates of 2,300 Westchester residents, mainly Quakers.

Rehoboth (Horace Greeley Barn)

33 Aldridge Rd., off King St., Chappaqua

"I should have been a farmer," wrote Horace Greeley in his autobiography. "All my riper tastes incline to that blessed calling. . . . Its quiet, its segregation from strife, and brawls, and heated rivalries, attract and delight me." As an outspoken opponent of slavery, editor of the *New York Tribune*, and candidate for President against Ulysses S. Grant in 1872, Greeley knew well the "strife" and "heated rivalries" of the mid-nineteenth century. But

he also had a chance to sample the "blessed calling" in Chappaqua.

Greeley began to purchase land in 1852, increasing his holdings parcel by parcel until he owned 78 acres. Here he built the isolated "House in the Woods," to which the notables of the day journeyed. It later burned down.

Greeley also designed and built "The Old Stone Barn" in 1865. He wrote later: "Building with concrete was a novelty when I built my barn. I calculate this barn will be abidingly useful long after I have been utterly forgotten and that had I chosen to have my name lettered on its front it would have remained there to honor me as a builder after my name had ceased to have any other signature."

Horace Greeley Barn in 1872

Temple Beth El of Northern Westchester

220 Bedford Rd. (Rte. 117), Chappaqua

Clerestory windows light the central space of this extraordinary synagogue designed by Louis Kahn in 1972. Two levels afford entry to the octagonal-shaped structure.

49

*Temple Beth El of Northern Westchester,
Chappaqua*

On the upper level, a poured-concrete portico serves as the formal entry. Below, gaps in the façade welcome children attending religious instruction classes.

Great concrete beams articulate the structure. The walls are simple planks, and expanses of glass reflect the wooded setting.

Reader's Digest

Roaring Brook Rd., Exit 33 of Saw Mill
River Pkwy., Pleasantville
OPEN: Mon.–Fri., 10 a.m.–3 p.m., for
    guided tour of art collection
PHONE: (914) 769–7000

An international publishing empire built on an unequaled ability to discern the tastes of the average reader has its headquarters, almost symbolically, in Pleasantville. The Georgian-style campus plan was designed in 1939 by William McKenzie to house the expanding company started by DeWitt and Lila Acheson Wallace, which moved to Pleasantville in 1923. A collection of about twenty paintings—mainly French Impressionist —is open to the public.

Main Street, Mount Kisco. Shingle and clapboard houses, their ample porches shaded by trees and shrubs, line the streets north of Main St. between the railroad station and the Saw Mill River Pkwy. (Hillside Ave., Prospect St., Willets Rd.); 83 Hillside Ave., with crisp carpenter trim on jerkin-head gables, is characteristic of the many fine buildings of the 1860's to 1890's.

St. Mark's Episcopal Church (Main St. and Bedford Rd., Mount Kisco). This is not the simple English country church it pretends to be. Its true age is revealed by its affinities to the sophisticated simplicity of the early twentieth century. The church itself was designed in 1909 by Cram, Goodhue & Ferguson. Goodhue added the tower and vestibule in 1919. Limestone trim and window surrounds make an elegant foil to the coursed fieldstone. The interior is exquisitely furnished. An elaborately carved choir screen is set off by the smoothness of the walls.

St. Mark's Episcopal Church, Mount Kisco

United Methodist Church, Mount Kisco

United Methodist Church (300 Main St., at Smith Ave., Mount Kisco). Alterations and additions have not destroyed the expressive quality of this asymmetrical Stick-style church. The more massive of its two towers is square, crowned by a belfry and tall spire whose overhang is supported by exposed wooden ribs.

Fox Lane Middle School

Rte. 172, east of intersection with
Rte. 684, Town of Bedford

Set in a wooded area on sharply rising rock ledges, the Fox Lane Middle School building plan grew out of the educational program. Three schools-within-a-school are located in separate academic "houses," which are grouped around a three-story octagonal central-facilities

building. Interior spaces easily adaptable to a variety of uses meet the needs of the 11–14-year-old pupils. The school is the imaginative design of The Architects Collaborative and was completed in 1966.

Bedford Village Green

Rte. 22
*OPEN: Bedford Court House and
Museum, and Schoolhouse:
Wed.–Sun., 2–5 p.m.
PHONE: (914) 234–9328

Until 1870 Bedford and White Plains were both county seats, alternating each year as the site of county court sessions. But the New York & Harlem Railroad made White Plains a bustling commercial and governmental center, and left Bedford a quiet country village with only a milk train to carry its dairy products to market.

This is no whistle stop, however, but the very model of exurban exclusivity. Its nineteenth-century atmosphere is carefully nurtured, even though heavily trafficked Rte. 22 disturbs its peace and a "Colonial" shopping center threatens its integrity.

Land usage in Bedford, unlike most of Westchester, developed along the typical New England town plan. In 1680 the twenty-two original settlers from Stamford divided up the 7,000 acres of their purchase from the Indians into more or less equal shares according to the European tradition of three-field crop rotation. In a forerunner of modern zoning practice, the group determined that "no man's house lot shall be less than three acres." The house lots were clustered together for safety. Three acres were set aside as a

Court House, Bedford.

"common," where the cattle, branded to identify their owners, were pastured.

Around the commons, or the Bedford Green, as it is called, and the historic roads which lead to it, are public and private buildings, which, though of different periods and architectural styles, combine to create a strong sense of Bedford's history.

The oldest building is the Bedford Court House and Museum. Built in 1787, it has been extensively restored to its early-nineteenth-century appearance. It is a two-story building with a gambrel roof, a columned portico, and a belfry atop. The first floor contains a courtroom restored to the period when William Jay, son of John Jay, presided on the bench. Aaron Burr, later vice president, argued cases here, and his portrait hangs on the wall, along with those of Jay and other attorneys. Upstairs are two old jail cells and the Bedford Museum, which contains exhibits of 300 years of local history.

The Bedford Free Library, built in 1807, was originally the Bedford Academy, and its pupils included John Jay II, grandson of John Jay, and William Vanderbilt.

The Post Office, built in 1838, was moved from its original site on Pound Ridge Rd. to its present location in the 1890's. An amusing counterpart is its twice-as-large next-door neighbor, built as an A&P in 1906.

The verticality of the Bedford Presbyterian Church, built in 1872, shows the Gothic trend of that time. Board-and-batten siding emphasizes the soaring lines; fanciful wood moldings enrich the façade; the towers rise steeply, but unevenly, into the sky.

A tiny, stone one-room schoolhouse, which was Bedford's public school from 1829 until 1912, is now restored and open as a museum of the history of education in Bedford. It is on the south side of the Green.

On the north side is the Old Burying Ground, in use as early as 1681. A good view of the Green and the bordering buildings rewards those who climb to the top of the hill.

Historical Hall, next to the Old Burying Ground, was at the time of its construction in 1806 a Methodist church. It is now the headquarters of the Bedford Historical Society.

St. Matthew's Episcopal Church (Rte. 22, north of Bedford Village). John Jay, Founding Father, was also a pillar of the Bedford community when he built his retirement home there. He was instrumental in the founding of nearby St. Matthew's, advancing the purchase money for the land to the congregation. Until this church was built in 1810, the common form of worship was Congregational, reflecting Puritan origins. The structure is delicately scaled, with fine detailing; it is built of brick painted to resemble stone, according to the tastes of the Federal period. The steeple and belfry were rebuilt in the 1880's, and in 1914 the porch was extended to include the whole tower.

John Jay Homestead (Bedford House)

Jay St. (Rte. 22), Katonah
OPEN: Daily, except Mon. and Tues.,
   9 a.m.–5 p.m.
PHONE: (914) 232–5651

Even for John Jay—president of the Second Continental Congress, minister to Spain, first chief justice of the United States, and governor of New York—it was no easy task to get a house built in the country. In May 1801, in a letter to his wife, Sally, he complained that work on their long-awaited retirement home in Bedford "proceeds with a far slower pace than in the cities. In the latter materials are purchased on the spot in a state of preparation and nothing is to be done but to put them together. In the country the stones are to be broken, the bricks and lime to be burnt, the timber to be felled and hewed and everything to be drawn from a distance. Besides workmen are scarce, sensible of their own importance, extortionate, and lazy."

Nevertheless, Bedford House—en-larged from an existing farmhouse—was completed in the summer of 1801. Jay planned the addition himself, after some consultation with the more experienced Thomas Jefferson. Sally Jay died the following year, but John Jay lived in the house with his children and grandchildren until his death in 1829, at the age of eighty-three.

The house, set well back from the road overlooking a broad expanse of land, is a two-and-a-half-story rectangular clapboard structure with five bays and side wings. A stone ell was added in 1924 as a fireproof repository for the family collection of American paintings by Gilbert Stuart, John Trumbull, and others. Also on the property is a two-story brick cottage, originally designed by Jay for his farm superintendent. Jay and his daughter stayed in this cottage while supervising construction on the main house. Two stone barns still stand as well.

Members of the Jay family occupied the homestead until 1954; the property is now maintained by the New York State Division for Historic Preservation. Many furnishings from the family collections fill the interior.

Residence of the Hon John Jay.

Caramoor

Rte. 137, off Rte. 22, between
Bedford Village and Katonah
*OPEN: By appointment only,
        Tues.–Sat., April–Nov., and in
        certain periods during winter
        months
PHONE: (914) CE2–4206 for tour
        reservations and information
        about Caramoor Summer Music
        Festival

The eighteenth-century Swiss wrought-iron entrance gates, flanked by pylons supporting Pegasus heads sculpted by twentieth-century artist Malvina Hoffman, announce that Caramoor is a highly personal creation. It reflects the individual tastes of one man—the late Walter T. Rosen, banker, lawyer, international financier, and passionate collector. He built Caramoor in 1928 as a house–museum in a garden setting to form a "compatible background" for the art and antiques he had collected in Europe. Rosen's exquisite collection of paintings, furnishings, sculpture, and art objects, including many fine Italian and Oriental pieces, is displayed in a series of spectacular period rooms and galleries.

The Walter and Lucie Rosen Foundation, which maintains Caramoor as a "center of music and art," presents outdoor chamber music and opera performances in a large Venetian theater and the more intimate Spanish courtyard. The house, however, is not open to visitors during the music festival.

Bedford Road (Rte. 117), Katonah

The alternatives facing Katonah in 1894, as the secretary of the Village Improvement Society put it, were "No Katonah" or "New Katonah." The crisis was precipitated by the New York City Board of Water Supply's decision to flood the area to create a reservoir of Croton Lake.

The decision was made in favor of "New Katonah." Part of the plan involved moving houses to the new area—a task that meant lifting each house from its foundations by jacks and towing it along a set of timber tracks lubricated with yellow laundry soap. Horses pulled the buildings along the tracks, which were picked up behind the buildings and laid down ahead to make a new section of runway. While this laborious procedure was under way, life went on as usual. Families lived in transit; children went to school in the morning to find their homes in a different spot each day when they returned.

Another part of the plan was the creation of a new and more beautiful village center, envisioned this way: "On the map the street is laid out 100 feet in width. The intention is to have a center strip devoted to flowers, and a wagon path on either side. Paved and curbed gutters, flagging for the sidewalks, and rows of trees are to be among the other improvements."

Bedford Rd. still has that turn-of-the-century expansiveness, enhanced by buildings of the period. The Methodist Episcopal Church is a cobblestone structure of imposing proportions. Its square tower has an open belfry. The rectory is an outstanding example of the Queen Anne style of the late nineteenth century.

The First Church of Christ, Scientist (13

Bedford Rd. at the corner of The Parkway) was originally the residence of William Henry Robertson, a leading Gilded Age Republican. One of his prize political plums was the post of collector of the Port of New York, to which he was appointed by President Garfield.

Robertson's residence in Katonah befitted his stature. A large and imaginatively massed example of the Shingle Style, it is now painted white and thus robbed of its appropriately somber quality.

The newer buildings fit in comfortably. The Katonah Library (Bedford Rd. and The Parkway) is a well-proportioned, finely detailed Georgian Revival structure, ingeniously adapted to its corner location by the architect, Kerr Rainsford. It was built in 1930 of fieldstone, with brick quoins and a semicircular wooden portico.

The Katonah Gallery, at the rear of the library, uses the same building material—fieldstone—and a restrained contemporary design, both to set off the library to good advantage and to make a forthright statement of its own. The gallery is small, but the frequently changing exhibits are presented with rare taste. Phone: (914) 232-4988.

Thomas J. Watson Research Center, IBM

Rte. 134, east of Taconic Pkwy., Yorktown

This huge three-level building, designed by Eero Saarinen, is in the form of an expansive smoked-glass arc. Opened in 1961, it can house 1,500 employees. The extraordinarily powerful and yet subtle modulation of forms is a sure mark of a master. At the rear of the 240-acre land-

Watson Research Center, IBM

scaped site are intimate Japanese gardens, surrounding a chipped-marble lagoon. The parking areas, out of sight from the sunken gardens, are connected to the structure by ramps.

Wiltwyck School for Boys

Illington Rd., off Rte. 134, Yorktown

Architect Richard Stein designed for the Wiltwyck School a facility that encourages comfortable patterns of living and working for the emotionally troubled urban boys who reside on the campus.

The concrete-framed central facilities are boldly massed and assertive, imposing a sense of discipline without rigidity. One-story brick dormitories, more intimate in scale, are set apart on the hilly, wooded site.

The new campus was completed in 1967, but the school had been founded in 1939. Claude Brown, an alumnus, dedicated his book *Manchild in the Promised Land* "To the late Eleanor Roosevelt, who founded the Wiltwyck School for Boys, and to the Wiltwyck School which is still finding Claude Browns."

Town of Yorktown Museum (1886 Hanover Ave., Yorktown Heights). Changing exhibits of local interest are displayed in this mid-nineteenth-century house, along with a permanent collection of dolls and dollhouses. The museum is open Tues.–Thurs., Sun., 2–4:30 p.m. Phone: (914) 962–2970 or 962–7282.

Christal Farms (Hanover Ave., Yorktown Heights). Before the recent housing boom in Yorktown, the area was primarily rural. This quality still exists on the outskirts of town. One example is Christal Farms, where Morgan horses and Guernsey cows are raised.

Davenport House (Croton Heights Rd., off Hanover Ave., Yorktown Heights). Built about 1750, Davenport House was a command post held by Washington's troops throughout the Revolution. In 1781, it was the site of a skirmish between the American regulars, commanded by Col. Greene, and a party of 200 "cowboys," American guerrillas loyal to the British. Greene and 20 of his men were killed in what has been considered an unjustified attack, since Greene had agreed to surrender. Historians now believe, however, that someone within the house fired a shot, accidentally or impetuously, setting off the barrage. Some of the victims are buried in the Yorktown Burying Ground.

Davenport House is currently being restored by the Westchester County Historical Society.

Peter Pratt Inn (across from Davenport House on Croton Heights Rd., Yorktown Heights). The central portion of this inn, formerly a below-grade barn, was built about the same time as Davenport House. The rest of the building was added in the 1850's.

Gilbert Beaver Conference Farm (Rte. 118 and Underhill Ave. [Rte. 131], Yorktown Heights). Edward Underhill's 1881 remodeling transformed a modest eighteenth-century farmhouse into an elaborate Victorian status symbol. He added a two-story section and built a new barn. Iron urns were set upon cut-stone gateposts. Scrollwork and a tower were other flourishes.

A large number of the outbuildings of this once-prosperous farm still remain to document a vanishing mode of living. The house itself is now used for religious retreats.

Somers Town Hall (Elephant Hotel)

Intersection of Rtes. 100 and 202

The Elephant Hotel has a ponderous name that belies the grace and elegance of its construction. It was built about 1825 by Hachaliah Bailey and named to commemorate Old Bet, an African elephant he had purchased in 1815 and launched on a tour of the countryside.

Menageries were an early form of American entertainment. Even before the Revolution, as part of a quasi-scientific curiosity, small collections of lions, camels, leopards, and other animals were exhibited in cities. But Bailey, a shrewd entrepreneur, was the first to include an elephant—an animal that captured the public fancy—and the first to organize a

Beaver Conference Farm

"rolling" show that went from town to town. Furthermore, he had a talent for publicity.

His business acumen was also applied to other areas. Bailey built a hotel at the junction of two main toll roads, which was a stagecoach stop on the New York, Danbury, and Boston line. Cattle drovers stopped here, as well as notable social and political figures, such as Martin Van

Buren, Aaron Burr, Horace Greeley, and Washington Irving. The hotel also housed the Farmers' and Drovers' Bank, which Bailey founded in 1839. The hotel was a commercial success until the advent of the railroad in the 1840's.

The building was purchased in 1927 from the Bailey family by the Town of Somers and now serves as the Town Hall. As headquarters of the Somers Historical Society, it also contains historical collections and a museum dedicated to circus history; open Fri., 2–4 p.m.; Sat., 10 a.m.– noon; and by appointment. Phone: (914) 277–4977.

Its past was flamboyant, but its styling is conservative, with fine brickwork and crisply cut granite trim. The low, hipped roof is marked by a chimney stack at each end. At the third-floor level, a half-round window encloses pointed arches.

Facing the hotel is a replica of the elephant statue that Bailey had constructed in 1827 to memorialize Old Bet. The great beast herself had been shot by an angry farmer.

St. Luke's Episcopal Church (Rte. 100, Somers). This Greek Revival church, built in 1842, is one of the two monumen-

Elephant Hotel

St. Luke's Episcopal Church, Somers

57

tal structures (the other is the Elephant Hotel) that are the focus of the intimately scaled main street of Somers, popularly known as "100."

Stone House (Rte. 100, north of Somers). This two-and-a-half-story cut-stone mansion of the prosperous farmer and circus entrepreneur Gerard Crane was built in 1849. It was distinguished by the use of the finest workmanship and materials. Even the privy was granite!

Croton Falls Baptist Church (Rte. 22). The fantasy of this Stick-style church soars above a placid street lined with small wooden cottages. Built in 1872, it is a high point of American carpenter-Gothic design. Wooden members are pierced, carved, punched, and cut in a remarkable display of woodworking virtuosity.

Main Street, Purdy's

Rte. 22, at Rte. 116

In the 1840's Isaac Hart Purdy offered part of his large farmland to the New York & Harlem Railroad to build a new station at the end of the line. The prosperous village that grew up was named Purdy's Station in honor of its founder. However, in 1900, it was feared that the Croton Reservoir would overflow and flood the village, and the decision was made to move to higher ground.

In its few blocks Purdy's encompasses the intimate scale of a late-nineteenth-century hamlet, in which no structure dominates but each seems to enhance its neighbor. One example: a tiny stable with board-and-batten siding and scrollwork at the eaves, on Mills Rd. past First St.

Croton Falls Baptist Church

Box Tree Restaurant (junction of Rts. 22 and 116, Purdy's). Standing serenely at the busy intersection, as if its cast-iron fence could keep out modernity, is the Purdy Homestead, built in 1775 and now a restaurant. During the Revolution, Joseph Purdy led a band of patriots who apprehended a local Tory. Even though they strung him up three times, he refused to divulge the name of a companion. Finally they let him go with a warning to leave the county. Soon afterward, all the known Tory sympathizers decided it was politic to leave as well.

The form of the original dwelling—two stories and five bays with a central, double-leafed door—is embellished by mid-nineteenth-century adornments. Among these are a richly detailed cast-iron fence, an ornamented porch, and carved brackets supporting the overhanging eave.

North Salem Town Hall

Rte. 116, Salem Center

In its 200-year life, this building has served as manor house, jail, courthouse, academy, and town hall. It was originally built in 1773 for Stephen DeLancey, a leading Loyalist. His property was confiscated during the Revolution, and the house used as a courthouse and jail for spies, Tories, cattle thieves, and other disturbers of the peace. Rochambeau and his officers, on their way to join Washington, camped here for two days in October 1782.

After the Revolution the building reverted to more peaceable purposes—it became the North Salem Academy in 1786, and among the pupils in its century as a school was Daniel D. Tompkins, who became governor of New York and vice president of the United States.

In 1886 the Town of North Salem purchased the building, and in the 1950's it was restored and remodeled. In style, the building is a country cousin to fashionable English taste of the time. Modillions are carved below the eaves, and a tiny gable adorns the façade; a delicate cupola surmounts the roof. The second floor, with its high ceiling under the gambrel roof, serves as the town library.

North Salem Town Hall

Tool Shed and Herb Nursery (D. O. Mills House) (Mills Rd. and Turkey Hill, off Rte. 116 at reservoir, Salem Center). Darius Ogden Mills, who was born in this house (which had been built in 1725) and spent his boyhood in North Salem, made his fortune in the West. "Lucky Ogden," as he came to be called, went to California in 1848, like many other gold-hunters. But, shrewdly assessing the poor risks of prospecting, he decided to sell merchandise and food to prospectors in return for their gold dust. After establishing himself as a successful merchant, he set up the D. O. Mills and Company Bank, one of the most prominent in California.

Merryweather (Grant Corners, junction of Rtes. 121 and 124). Ulysses S. Grant visited his son and daughter-in-law frequently at Merryweather, an ample Shingle-style mansion which had been a wedding present in 1881 from the bride's father, Senator Jerome Chaffee of Colorado. On his visits here, Gen. Grant paraded his high-spirited Arabian horses, which he had received as a gift on a goodwill tour around the world.

June Farm

Rte. 124, north of junction with
Rte. 116, North Salem

In the 1820's, soon after Hachaliah Bailey of Somers bought the elephant Old Bet and started a touring show that fascinated the local townsfolk, four of North Salem's solid citizens—John J. June, Lewis B. Titus, Caleb Sutton Angevine, and Jeremiah Crane—fell prey to circus fever too. They pooled some money and founded a rolling menagerie show, called the Zoological Institute, which soon played small towns around New York and Philadelphia. Daniel Drew of Carmel in Putnam County held the job of barker before he became a partner of Wall Street sleight-of-hand financial experts Jay Gould and Jim Fisk (also a former menagerie man).

Many other businessmen in the area followed their lead and set up circuses. June and a group of his partners, under the tutelage of Drew, formed a syndicate to import wild animals to supply the growing demand. To a would-be rival company they announced: "We put our foot down flat and shall play New York; so watch out." From this warning they became known as the "Flatfoots" and were the most powerful circus syndicate for many years.

The June Farm, a handsome Greek Revival house, is now a plant nursery; its distinguished air gives no hint of its exotic associations with the past.

Hammond Museum and Oriental Stroll Garden

Deveau Rd., off Rte. 124, ¼ mile north
of intersection of Rtes. 116 and 124,
North Salem
*OPEN: Wed.–Sun., 11 a.m.–5 p.m.,
    end of May–end of Oct. (for
    gardens), –end of Dec. (for
    museum)
PHONE: (914) NO9–5033;
    NO9–5135

On top of a hill, formerly a cow pasture, overlooking Lake Titicus and Hunt Mountain, with the Berkshires in the distance, is the Hammond Museum and Stroll Garden, inspired by a seventeenth-century Japanese form. The Stroll Garden—actually fourteen small interconnected gardens—recreates in miniature an entire landscape, complete with mountains, lakes, valleys, and rivers. The gardens were designed by Natalie Hays Hammond, a painter, miniaturist, costume designer, and needlepoint expert.

The Guildhall, a modern cinderblock building, contains permanent exhibits devoted to various historic periods and offers changing exhibitions, lectures, and concerts as well.

Woolner House

Woolner House (Baxter Rd., off Rte. 124, North Salem). This gleaming white arched structure, something of a surprise in this rural area, was originally conceived as a prototype for a modular linear city which could, theoretically, stretch 50 miles or more. Supported by 20-foot-high wooden arches, the rear half (away from the road) is sheathed merely in clear plastic, so that moonlight, sunlight, and dusk's reflections form an ever-changing wall. The house was designed by Anne and Anthony Woolner as their residence.

60

Peach Lake Meeting House (Rte. 121, at Putnam County border). No frills encumber this simple brown-shingled building set back from the road and the small nearby graveyard. It was built in 1763 for the Friends of the Peach Pond Meeting and enlarged to its present size in 1778. The Meeting joined a larger group in 1810 and the double doors open only once each year, for an annual meeting in late August.

The beautiful stone-and-shingle dwelling adjacent to the meeting house is a worldly contrast.

Main Street (Rte. 33), Ridgefield

"Ridgefield is not merely shining and well improved," wrote historian Allan Nevins, "it has a distinct touch of old-fashioned gentility." Nowhere is this more evident than on Main St., a gracious, wide, tree-lined avenue. An elegant tone is set with the formal Renaissance styling of the brick-and-limestone Ridgefield Library and Historical Association (corner of Main and Prospect sts.). St. Stephen's Episcopal Church, built in 1915, is a combination of fieldstone and wood, with a square tower and open belfry. Across the street, in Veterans Memorial Park, is the Ridgefield Community Center, formerly the retirement residence of Governor Phineas T. Lounsbury. Grove Lawn, as he called it in 1896, was modeled after the Connecticut State Building at the 1893 Columbian Exposition.

High Ridge Rd., behind Main St., is equally impressive. Amid the spacious turn-of-the-century homes, No. 15 is a

small-scale reminder of earlier times. It was once the home of Samuel Goodrich, a Ridgefield author who, under the pseudonym of Peter Parley, achieved great popularity in the early 1800's. The cornerstone of the Catholic Church (Catoonah and High Ridge rds.) dates from 1896. Built of yellow brick and cobblestone, it is a full-blown example of the Shingle Style.

Peter Parley House in 1878

The Aldrich Museum of Contemporary Art

258 Main St., Ridgefield
*OPEN: Sat., Sun., 2–5 p.m.,
mid-April–mid-Dec.
PHONE: (203) 438–4519

In the late nineteenth century Ridgefield attracted many artists, among them Frederic Remington and J. Alden Weir. A new kind of artist is represented here today, in works if not in person—the avant-garde of contemporary art. Larry Aldrich, couturier and collector, has created a showcase for those artists in a stately three-story, gambrel-roofed mansion on Main St. that started life in 1783 as a store and became a Christian Science Reading Room in the twentieth century. "Old Hundred," as the building was called, has adapted to its new role with grace, its white walls showing off the bold canvases to good advantage. The expansive lawn in the rear is used to display contemporary sculpture, which weathers the New England winters and basks in the summer sun. The museum presents two shows a year.

Keeler Tavern

25 Main St., Ridgefield
*OPEN: Wed., Sat., Sun., 2–5 p.m.
PHONE: (203) 438–5485

As early as 1644 the Colony of Connecticut recognized the necessity of a tavern to the wellbeing of a town. Any settlement that did not have a tavern was liable to a fine of 40 shillings a month. The spirit of that law was no doubt in effect in 1769 when Timothy Keeler, Jr., bought a house and then turned it into an inn three years later. The house, a two-and-a-half-story, gambrel-roofed building with a large central chimney, had been built about 1760.

"This particular tavern had special claims to notice," wrote Peter Parley. "It was, in the first place, on the great thoroughfare of that day between Boston and New York and had become a general and favorite stopping place for travelers. It

was, moreover, kept by a hearty old gentleman [Squire Keeler], who united in his single person the various functions of publican, postmaster, representative, justice of the peace, and I know not what else."

The Keeler Tavern was operated as an inn until 1907, when architect Cass Gilbert bought it. He lived in it until his death in 1934; the section at the back was added during his residence. Maintained by the Keeler Tavern Preservation Society.

Spring Street, South Salem

Spring St. has been bypassed by Rte. 35, and so its charm has been little changed. The burial grounds form the central green space in the town (the church was burned and a new one will be built in its stead). An 1840 meeting house, a simple gabled structure, faces it. The Horse and Hound Inn is nearby; this low, two-story structure, built in 1749 and extensively remodeled over the years, is adjoined by blacksmith shops. "Antiques on Peaceable Street," a red salt-box with two doors, hugs the roadside.

St. John's Episcopal Church is a diminutively scaled country church dating from 1853. Built of crudely laid stone, the church has a square tower with pointed-arch door and window openings. Its simplicity is affecting.

Route 35 from South Salem to Cross River. Many old farm structures create a bucolic ambiance; nevertheless, sophisticated accents, such as Le Château, a restaurant which occupies the baronial mansion built in the early 1900's by J. P. Morgan, seem equally at home.

Conant Hall

Westchester Avenue (Rte. 137), Pound Ridge. Pound Ridge has an air of special charm, with buildings from past and present mingling with rare grace. In the center of the town, the pedimented Town Hall is an example of monumentality on a small scale. Next to it, Conant Hall, more flamboyant, has a spiky spire crowning its open belfry.

Hiram Halle Houses

Trinity Pass, Westchester Ave., and Salem, Stone Hill, Pound Ridge– Bedford, and Old Mill River rds., Pound Ridge

Hiram Halle, an architect, loved old houses and barns, so much so that whenever he saw an attractive one in the New York or Connecticut countryside, he would buy it and have it dismantled with great care and shipped to Pound Ridge. There he hired local carpenters to reassemble the structures according to his plans.

A great many of Halle's reconstructions, completed in the 1930's and early 1940's, are visible in Pound Ridge, easily identifiable by the Halle hallmark: the second course of bricks at the top of the chimney is painted black.

Wilton High School (Rte. 7, in northern part of Wilton). A sense of movement and activity pulses through the Wilton High School, built in 1972 by Schofield & Colgan, and Earl R. Flansburgh. The library-resources center and the field house are connected to the three-story main building by ramps. The whole is a pleasing combination of warm-hued brick, concrete, smoky glass, and buff-colored aluminum panels.

Congregational Church (70 Ridgefield Rd., Wilton). Another of the sturdy Congregational churches that stand as eloquent reminders of Connecticut's theocratic origins, this simple structure with double tiers of windows was built in 1790 and altered in the 1830's. The parsonage (77 Ridgefield Rd.) was constructed at the later time. Across the street is the Wilton Garden Club (69 Ridgefield Rd.), built in 1828 as the Wilton Academy and later used as a town hall.

Wilton High School

63

Heritage Museum

249 Danbury Rd. (Rte. 7), south of
intersection with Rte. 33, Wilton
*OPEN: Sat.–Sun., 2–5 p.m.
Closed Aug.
PHONE: (203) 762–7257

The proper name for this clapboard dwelling should be the Raymond–Fitch House. Clapp Raymond built it in 1757, and the Fitch family lived in it from 1846 to 1933.

The name chosen by the Wilton Historical Society—Heritage Museum—seems appropriate, though. First, it is a particularly fine Colonial dwelling, small in scale and simple in form. The Georgian detailing—beaded clapboards, paneled doors, and fluted pilasters flanking the entrance—seems especially charming in contrast. Second, the building is used to display collections of antiques, clothing, and other objects and to conduct educational programs. The interior is sparsely furnished—accurately, because there is little evidence to justify the large amounts of furniture found in many restorations.

Lambert House and surrounding buildings

150–154 Danbury Rd., Wilton
OPEN: Tues.–Fri., 9 a.m.–noon,
1–5 p.m. Closed July and Aug.
PHONE: (203) 762–7257

The question of how to utilize historic buildings, once they have been saved, has been solved by the Wilton Historical Society in a financially practical and aesthetically pleasing way. Four structures have all been "recycled," or converted to a suitable modern use. The Lambert House, built in 1724, and the only one originally on the site, is leased, in part, to the Hitchcock Chair Company as a sales outlet and also serves as library and office for the Historical Society. The Kent School, built in 1843, is an architect's office; the tiny Batchelder House, built in 1829, is a real-estate office; and the Hurlbutt St. Post Office and General Store, dating from the 1890's, will serve as the Society's own Antique Consignment Shop.

The Lambert House was owned by one family for over 200 years, and in 1963 was

Lambert House

acquired by the Historical Society. It is an ample clapboard structure with a gabled portico, five bays, and 12-over-12 windows. The gambrel roof has been raised in the rear. The beaded clapboard façade adds a note of refinement.

The house survived the march of Gen. William Tryon in April 1777, so the story goes, because the ladies of the house provided the soldiers with fresh-baked bread. Before the Civil War, Lambert House was a station on the Underground Railroad.

Merritt Parkway

One of the two main highways along the Connecticut coast (the other is the Connecticut Tnpk.), the 38-mile-long Merritt Pkwy. is an important example of "greenbelt" parkway design, in which continuous landscaping of the road system provides a scenic outlook and, just as important, reduces the monotony of highway driving.

The bridges over the road are chunky concrete forms typical of the Art Moderne style popular in the 1930's when the parkway was constructed. Its designers called it the "Queen of the Parkways." Each bridge is decorated with a different decorative motif and symbol. Some examples: Riverbank Rd. has futuristic concrete forms; Newfield Rd. has reeded piers with decorative motifs on the span; White Oak Bridge Rd. has a spiral motif; and Comstock Hill Rd. has a Pilgrim motif.

Sadly, the design challenges met by the Merritt Pkwy. have not been exploited in contemporary highway plans, and the greenbelt of this parkway has been threatened by proposed expansion.

Little Red Schoolhouse (Carter St., near corner of Clapboard Hill Rd., off Rte. 106, New Canaan). A one-room schoolhouse, painted red, has been restored to show what school was like in the late nineteenth century. The school was built in 1865 and used until 1958; one teacher taught classes here for the last forty-nine years of its service. It is open by appointment. Phone: (203) 966-0198.

Hanford–Silliman House

33 Oenoke Ridge (Rte. 124),
New Canaan
*OPEN: Tues.–Fri., Sun., 2–4 p.m.
PHONE: (203) 966-5598

Originally the principal tavern of the parish of Canaan, the Hanford–Silliman House was built in 1764; a half-round window in the center gable is an elegant detail of its construction. The house is furnished in the Colonial and post-Revolutionary periods, with antiques and a superb collection of pewter on display.

Also in the museum complex are a tool museum, costume museum, and the New Canaan Hand Press, a re-creation of a nineteenth-century printing office with a working 1822 press. The New Canaan Historical Library (13 Oenoke Ridge) has a fine reference collection; a wing is devoted to a re-creation of New Canaan's first drugstore. The one-room Rock School, built in 1799, has been moved to the grounds and is being restored. Craft demonstrations, tours, and research services are provided to bring these structures to life.

Among the restrained Colonial buildings is one small reminder of the sentimentality that engulfed Victorian America. This is the studio–cottage of John Rogers, renowned as the "master of plaster," whose mass-produced statuettes were *de rigueur* in every respectable American parlor from the 1860's to the end of the century.

Rogers achieved his first success in 1859 with "The Slave Auction," and went on to create similar touching and appealing vignettes. Rogers groups sold for $6 to

$25 each, and came with instructions for repainting if the surface was damaged.

Rogers spent summers in New Canaan and then lived here all year round until his death in 1904. He frequently used local residents as well as his own family for models. His house on Cherry St. was destroyed in 1962, and the studio moved to its present location, where it now contains a representative display of Rogers groups.

Church Hill (triangular section between Park and Main sts., New Canaan). Across from the New Canaan Historical Society's complex is the original center of Canaan Parish, the burying ground that was called Church Hill in the eighteenth century and dubbed "God's Acre" in the 1880's by a homesick New Canaanite.

St. Michael's Lutheran Church (formerly St. Mark's Episcopal), next to the Historical Society Library, was built in 1833; its Greek Revival features were given an Italianate flavor in 1857 by the addition of a porch, tower, and spire and by the change of the window openings from flat- to round-headed. On top of Church Hill is the Congregational Church, designed in 1843 on the model established by Minard Lafever, an English-trained architect whose published plans made possible the execution of high-style structures by country craftsmen.

New Canaan Railroad Station (Pine and Park sts.). Commuters have been waiting at this station since 1868, when the railroad came to New Canaan and revolutionized country life. This station, in a fine state of repair, has board-and-batten siding; the gable end is decorated with a charming finial.

New Canaan "Modern"

One of the most extraordinary houses built in the post–World War II period is the glass house that Philip Johnson designed for himself in New Canaan in 1949. Located on Ponus Ridge Rd., near Wahackme Rd., it is in an idyllic setting, surrounded by woods and overlooking a small lake. In a class by itself, this trendsetting house sets a standard for purity of form and elegance and finesse of details, aspects that have made it one of the most famous homes in America and have attracted throngs of curious viewers. (Landscaping now obscures it to the outsider.)

Along with Johnson, four Harvard associates—Eliot Noyes, Marcel Breuer, Landis Gore, and John Johansen—as well as Victor Christ-Janer, were attracted to New Canaan around the same time by its favorable zoning, proximity to New York, and the availability of land. They designed several dozen innovative dwellings which can be glimpsed in their wooded settings. One by Marcel Breuer is at 628 West Rd., north of West Hills Rd.; others are on Cross Ridge Rd., Weed St., and Wahackme, Valley, Woods End, Laurel, West, and Country Club rds.

High Ridge Park (High Ridge Rd. [Rte. 137], Exit 35 of Merritt Pkwy., Stamford). Some of the half-dozen or so structures in this curvy corporate enclave of scallop shells, waterless moats, and space-ship instrument panels were built speculatively, others designed especially for their tenants. Each of the steel-frame structures set around a small lake is trimmed with its own thematic element, in some cases suggesting the product or activity of its occupant. In this corporate "What's My Line?" game, who else would occupy a building that looks like a clock's gear but General Time?

Among these outsize rhebuses, the building of Conoco Headquarters differs radically; its well-proportioned and sweeping forms are sheathed in softly tinted reflecting glass. On its façade, crisp reflections of the woods behind or of clouds communicate congenially with the countryside.

Combustion Engineering (900 Long Ridge Rd. [Rte. 104], Exit 34 of Merritt Pkwy., Stamford). A civilized example of corporate design, this concrete building by architect Benjamin Hunter crests its sloping site. With its irregular buttressed silhouette, it seems a modern-day castle for the knights of industry.

Reid Hall, Manhattanville College

Purchase St. (Rte. 120), south of Anderson Hill Rd. (Rte. 18), Purchase

---

Everything Ben Halladay, a self-made Western transportation magnate, touched turned to gold—or silver. He even won part of the Ophir silver mine in Nevada in a poker game, and in 1864 he built Ophir Hall, back East, in Purchase. After his fortunes failed, the property eventually passed to Whitelaw Reid in 1887.

A fire the next year leveled the opulent residence. Little daunted, Reid, diplomat and publisher of the *New York Tribune*, commissioned an equally lavish castle– residence, broad and solid, with imposing battlements. The library wing was added by Stanford White in 1912.

The Reid family owned the mansion until 1949, although it was vacant for many years. It was purchased by Manhattanville College, renamed Reid Hall, and restored as an administration building.

Read Memorial Community House (Purchase St., Purchase). This community center had its inspiration during World War I in response to the social needs of soldiers. Built after the war, it was intended to commemorate the dead while providing well-planned leisure spaces for the living. Donn Barber was the architect.

PepsiCo World Headquarters

Anderson Hill Rd., Purchase
OPEN: Grounds and sculpture garden
always open

Good corporations make good neighbors, or so PepsiCo set out to prove in 1970 when it opened its new headquarters on the 112-acre former Blind Brook Polo Club. Edward Durrell Stone's series of seven interconnected buildings, each joining the next at the corner, is above all polite. The buildings take up only a small portion of the site, and the softly rolling hills are allowed to dominate.

This beautiful "natural" landscape—artfully designed by Edward Durrell Stone, Jr.—serves as a serene setting for PepsiCo's fine collection of outdoor sculpture. Henry Moore is represented by three works, one a massive, mysterious bronze nude called "Reclining Figure." She rests on a stone slab against a backdrop of water playing from fountains. Three surrounding sunken gardens—each a sculpture in itself—also contain sculpture.

Alexander Calder's "Hat's Off" is a cheerful red stabile that towers at the edge of a pond at the back of the building. Other sculptors represented are David Smith, Arnaldo Pomodoro, Jacques Lipchitz, Henri Laurens, Seymour Lipton, and Alberto Giacometti.

State University of New York at Purchase

Anderson Hill Rd.

The farmlands of Anderson Hill Rd. have been transformed by two twentieth-century giants—one a corporation, the other an institution of higher education.

The SUNY campus at Purchase is part of a vast state building program. When completed, the 500-acre campus will provide instructional facilities for 6,000 students at a College of Letters and Science and a School of the Arts, and living facilities for half of them.

A team approach, directed by Edward Larrabee Barnes as master planner and

participating architect, has utilized a "who's who" of many contemporary architects, including such diverse talents as Robert Venturi, Paul Rudolph, Gunnar Birkets, and Philip Johnson.

Recalling the classical agora and the civilizing effect of close human contact, Barnes has turned away from traditional campus design in favor of a city "grid" plan. In the center of a vast green space, a 900-foot-long pedestrian mall serves as the focal point of the campus. Vehicles are routed around it or, along with a host of service activities, under it.

Uniform in height and in their use of brown-brick sheathing, five classroom buildings are arrayed on either side of the mall on lots 130 feet wide. Fronted by covered arcades and rows of trees, the individuality of each structure cannot be grasped from the mall. It is only in the alleys formed between each building, 32 feet in width, that the unique quality of each structure and the often exciting inter-relationships can be perceived. One example is the contrast between the genteel wall of Venturi's Humanities Building and the checkerboard of Johnson's Neuberger Museum of Art. (The museum presents changing exhibitions in its gallery.)

A great court, in the center of the mall, is defined by the arcades on either side. Its space is dominated by the massive forms of the library, post office, and a four-part theater complex. Dormitories and various student activity centers are set somewhat apart from the central hub.

The monumental scale and rational organization of the components of the Purchase campus are surely impressive. But is this an environment that encourages the flowering of the human spirit? Only when the campus is fully utilized will the answer be clear.

State University of New York, Purchase

Main Street, Southport

3 | Long Island Sound: New York and Connecticut

The shoreline of Long Island Sound covered in this section—from Pelham Bay to Bridgeport Harbor—has been both a center of commerce and a residential area for three centuries. Remarkably, buildings from every significant period—even the earliest—survive, providing a striking diversity of architectural forms and functions.

Among the contrasts are simple salt-box dwellings and stately Federal and Greek Revival mansions, comfortable taverns and once-lavish resort inns, handsome commercial buildings of the nineteenth century and their angular modern counterparts, the headquarters of giant corporations.

The area offers more than a collection of individual buildings, however notable. Whole sections of towns retain distinctive period flavors—for example, the rural but sophisticated charm of the mid-1800's may still be felt in Fairfield's three historic districts, while the combination of elegance and utility of the late 1800's remains in the industrial areas of Bridgeport.

Throughout, the Sound is pervasive but changeable—a peaceful vista from a broad-lawned estate, a bustling harbor, a secluded marina. The historic Boston Post Rd.—Rte. 1—is heavily commercial now, but bordering it is a host of pleasures.

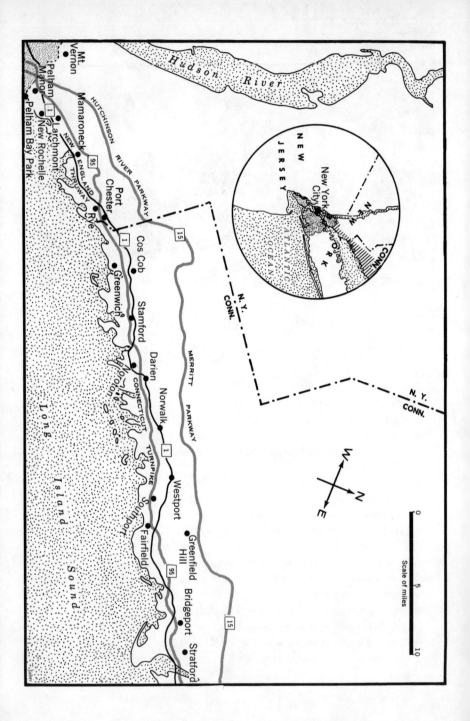

Bartow–Pell Mansion

Bartow–Pell Mansion

Shore Rd., Pelham Bay Park, Bronx.
North of Orchard Beach Exit of
Hutchinson River Pkwy.
*OPEN: Tues., Fri., Sun., 1–5 p.m.
PHONE: (212) TT5–1461

A two-story, dignified gray stone building, the Bartow–Pell Mansion presents a cool, even remote, façade to the twentieth century. Technically it's in the Bronx, but its historical ties are to Westchester and, until the boundaries were changed in 1895, it was on Westchester land.

The house was built between 1836 and 1842, but the architect is not known. The owner, Robert Bartow, was a descendant of Thomas Pell, who bought the land from the Siwanoy Indians in 1654 and whose sons became lords of the Manor of Pelham.

The house is a distinguished example of a Greek Revival dwelling. Conservative in style, it follows the five-bay plan of earlier designers; only the double-leafed door and arched window openings above it hint at the sophisticated Italianate style

soon to become popular. Built of cut fieldstone, the window and door surrounds as well as corner quoins are marked by smooth granite blocks. Decoration at the eaves is also restrained—an unadorned frieze and wooden dentils. The flourishes of cast-iron balconies and the gentle curve of the stair relieve the stark geometry of the façade. Three iron gates lead from the formal garden behind the house—one to the woods, one to Long Island Sound, and one to the Pell family cemetery.

The Bartow–Pell Mansion has been owned by the City of New York since 1888. Furnished with a superb collection of antiques, it is maintained by the International Garden Club, which has its headquarters here.

The house is in a secluded location, much as it was when the area was sparsely settled. The towers of Coop City are just beyond view, but the isolation and the garden setting give the mansion its special evocation of nineteenth-century serenity.

St. Paul's Church, Eastchester

897 S. Columbus Ave. (Rte. 22),
Mount Vernon
OPEN: Sunday services at 9:30 a.m.
Guided tours by appointment
PHONE: (914) 667–4116

St. Paul's Episcopal Church, Eastchester (actually it's in the City of Mount Vernon), is a religious edifice that has been intimately involved with the secular side of American history. The area now hemmed in by fuel oil depots, factories, and a Salvation Army warehouse was once the Village Green of Eastchester. Here the first St.

Paul's Church, a small wooden structure, was built in 1665 by early Nonconformist settlers—Presbyterians, Congregationalists, and Quakers. (This is the area where Anne Hutchinson came to seek religious freedom, was massacred by the Indians, and is today memorialized by a river and a parkway.)

In 1733 an election for representative to the Provincial Assembly between the

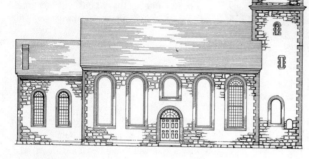

St. Paul's Church, Eastchester, Mount Vernon

royal governor's candidate and a popular opposition leader was held on the Green. The local residents were so outraged by the blatant mishandling of the election that John Peter Zenger, a German printer, wrote scathing accounts of it in his New York *Journal*. Because he continued his denunciations of the governor, he was arrested, tried for libel, and later found innocent by a jury. The principle of freedom of the American press, later incorporated in the Bill of Rights, was established by this trial; and St. Paul's Church has claimed fame by association ever since.

Another link to the traditions of American freedom is the church bell. It is an exact duplicate (except for the crack) of the Liberty Bell in Philadelphia; both were cast at the Whitechapel Foundry in London. The bell, which can be viewed inside the tower, still peals each Independence Day.

The original building was torn down, and in 1765 a new structure was begun. It was still unfinished when the war broke out. Nevertheless, during the fighting the church served intermittently as a hospital for British and Hessian soldiers. Many of the wounded died and were buried in a common grave in the churchyard. The marker is one of the many Revolutionary-period gravestones in the cemetery, which contains interesting stones from other periods as well.

The structure represents a blending of various traditions. The tower in front of the nave is a late provincial echo of the English Georgian tradition, while the entrance in the middle of the long side recalls the form of the Colonial meeting house.

The church is constructed of coursed rubblestone with brick surrounds on arch-headed window and door openings. Corners are marked by brick quoins. The tower has been enlarged several times, most recently in 1887, when a brownstone belfry, providing a late-Victorian flourish, replaced the earlier wooden one.

Sara Delano Roosevelt, indefatigable mother of FDR, took on the restoration of the church as a personal crusade. Her husband's ancestor James Roosevelt owned a pew in the early 1800's. It was largely through Mrs. Roosevelt's efforts that St. Paul's was made a National Historic Site in 1943.

Christ Church (Priory Lane, at Pelham Rd., Pelham Manor). Rev. Robert Bolton was rector of St. Paul's Church, Eastchester, until this fine church, an early example of the English parish–style revival, was built for him in Pelham in the mid-1830's. The stained-glass windows were made by his sons, who introduced the craft to America. Stone walls visually link the church to his home, the Priory, built in 1838. His friend Washington Irving contributed yellow bricks from the Old Dutch Church at Sleepy Hollow to outline the date of construction over the door. The brick tower of the mansion, which was substantially rebuilt after a fire, is visible from the street.

Leland Castle, College of New Rochelle (Castle Place, off Elm St., near Pelham Rd., New Rochelle). Simeon Leland, a hotelier of the mid-nineteenth century, took seriously the adage that "Every man's home is his castle." William T. Beers, his architect, followed contemporary fashion in 1855 by designing a picturesque Gothic mansion with towers, gables, turrets, and battlements. A contemporary commentary on the sixty-room house, true to the ethic of self-betterment, stated: "In other lands, the sight of such magnificence may create envy, but in our land it arouses only ambition, and stands as a monument to every poor and honest man, who can solace himself with the thought that nothing save his own fault can keep him some day from being a master of just such a place."

Leland Castle is now undergoing renovation to become a center for administrative and faculty offices of the College of New Rochelle, which has owned it since 1897. Although many changes have been made over the years, some of the original ornamentation of the period remains.

Trinity Episcopal Church (311 Huguenot St., at Division St., New Rochelle). Brownstone trim makes a lively punctuation mark to this exquisitely proportioned granite church designed in the 1860's by the office of Richard Upjohn.

First Presbyterian Church and Pintard Manse (50 Pintard Ave., New Rochelle). An extraordinarily imaginative Georgian Revival church, designed in 1928 by John Russell Pope, this building was the successor to one erected by the Huguenot French Reformed congregation. A graceful tower and richly detailed and well-proportioned spire crown the transept; colossal Ionic columns support a triangular pediment on the principal façade. The craftsmanship, in wood and stone, is of impeccable quality.

East of the church is the Pintard Manse, a one-and-a-half-story Georgian Colonial dwelling. It is a graceful neighbor to the imposing church next door, with white-shingled walls and a carved cornice. The porch and dormers were probably added in the nineteenth century.

Wildcliff Natural Science Center

Wildcliff Rd., New Rochelle
*OPEN: Daily, except Fri., 1–5 p.m.
PHONE: (914) 636–2108

In a scenic location overlooking Echo Bay off Long Island Sound, the Wildcliff Natural Science Center is both a nature preserve, with outdoor and indoor educational facilities in the natural sciences, and a museum and sculpture gallery.

Wildcliff was one of the several dwellings in New Rochelle designed by A. J. Davis in the 1850's. (Another, just able to be glimpsed beyond high hedges, is on Davenport Ave.) Davis' hallmark in these country retreats was cross gables, steeply pitched and elaborately decorated with fanciful bargeboards. However, Wildcliff was drastically remodeled in 1919 and so today represents an interesting amalgam of two periods.

Larchmont Shore Club (1 Oak Bluff Ave.). The many gables of the Tudor-style clubhouse of the Larchmont Shore Club—once the home of the beer dynasty Schaefers—are a striking note among the more restrained late-nineteenth-century dwellings which surround it in the shorefront area (Pryor Lane, and Larchmont, Beach, and Ocean aves.).

Emelin Theatre (Library Lane, Larchmont). Hardy Holzman Pfeiffer Associates were the architects of this versatile theater complex completed in 1972.

Mamaroneck Beach Cabana and Yacht Club (S. Barry Ave., east of Boston Post Rd. [Rte. 1]). Restorations following a recent fire have stripped the clubhouse of the Mamaroneck Beach Cabana and Yacht Club of many of the grandiloquent details it displayed when it was the home of Charles J. Osborn, a financial intimate of Jay Gould. However, the imposing mass and dynamic composition, the work of Stanford White in 1884, can still be grasped. The structure, though mutilated, remains a rare monument of the Shingle Style.

White's inventiveness was apparently allowed even freer rein in the dependencies that were part of the estate—the stable, icehouse, gardener's cottage, and gatehouse. Dark shingled surfaces are capriciously interrupted by towers, gaping voids, and rows of spindles. The gatehouse is of stone, but no less imaginative.

VFW (189 Prospect Ave., Mamaroneck). A Greek Revival structure with smooth matchboard sheathing and columns supporting the gabled pediment, this building began life as a town hall and was subsequently a church.

Melbourne Avenue, Mamaroneck. This is a street of carpenter-crafted mid-nineteenth-century dwellings. Neatly aligned, they create an ambiance of comfortable dignity, in spite of modern construction on many once-spacious lots.

Larchmont Avenue, Larchmont

United Methodist Church, Mamaroneck

United Methodist Church (Boston Post Rd., Mamaroneck). This charming Stick-style church dates from 1859. Because of the extraordinarily fine design and joining of wooden framing elements, it is supposed to have been built by ships' carpenters. A tall spire and an abundance of gables, pinnacles, and finials create a delightfully lively silhouette.

Board of Education Administrative Headquarters (740 W. Post Rd. [Rte. 1], Mamaroneck). This typical late-Victorian schoolhouse, built in 1888, represents a vanishing architectural form. Now set among the undisciplined sprawl of commercial strip development, it is a prim reminder of more ordered days.

De Lancey House (404 W. Post Rd., Mamaroneck). The Neutral Ground—the territory neither rebels nor Redcoats controlled—was the subject of James Fenimore Cooper's writings about the Revolutionary period. Cooper himself lived in Mamaroneck for a time, after he married Susan De Lancey in 1811. She was the granddaughter of Col. Caleb Heathcote, lord of the Manor of Scarsdale, who called Westchester "the most rude and heathenish country I ever saw in my life."

Cooper and his bride lived in the De Lancey House, known as Heathcote Hill, built in 1792. The building has suffered numerous indignities since then—it was sold at auction for $11 and moved from its original site overlooking Long Island Sound to commercial Post Rd., and has been used as a gas station and restaurant for over thirty-five years. Perhaps the colonel had a point.

Rye Playland

Playland Pkwy., off Rte. 1. New England Thruway, Exit 11; Hutchinson River Pkwy., Exit 25
OPEN: Early May–Labor Day
PHONE: (914) 967-2040

Planning an amusement park, particularly one "possessing artistic merit," is not all fun and games. This was the assignment of Gillette & Walker, architects, and Gilmore D. Clarke, landscape architect, in 1923, when the Westchester County Park Commission decided to develop over 200 acres of shore front on Long Island Sound.

Above all, the designers wanted to avoid the garish, unplanned, and tawdry atmosphere of "Coney Island architecture," an example of which existed in the amusement park already on part of the site. The design team (including architects, landscape architect, engineers, amusement-park expert, lighting specialist, swimming-pool designer, and

others) embarked on the task with enthusiasm but some trepidation. Such a
wedding of showmanship and art had not
been attempted before.

An important feature of the plan was a
curved beach and boardwalk about a
quarter of a mile long, with a bathhouse
nearby. The amusement-park area extended from one end of the boardwalk to
an 80-acre lake.

Throughout the complex the designers
strove for a "holiday spirit." They used
simple, playful designs. Decorative friezes
adorned the colonnades, with cheerful,
partly stylized figures with a distinctive
'20's air. Outline and indirect lighting, in
combination with colored lights, created a
"fairyland" atmosphere. Musical equipment, innovative for the times, avoided
the din of competing calliopes and bands
and provided separate units for different
areas. Landscaping was designed to unify
the site, and flowering shrubs, annuals,
and perennials added gaiety and color to
the scene.

The designers felt that in their work at
Playland, which opened in 1927, they

Kirby Mill

had raised the amusement park to a
"higher plane, and made of it a place
where people of refinement may go in
quest of pleasure heretofore only found in
environments lacking in art and culture."

Playland, which is maintained by the
Westchester County Playland Commission, has made some changes over the
years, not all of them in keeping with the
original design and intent. Still, the basic
concept and plan are there, and so are
many of the original details.

Kirby Lane, Rye. The simplicity of the
eighteenth-century Kirby Mill is a fine foil
for the grand houses that surround the old
millpond and the lane that leads to it. The
old frame mill, once powered by the tides,
now serves as a boatyard.

Manursing Island, Rye. Especially
notable among many fine late-nineteenth-
century to present-day dwellings in this
favored location is the formal contemporary design at 81 Manursing Way.
Ulrich Franzen was the architect.

Rye Golf Club (Boston Post Rd. [Rte.
1]). Another A. J. Davis building, designed in 1853, this is now a public

Bathing Pavilion, Rye Playland, in 1928

restaurant. Dark stone and low, heavy masses, barely relieved by the crenellated tower, contribute to its rather somber appearance.

United Methodist Center (Peter Jay House)

(210 Boston Post Rd., Rye). The Jay family, and its most illustrious member, John, had strong ties to Westchester. Their estate was originally purchased by John Jay's father, Peter—a total of 400 acres for the sum of 300 pounds. John Jay, his elder brother, Peter (blinded in youth from smallpox), and two sisters grew up here in a simple but large farmhouse called The Locusts, which served as the model for the one owned by the Wharton family in James Fenimore Cooper's novel *The Spy*. John Jay's son, Peter Augustus, inherited the property in 1838 and built the estate called Alansten, a name of unknown origin.

The house is a simple rectangle with a four-columned portico. In general, Peter Jay's builder seems to have been familiar with Minard Lafever's *Beauties of Modern Architecture*, published in 1835 as a guide to the details of the Greek Revival style.

North of the Jay family cemetery is Lounsberry, an impressive Greek Revival mansion.

Christ's Church–Rye and Rectory

(Boston Post Rd., near Rectory St.). The rectory, designed by the firm of McKim, Mead & Bigelow in 1878 (the year before Stanford White became a partner), is a prim, mid-Victorian, cut-stone structure, with steeply pitched gabled roof and dormers with curious inlaid floral motifs. The impressive stone church was built about twenty years earlier.

Square House (Rye Historical Society)

Purchase St. (Rte. 120), at Boston Post Rd., Rye
OPEN: Tues.–Fri., Sun., 2:30–4:30 p.m; and by appointment
PHONE: (914) 967–7588

When the Boston Post Rd. was the main route between Boston and New York, Rye was three stops (East Chester, West Farms, and Kingsbridge) from the end of the stagecoach line in lower Manhattan. Weary travelers often sought refuge at taverns along the way.

The Square House in Rye, 32 miles from New York, was such a tavern, though grander than most, from 1760 to 1830. Although it served many owners before and since, it is this aspect of its history that is most intriguing and it is to this era that it has been superbly restored.

The exact date of its construction is not known. The oldest part (about two-thirds of the present building) was probably built in the early 1700's, hard by the Post Rd. The serenity of the present form at first

Square House

conceals the fact that it is the result of a series of additions and modifications. Beaded clapboards, round-butt shingles, leaded transom lights, gambrel roof, porch—all testify to the continuous development of Square House over a century or more.

In 1760 Dr. Ebenezer Haviland, a leading citizen, bought the house and turned it into a tavern. He sold it in 1775, leaving himself free to pursue the Revolutionary cause as a surgeon in the New York regiment of the Continental Army. Dr. Haviland died during the war, but his widow, Tamar, returned to Rye, repurchased the inn, and went back into business.

She was apparently a good businesswoman, for many travelers wrote of their favorable impressions. In 1788 a French traveler, J. P. Brissot de Warville, called it "one of the best taverns I have seen in America." George Washington gave Haviland's a somewhat less enthusiastic review in 1789, calling it a "very neat and decent inn."

About 1830 the Square House ended its career as a public house and reverted to private status. The house was acquired in 1905 by the Village of Rye and served until 1965 as Rye's municipal building. Scholarly restoration began at that time. The restoration has been carefully recorded, and examples of the original construction are visible through specially designed doors and panels. The Rye Historical Society now leases the building and maintains it as a museum and community center. Changing displays of Colonial arts and crafts add a lively note to the permanent exhibits.

Bush Homestead (479 King St., [Rte. 120A], in Lyon Park, Port Chester). The Bush Homestead, in the heart of the Neutral Ground during the Revolutionary War, was witness to the violent struggles between Tories and patriots. It was the home of the Bush family, descendants of Justus Bush, a New York City merchant who purchased land near Sawpit Landing (renamed Port Chester in 1837). The house was built in three different sections, the oldest probably dating from the late eighteenth century. Surrounding outbuildings recall its historic configuration. It is now owned by the Port Chester Parks Department and serves as the residence of the Superintendent of Parks. Open Thurs., 1:30–4 p.m. Phone: (914) 939–2770.

Congregation Kneses Tifereth Israel (575 King St., Port Chester). Philip Johnson designed this rigidly disciplined steel-framed structure in 1955–56. An oval entryway leads to the main body—an open, rectangular space which can be divided by movable screens for special purposes. The angular severity of the interior is relieved by the graceful curve of the tentlike plaster ceiling and by the light shining through the vertical slots of colored glass set between the concrete panels.

Ward House (Comly Rd., off Rte. 1 and King St., Port Chester). Dramatic in appearance, the Ward House is something more—a truly revolutionary building. It is

Congregation Kneses Tifereth, Port Chester

Ward House

the first reinforced-concrete home in America, and probably the first in the world.

William E. Ward, a tool manufacturer of daring and originality, hired architect Thomas Mook to design his mansard-roofed dwelling in 1871 but personally supervised every step of its construction. Fascinated by the properties of iron rods in combination with poured concrete, Ward observed that together they could perform far greater tasks than each could alone.

Ward built his entire mansion—floors, walls, tower, porches, dormers, steps; everything except doors and window frames—of reinforced concrete. The strength of the floors was so great that a test load of 26 tons placed on them for a period of several months had no significant effect.

The house that Ward built is imposing indeed. Gleaming white, it sits on a high knoll, lawns spreading out in all directions. A soaring four-story tower breaks away from the confines of its square mass. The notched edges of crenellations in the upper stage of the tower add a theatrical note. A semicircular loggia with paired columns boldly wraps around the base of

the tower. An aggressive structure, this, well suited to the strength of its materials and its technological originality.

Life Savers Factory (Rte. 1, Port Chester). Larger-than-life candy packages projecting from the first floor announce the sugary product of this large-scale factory. It was designed in 1926 by the architect–engineers Lockwood Green Engineers as the latest in efficiency. Imaginative details relieve the scale: smoky-green tiles sheathe the window spandrels, a tiled roof is supported by sculptured brackets, and delicate vegetable motifs encircle the door. Peeking out from among the vines on the door surrounds and dangling beneath the eaves are carved candies-with-a-hole.

Greenwich

Greenwich, just over the New York State border into Connecticut, marks the beginning of a different kind of landscape—large corporations have become the neighbors of the comfortable suburban residences and large estates that characterized Connecticut-on-the-Sound for decades.

Greenwich Hospital (Perryridge Rd.). Built in 1947 by Skidmore, Owings & Merrill, this hospital was decidedly modern in its day, and it is still impressive for its fine scale and chaste forms. Crisp treatment of surfaces—white brick with chrome trim—and horizontal bands of windows are evidence of the impact of the International style on post–World War II American architecture.

Town Hall, Greenwich

Town Hall (Greenwich Ave., at Arch St., Greenwich). An impressive brick-and-granite structure, Greenwich's Town Hall was completed in 1905. Employing Beaux Arts principles, it has a full range of Classical motifs, careful proportions, and symmetrical design.

Second Congregational Church (W. Putnam Ave. [Rte. 1], Greenwich). This well-proportioned Gothic Revival stone church, constructed with masterly craftsmanship, is on Greenwich's main street. It was built in 1854. Mead House, its original parish house (48 Maple Ave., off W. Putnam Ave.), is a high-style Italianate design translated into a local vernacular. It was built by Solomon Mead in 1858 and is now used as a community center.

Greenwich Library (W. Putnam Ave.). A department store of the 1920's has been converted into an impressive library complex by the 1969 addition of a boldly articulated concrete annex, designed by Sherwood Mills Smith Partnership. The discreet placement of the modern structure —to the rear and side of the earlier building—restrains it from overwhelming the dignity of its neighbor or the streetscape.

First United Methodist Church, Greenwich

First United Methodist Church (W. Putnam Ave., Greenwich). The great stone masses of the Gothic builders were often translated into thin wooden skeletons by resourceful American carpenter–builders. The framing members of this church, built about 1865, have a matchstick quality and define the space nervously. Remarkably, the original glass—mostly clear with etched red or blue pieces set at intervals —remains. Behind the church, on William St., is a fine grouping of early- to mid-nineteenth-century buildings.

YWCA (259 E. Putnam Ave. [Rte. 1], Greenwich). A novelty on this staid historic roadway is this dynamic concrete complex, designed by Victor Christ-Janer and completed in 1970.

Mead House

Putnam Cottage (243 E. Putnam Ave., Greenwich). A good story does a lot for a house. When this house was Knapp's Tavern in 1779, Gen. Israel Putnam of the Continental Army was a guest. "Old Put" learned suddenly that the British were coming and was forced to cut his visit short, so short in fact that he dispersed his few companions and rode to Stamford for reinforcements, taking a daring leap on horseback down a steep precipice nearby to escape Gen. William Tryon.

That story has probably saved this typical three-bay, shingled Connecticut house from destruction. It is now owned and maintained by the Putnam Chapter of the DAR and is being restored to its eighteenth-century appearance.

Is the story true? Historians doubt it. But the legend has persisted, and Gen. Putnam was indeed a popular leader of the Revolutionary cause. More important, it's a charming house. Phone: (203) TO9–8034, for scheduled opening and guided tours.

Museum of Cartoon Art

384 Field Point Rd., Greenwich
OPEN: Tues.–Sat., 10 a.m.–5 p.m.;
    Sun., 1–5 p.m.
PHONE: (203) 661–4501

The turn-of-the-century, three-story, stone Mead Mansion, overlooking Greenwich Harbor, has been converted into a museum of one of the liveliest of the arts—cartoons and comic strips. Next door is the Homestead Inn (420 Field Point Rd.), built in 1799 as the Augustus Mead farm and remodeled in the Italianate style in the 1840's.

This section of Greenwich abounds in exuberant Shingle-style mansions of the late nineteenth century.

Steamboat Road, Greenwich. On Steamboat Rd., a short stretch leading to Long Island Sound, the apartment house and corporate office building are now claiming equal rights with the gracious country homes that once presided exclusively over the view to Greenwich Harbor.

Harborside, which marks the beginning of the road, is one such luxury condominium apartment building. Farther down the road is the home of Buster Brown Textiles, finely and imaginatively crafted and well proportioned. Next to it, at 666 Steamboat Rd., is the Berni Design Center, built in 1972 to the plan of Alan Berni with Michael Spector Associates; it is notable for its pleasing scale, the delightful variety of window size and shape, and its jaunty nautical air.

Bush–Holley House

39 Strickland Rd., Cos Cob. South of
Rte. 1, overlooking Cos Cob Harbor
*OPEN: Tues.–Sat., 10 a.m.–noon,
    2–5 p.m.; Sun., 2–4:30 p.m.
PHONE: (203) 869–9849

A recurrent problem facing preservationists is determining which period a restoration should cover and what to do

Berni Design Center

Armory Show Barn, Bush–Holley House

with elements of other periods. The Bush–Holley House is an example of a fitting and beautiful solution: in the house elements are preserved of the four major periods that influenced it—early Colonial, Revolutionary, nineteenth century, and early twentieth century. These elements blend together harmoniously despite their differences.

Although the exact date of construction and the first owner are not known, the original salt-box was no doubt built before 1700. The first owners of record were the Bush family, who lived in the house from 1738 to 1844. During the Revolutionary period the house served as office for a tidal mill as well as a dwelling. Additions and alterations were made to accommodate the changing needs of the family. In the 1850's, when it was a boardinghouse, further alterations were made to the Victorian taste.

Edward Holley purchased the house in 1882 and began its greatest period—the Art Colony days. Emma Constant Holley, his daughter, married the artist and sculptor Elmer Livingston MacRae, and they made the Holley Inn a congenial place for their writer and artist friends to live and work. Some of the most prominent turn-

of-the-century artists stayed at the Holley Inn—John Twachtman, Lewis Comfort Tiffany, Childe Hassam, Walt Kuhn, and George Bellows. Ernest Thompson Seton, Willa Cather, Jean Webster, and other literary figures added to the lively atmosphere.

In his *Autobiography*, Lincoln Steffens recalled that "the Holley House was a great, rambling, beautiful old accident— so old that it had its slave quarters up under the roof; and it looked out from under elms as high as oaks upon the inner harbor and an abandoned boat-building house with sail lofts. There was a long veranda where the breezes came down from the river, up from the Sound, and cooled the debaters."

The impressions of the house recorded by the Art Colony residents were a valuable record for the Greenwich Historical Society when it began its restoration in 1957, four years after Elmer MacRae died and his widow sold the house to the Society, which maintains it as a museum and opens it to the community for special events.

Throughout the house are fine examples of American decorative arts. Behind it are two other buildings of interest: one housing an extensive collection of John Rogers groups, the putty-colored statuettes that were the rage of the late 1800's; and the Armory Show Barn, which served as the headquarters of the organizing committee of the 1913 Armory Show which stunned the American art world. Elmer MacRae served as treasurer of that committee.

Condé–Nast Press (E. Putnam Rd. [Rte. 1], west of Havemeyer Lane, between Greenwich and Cos Cob). The Condé–Nast Press brought glamour to the suburbs with its futuristic headquarters, built in the 1920's. Expansively sited on both sides of Rte. 1, its territory is marked off by massive pylons proudly bearing the names of the periodicals of this once-great publishing empire—*Vogue, Harpers Bazaar, House Beautiful*. A massive tower seems to guard the main structure—three stories of concrete and glass. Across the road, the forlorn garden is graced by a miniature tempietto and two stone sphinxes—one minus its head.

Condé–Nast has since moved, and the building is now occupied by a variety of firms.

Sound Beach area of Old Greenwich

(south of Rte. 1). Sound Beach Ave., which runs from the main roads to the harbor area, contains many fine buildings from different eras.

The Perrot Library, built in 1931, is a neo-Georgian brick building with a cupola surrounded by a balustrade. Less refined is the Albertson Memorial Church, a wooden carpenter-Gothic building with a cobblestone foundation.

Sound Beach Ave. leads to Shore Rd., in the early 1900's a thriving resort area. The Old Greenwich Lodge and the more imposing Old Greenwich Inn (across from it

Perrot Library

on Shore Rd. and Wahneta St.) were built around the turn of the century. An airy veranda encircles the inn and there is a large and inviting reception room.

Dark shingled dwellings, once summer homes, with wide verandas and lozenge-shaped windows, abound in the neighborhood. Two fine examples are at 207 Shore Rd. and 165 Wahneta St.

Stamford

The bold new shapes of downtown Stamford include the ten-story General Telephone and Electronics Building (five levels of smoked glass in the form of an inverted pyramid), the twenty-one-story Landmark Towers (finlike projections at the corners flare out and form the base of the structure), and the three tall, circular forms of St. John's Towers (where the children play, à la Corbusier, in elevated playgrounds). Since 1965 Stamford, once a small town, has been transformed by the immigration of more than forty corporate headquarters.

Hoyt–Barnum House

713 Bedford St., Stamford
*OPEN: Tues.–Fri., 1–5 p.m.,
and by appointment
PHONE: (203) 323–1975

A little red salt-box tucked away in the middle of downtown Stamford stands as a neat reminder of the city's early settlers, among them the Hoyt family. Isaac Hoyt built this one-and-a-half-story farmhouse with its massive central chimney about 1690, a date suggested by the heavy

Hoyt–Barnum House

framing members, which are mortised and pegged, and chinked with clay.

Why are some early homes preserved and so many others destroyed? Long ownership by one family—the Barnums and Hoyts were related—is definitely an asset. The Stamford Historical Museum acquired the house in 1942 and maintains it with exhibits of early Stamford history.

First Presbyterian Church (1101 Bedford St., Stamford). Rising dramatically from the downtown area of "renewed" Stamford is the 260-foot carillon tower of the First Presbyterian Church. The tower, like the church itself, was designed in 1956 by Wallace Harrison of Harrison & Abramovitz. Harrison's aim was to build "a church today which might be the same light structure of stone and glass achieved so marvelously in the Middle Ages," but to achieve this effect he used twentieth-century design and materials.

The structure is actually a complex geodesic. Sloping triangular precast-concrete panels converge at the high peak of the sanctuary and extend through its full length, without supporting pillars. Stained-glass windows are embedded in the concrete panels. The roof and long

slanted walls are covered, except for the window areas, by gray slate shingles.

This church is often called the "Fish Church," because the floor plan of the sanctuary resembles the earliest symbol of Christianity.

Shippan Point area, Stamford. This section, with a lovely view of Long Island Sound, has been a resort area since the 1840's. Fine late-nineteenth-century mansions are set on spacious grounds; for the most part, they can only be seen from the rear.

Old factory area, Stamford (Henry and Pacific sts.). Though overrun with decaying tenements, this area still has some interesting examples of Stamford's first period of industrialization. The Yale and Towne Company, noted key manufacturers, was located here, and there are good examples of nineteenth-century factories still standing. Projecting piers which mark the rhythm of the bays and brick corbeling at the cornice level are typical features.

First Presbyterian Church, Stamford

Bates–Scofield Homestead

Bates–Scofield Homestead

45 Old King's Highway N., Darien
OPEN: Wed., Thurs., 2–4 p.m.;
       Sun., 2:30–4:30 p.m.;
       and by appointment
PHONE: (203) 655–9233

Darien boasts a large number of Revolutionary and early-nineteenth-century buildings. This characteristic Connecticut farmstead, a modern addition to which also serves as the headquarters of the Darien Historical Society, is the only one open to the public.

Apparently no house was built on this site until the 1740's, when John Bates formally deeded his son John, Jr., 45 acres, identified as that land "whereon my . . . son's mansion house stands." The house stayed in the Bates family only until 1774, then passed through several owners and was bought in 1825 by the Scofields, who lived in it for one hundred years. It was saved in 1964 by the Darien Historical Society and moved from its original site across the street.

Several wings and a front porch were removed, and the roof line restored to its original salt-box slope. Fortunately, few changes had been made to the interior over the years. Like many Connecticut homes of the period, the house is built around a large chimney stack, which is nine by ten feet at the base. The interior is furnished in the period. Behind the house is an eighteenth-century herb garden.

Darien Ice-Skating Rink (Old King's Highway N.). This stunning rink, designed by Sherwood Mills Smith Partnership, is an echo, in twentieth-century terms, of the bold geometric patterns and stark simplicity of the nearby Bates–Scofield Homestead. The rink was opened in 1973.

Boston Post Road (Rte. 1), Darien. On both sides of Boston Post Rd. near the railroad, Darien's "downtown," there is a strong nineteenth-century flavor. Among the gems are the Town Hall (Academy St. and Boston Post Rd.), an imposing red-brick structure with nice detailing; the Unusual Country Store, a Shingle-style building with particularly imaginative woodworking detail, dating from 1901; and a number of store fronts of the mid-nineteenth century.

Darien Ice-Skating Rink

First Congregational Church (Old King's Highway N., at Brookside Rd., Darien). This simple and substantial brick structure, built in 1837, has four fluted columns supporting a wooden pediment surmounted by a squat square tower. A plaque commemorates the Tory raid of July 22, 1781, in which Rev. Moses Mather and fifty men of his congregation were seized by the British, imprisoned in New York, and "jeoparded their lives unto the death."

Great Island Farm

Field Point Road, Noroton. The dwellings at 188, 190, 192, and 194 Field Point Rd. bear the inimitable mark of Lurelle Guild (rhymes with "wild"), a twentieth-century Renaissance man. An actor in early motion pictures (he played in films with Mary Pickford and Rudolph Valentino), a producer, photographer, painter, magazine illustrator, and a pioneer in the field of industrial design in the 1930's, he has also been passionately involved with early American architecture. When Guild found eighteenth-century buildings threatened with demolition, he acquired them with the goal of establishing a Williamsburg-like complex on Swift's Lane in Noroton. Among the buildings he bought were a country store, a schoolhouse, a town hall, and several houses distinguished enough to be recorded by the Historic American Buildings Survey. He also collected parts of buildings as they became available—a doorway here, a column there, windows, doors, paneling, and other elements.

When Guild started to build houses of his own design, he incorporated these architectural elements in a completely uninhibited and freewheeling way, unencumbered by the demands of historical accuracy. The result is a collection of highly individualistic buildings with disparate elements of salt-box, mansard, Colonial, and Regency styles, assembled so that they "ring a bell" to Guild.

Each building is reduced to three-quarter scale (Guild also designed stage sets) to make the visitor feel comfortable. "You feel bigger than the building," he explains. "Scale is of the utmost importance, and in keeping with the spirit of the original." More precisely, it *is* the spirit of these buildings that is original.

Ring's End Landing, Noroton. A scattering of nineteenth-century buildings marks this section of Noroton, once the center of maritime and commercial activities in Middlesex Parish. The Old General Store, a board-and-batten building, was used as a post office and general store and is now a dwelling. Next to it is a recently restored red-shingle building, formerly a customs house. The remains of a gristmill are on the shore. Across the road at 85 Ring's End Rd. is a Federal-style five-bay house originally owned by a prosperous merchant.

Great Island Farm (Goodwives River Rd., Noroton). Ring's End Rd. crosses an arched stone bridge over the Darien River, where a gatehouse marks the entrance to

Great Island Farm. A stone structure with gables flaring at the eaves, its gatehouse has elaborate stone pillars.

The main house is not easily visible, but the massive, gambrel-roofed barn with its great stone tower makes an impressive sight behind the iron fence that surrounds the farm.

Lockwood–Mathews Mansion

295 West Ave. (Rte. 1), Norwalk. Directly off Connecticut Tnpk., Exit 14
*OPEN: Sun., 1–4 p.m.; Tues., Thurs., hours vary; group tours by appointment
PHONE: (203) 838–1434

In 1863 LeGrand Lockwood, having made a fortune in banking and railroading, commissioned the European-trained architect Detlef Lienau to design the most fashionable manor house in America. Lockwood's mansion no doubt fulfilled his dreams. Enormous in scale—there are more than forty rooms—it does not overwhelm because of its imaginative massing. A porte cochere announces the entrance; a veranda, enclosing rounded bays, wraps around the façade; richly molded pediments surmount the projecting dormer

windows. Dressed granite, carved in a tour de force of craftsmanship, forms exterior walls; the slate mansard roof is crowned by exquisitely detailed iron cresting.

Properly awed, a contemporary newspaper reporter noted that "it might be two country seats of English noblemen rolled into one, or it might be a palace of Ismail Pasha."

Inside, an extraordinary sense of space is achieved by the unusual plan—rooms are arranged around a central rotunda lighted by a skylight four stories high. Interior architectural elements—paneling, inlay, and moldings—were designed in unison with the furnishings and form a fascinating ensemble. Gilt, fresco, marble, rich coverings, and etched glass are orchestrated with splendid effect. The variety and richness of woods are dazzling.

Lockwood died in 1872, only four years after he had moved in to the mansion, and the landscaping designed by Frederick Law Olmsted was never completed. The Gold Panic of 1869 had nearly ruined Lockwood, and his widow was forced to give up the mansion in 1874. It was later owned by Charles Mathews.

The City of Norwalk bought the house in 1941 and used it for city offices and storage. Plans for its demolition in 1961 were stopped by the formation of a citi-

Lockwood–Mathews Mansion

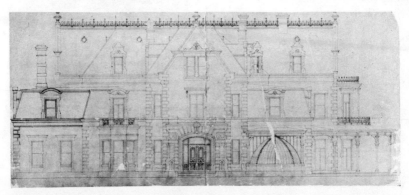

zens' group, which eventually won support for preservation through a referendum. In 1965 the Junior League of Norwalk–Stamford took a $1-a-year lease on the building and agreed to restore it. Restoration of the first-floor rooms is well under way, and the rotunda is used for art exhibits, as it was in LeGrand Lockwood's day.

Norwalk Harbor (near Water St. [Rte. 136], Steamboat Place). A number of elaborate late-nineteenth-century commercial structures remain around Norwalk's lively harbor. Among them is the vast Radel Oyster House, a reminder that oyster culture was one of Norwalk's earliest industries, learned from the Indians in the mid-seventeenth century.

Rogers & Stevens Building (Haviland St., off S. Main St., Norwalk). This is a rare example of a surviving building with a cast-iron façade. Typically, columns on one story are surmounted by columns on the story above. In this case, those on the first floor of this four-story building have been obscured by unfortunate modernization.

United Methodist Church (West and Mott aves. Norwalk). A large clapboard structure in the Italianate style, this church has twin towers with windows set in recessed arches. The effect is awkward but appealing.

Norwalk Library (across from the church). A handsome limestone entrance portico adorns this well-proportioned brick building, constructed in 1903. Rich detailing includes bands of glazed bricks, and decorated eaves and gables.

Mill Hill Historical Site

Mill Hill (E. Wall St.), Norwalk

The Norwalk Town House, a gabled Greek Revival structure of the 1830's, forms the nucleus of a set of reconstructed buildings of early Norwalk.

The Gov. Thomas Fitch Law Office has been reconstructed to its 1740 appearance, when it was used by the fourteenth governor of the Colony of Connecticut. The building is small—a lawyer's office and a clerk's office on the first floor, an attic with storage and clerk's bedroom above, and a cellar below.

Also being reconstructed is the Old Schoolhouse, a red clapboard structure with shingled roof, wide plank flooring, and vaulted ceiling.

An old jailhouse will someday be restored on the site, as will a replica of the Yankee Doodle House, once the home of

Rogers & Stevens Building

Norwalk High School

an officer in the French and Indian War whose shabbily dressed troops inspired a British surgeon to write the mocking lyrics of "Yankee Doodle Dandy."

Old Village Green, Norwalk (Park St. and East Ave.). A gracious, open space with stately trees, the Green on the east side of the Norwalk River is surrounded by mid-nineteenth-century homes. The columned First Congregational Church-on-the-Green has fine moldings in the style of the Greek Revival; its parish house has a fanciful cupola. At the north end of the Green is St. Paul's Episcopal Church, an impressive stone structure. From this Green in 1820 a hardy band of Norwalk settlers, whose homes had been destroyed in the Revolution by the British, set out for Ohio. The expedition had taken twenty-eight years to organize, and even at the last minute some pioneers decided to stay. Those who ventured west founded Norwalk, Ohio, and none returned to Connecticut.

Norwalk High School (County St., off Strawberry Hill Ave., off Rte. 1). This stunning structure, of glass and smooth and rough concrete, was built in 1970 from the designs of The Architects Collaborative.

Westport Congregational Church (Rte. 1). This simple white clapboard church, built in 1830, sits serenely on the crest of a gentle hillside. Four columns support a triangular pediment, and a two-stage octagonal belfry with arched openings surmounts the square tower and is crowned by a tall spire.

Town Hall (State St. E., Westport). This small-scale cobblestone structure with contrasting brownstone trim was built in the early twentieth century, when Westport's charm was far less sophisticated than today.

Westport Congregational Church

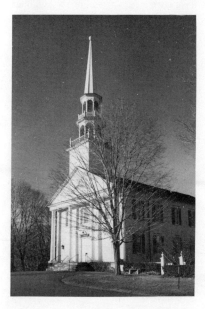

Southport Historic District

Harbor Rd. to Rose Hill Rd.

The burst of commerce and trade that followed the Revolution, and the need for new homes caused by the burning of Fairfield, spurred the growth of Southport. More shipping was owned in Southport, in proportion to its size, than in any other port between Boston and New York.

The surrounding countryside, however, remained farmland, and one of the principal crops was onions. A contemporary writer noted, "Nothing seems to grow but onions between Greenfield Hill and the sea. We pass many fields of five to ten acres each, and hear of growers who raise all the way from ten to twenty-five acres of the pungent bulbs." The onions were shipped from storehouses on the Southport wharves.

Today there is nothing commercial about Southport. The onion warehouses have been incorporated into the buildings of the Pequot Yacht Club; the harbor is now a marina filled with pleasure boats. The gracious homes erected by wealthy men of commerce, banking, and shipping still stand. In an area which includes more than 150 buildings, it is difficult to single

out any in particular. The total ambience of Southport—the gracious Federal, Greek Revival, and Victorian homes on streets rising from the harbor—sets it apart.

Harbor Rd. is surely special. The gracious Greek Revival house with four imposing Doric columns at No. 750 was a major addition to an older dwelling made in 1846 by Oliver Perry, a Connecticut legislator and one of the two Connecticut commissioners who finally settled the boundary dispute with New York. Its Corinthian-columned neighbor at No. 712 is equally impressive. The only building in Southport known to have survived the British raid is at No. 824, a two-and-a-half-story house with a large central chimney. The main part of No. 789 was built in the 1850's and was, in the 1890's, a clubhouse curiously called "Bachelor's Comfort and Married Men's Relief." Later it became the first clubhouse for the Pequot Yacht Club.

Public buildings also form an important part of the historic district. The Southport Savings Bank at 226 Main St. dates from 1854 and is an unusually fine survival of a mid-nineteenth-century commercial building. The Pequot Library at 720 Pequot Ave. is a neo-Romanesque building designed in 1894 by New York architect R. H. Robertson. The splendid board-

Pequot Yacht Club

Harbor Road, Southport

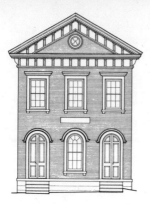

Southport Savings Bank

Pequot Library

and-batten Trinity Church at Pequot Rd. and Center St., rebuilt in 1862, has a slender spire that can be seen for miles and is a landmark for sailors even now.

THE GREEN, FAIRFIELD.

Fairfield Historic District

Old Post Rd. (Rte. 1), from Turney Rd. to Beach Rd.

In 1779 Gen. Tryon's troops raided Fairfield, burning and pillaging, so most of the seventy-five buildings in this historic district postdate the Revolution. A few earlier ones (the house at 349 Beach Rd. is an example) were saved because their own-

ers were Loyalists and/or they were used to quarter British troops.

The district covers most of the original town of Fairfield—laid out by Roger Ludlowe in 1630 along four squares of 25 to 30 acres each. This was the Fairfield where inns, homes, public buildings, and churches clustered around the Kings Highway (Old Post Rd.). Rte. 1 (New Post Rd.) bypasses the old section, avoiding the curves of the narrow thoroughfare marked out by Benjamin Franklin in 1753.

The focal point of the district is the Green, which was a drill ground during the Revolution. Bordering it are the Town Hall, rebuilt in 1794 and restored in 1937; the Rising Sun Tavern (1780), a five-bay structure with a gambrel roof (another stop on Washington's travels); and the Fairfield Academy, with a cupola on the roof and small, circular windows in the gables. The Academy was moved here from its original site.

The Burr Mansion (739 Old Post Rd.) was rebuilt in 1790. (John Hancock had been married in the original house in 1775 to Dorothy Quincy, who caused him no end of anxiety by her flirtation with Aaron Burr.) The mansion was remodeled by the addition of a heavy colonnaded portico in the 1840's. It is now

91

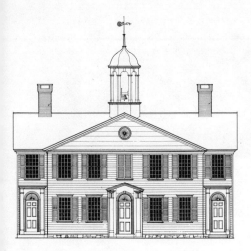

Fairfield Academy

an annex of the Town Hall and is open during business hours. One room is pleasantly furnished in the period.

The houses along Old Post Rd. in the historic district are mainly in the Federal and Greek Revival styles. The Sherman Parsonage (480 Old Post Rd.) was built in 1816 by Roger Sherman, nephew of the signer of the Declaration of Independence and an eminent jurist. The original house was built without the wing on the east end adorned with one Greek column. Mrs. Sherman, so the story goes, built that wing to accommodate the extra footage of velvet Wilton rugs she received by mistake from England.

The Old Burying Ground on Beach Rd. contains many pre-Revolutionary gravestones carved with the angels, skulls, weeping willows, and other designs popular with Connecticut stonecutters.

The Fairfield Historical Society (636 Old Post Rd.) contains exhibits and a library on Fairfield's past. Open Mon.–Fri., 9:30 a.m.–4:30 p.m. Phone: (203) 259-1598.

David Ogden House

1520 Bronson Rd., Fairfield
*OPEN: Thurs., Sat., 2–5 p.m.,
mid-May–mid-Oct.
PHONE: (203) 259-1598

One of the few remaining pre-Revolutionary houses in the Fairfield area, this dark-brown-shingled farmhouse was transformed from a square structure into a salt-box after its construction around 1700 by the addition of a second section in 1720 and a lean-to in 1750. It was restored in the 1930's by Mary Allis, an antiques dealer, who donated her house to the Fairfield Historical Society in 1974. She has left on extended loan her fine collection of folk art objects and paintings and antique furnishings.

Greenfield Hill Historic District

Area around Village Green and Meeting House Lane, Hillside Rd., and Old Academy Rd.

As Southport was the commercial heart of Fairfield, Greenfield Hill was its intellectual center. Its most famous resident was Timothy Dwight, pastor of the Congregational Church, who founded the academy here in 1783–84 and was its director for twelve years before he became president of Yale.

Dwight's Academy was open to both young men and women. Many of them came from outside Connecticut, a few from Europe. Dwight's successor at the academy, Jeremiah Day, also later became president of Yale, as did Theodore

Dwight Woolsey, one of his students. The original academy is gone, but the site is now marked by the Timothy Dwight Park (east of the Green and the church, between Hillside, Old Academy, and Bronson rds.). Many of the old homes in the vicinity have historic ties to the academy.

The focus of Greenfield Hill has always been the church on the Village Green. Timothy Dwight, in his long poem "Greenfield Hill" (1794), wrote:

There, turret-crown'd, and central stood
A neat, and solemn house of God.

The present structure is the fourth on the site and was built in 1855 in the same Colonial style as its predecessors, though the steeple is not as tall as the one that served as a lookout during the Revolution.

The house at 55 Meeting House Lane was built in 1823 and is supposed to have been designed by the young bride of Varick Dey, pastor of the church.

John Taylor Arms, an erstwhile architect who became well known as an artist, lived at 745 Old Academy Rd. from 1920 to 1950. Before he gave up the practice of architecture, he was the partner of Cameron Clark, who also lived in Greenfield Hill. Clark created superb replicas of early Connecticut houses; one three-bay example can be seen at 360 Old Post Rd. in Fairfield.

Many of Greenfield Hill's homes have been restored nostalgically, in keeping with the spirit of the past, if not always with accuracy.

A huge wooden windmill, recently restored, is on the grounds of 3015 Bronson Rd. It was built in 1890 to run a well on the Bronson estate, the first deep-drilled well in the area. A team of horses on a circular platform operated the drilling mechanism.

Greenfield Hill's idyllic atmosphere was elegized in these words in Dwight's poem, still apt today:

Thrice bless'd the life, in this glad region
spent,
In peace, in competence, and still content.

P. T. Barnum Museum

820 Main St., Bridgeport. Near Connecticut Tnpk., Exit 27, in downtown Bridgeport
OPEN: Tues.–Sat., noon–5 p.m.; Sun., 2–5 p.m. Closed Mon. and holidays
PHONE: (203) 576–7320

Everything P. T. Barnum did was flamboyant, and the museum dedicated to him, especially as it reflects his years in Bridgeport, carries on that tradition. When Barnum died in 1891, he provided in his will for an "Institute of Science and History" to be built, specifying that it was to overshadow the YMCA then standing across the street.

A local architectural firm created this highly original orange-brick edifice. The large dome that dominates the corner has eyebrow dormers which peek out from the red-tile roof. Brownstone and buff terra-

P. T. Barnum Museum

Brewster Garden Apartments

cotta brick trim the window and door openings. A frieze beneath the dome has five pressed terra-cotta panels with figures depicting Bridgeport's history.

It is a curious building, perfectly suited to its present purpose of housing curiosities—an unwrapped Egyptian mummy; circus memorabilia; mementoes of Barnum's famous attractions, such as Bridgeport's own Tom Thumb; an alpine village with 22,000 working parts; and a miniature animated circus.

Brewster Garden Apartments (Fairfield Ave. and Brewster St., in western section of Bridgeport). Some of the earliest public housing in America was built in Bridgeport shortly after World War I. Private efforts soon followed government projects. Brewster Garden Apartments was one such effort, built by a private developer for factory workers. Although designed in the neo-Georgian idiom, it was definitely forward-looking in planning concepts. The well-scaled, three-story structures fit easily into the preexisting urban fabric. Grouped around open courts, the red-brick apartment buildings define utility and pleasure spaces, walkways and service roads.

Industrial area of East Bridgeport. Across the Pequonnock River, East Bridgeport retains much of the scale and form of its late-nineteenth-century industrialization. East Main St., running down to the harbor, is lined by an incredible assortment of commercial and industrial structures, characterized by imaginative patterning of brickwork, and heavy—though impressive—scale. Particularly outstanding are the Bridgeport Brass Company (774 E. Main St.), now being renovated by the city, and the Bryant Electric Company (Hancock and Railroad aves.), a stunning, masterfully crafted red-brick structure.

Main Street, Stratford

Stratford's Main St. and the surrounding streets—Broad and W. Broad sts., Elm St., Academy Hill, Judson Place—maintain the orderly arrangement of dwellings, churches, and open spaces that belonged to the early nineteenth century. Many buildings of that period have survived, and newer buildings within the confines of this area seem to respect the existing scale and dignity.

The American Red Cross Building (2155 Main St.) is a four-square Greek Revival structure with eyebrow windows and a square tower with heavily articulated modillions. A remarkable Italianate mansion (1135 Broad St.), buff-colored with brown trim, is in nearly perfect condition. Its elaborate loggia with arched openings and fluted columns and beautifully modulated forms help to create a balance between imagination and order. The dwellings that line Elm St. have especially interesting carpenter detailing.

The First Congregational Church on Main St., a Stick-style structure from 1859, has particularly lofty proportions. (The tower has been altered considerably.)

Capt. David Judson was a prominent man in Connecticut Colony, auditor of the records and deputy to the General Assembly. His great-grandfather, William Judson, a founder of Stratford, had come to America in 1634 and built a house on this site five years later. The stones for the foundation of the Judson House were taken from the original home.

David Judson may have employed Thomas Salmon, who had come from England in 1717, to design the house, for it is similar to Salmon's design for the Second Episcopal Church.

The interior has been restored by the Stratford Historical Society, which now maintains the building. There are fine period furnishings throughout, some of which belonged to the Judson family.

Behind the Judson House is a recent addition which houses the excellent library of the Stratford Historical Society and a historical museum.

Captain David Judson House

967 Academy Hill, between Main and Elm sts., Stratford
*OPEN: Wed., Sat., Sun., 11 a.m.–
    5 p.m., April 1–Nov. 1
PHONE: (203) 378–0630

The Queen Anne doorway of this house is truly remarkable. It has a large, curved pediment with a richly profiled cornice and flanking fluted pilasters. Four small panes of bull's-eye glass are set in the transom.

The cruciform profile of the chimney is also unusual. The wide overhang of the gable is a particular Connecticut feature, and the round-butt shingles are also associated with the Sound area.

Doorway, Captain David Judson House

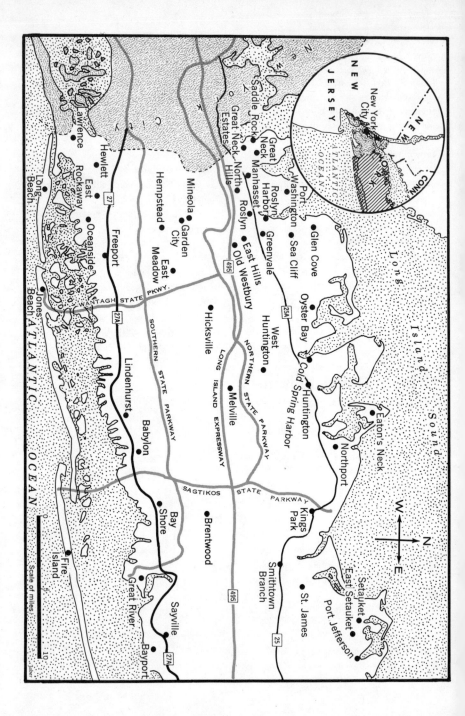

Bayard Cutting Arboretum

4 | Long Island

Bordered on the north by Long Island Sound and on the south by the open Atlantic, Long Islanders have been, since the days of the earliest Dutch and English settlers, influenced by the sea. The hardy farmers who worked the fertile soil and the fishermen who plied the bays and ocean were joined in the late nineteenth century by wealthy city-dwellers who created extravagant estates along the bluffs of the North Shore and, to a lesser extent, beside the sandbars of the South Shore.

The intensive suburbanization that followed World War II changed the face of Long Island nearly beyond recognition. Nevertheless, the flavor of its agricultural and maritime past can still be captured, particularly in the coastal villages. Most of the great estates that have survived have been converted to public uses, and many fine examples of typical Long Island architecture, in dwellings and churches, have been preserved.

This section is divided into two parts: the first follows the North Shore, with sites located on both sides of Rte. 25A from Great Neck to Port Jefferson; the second follows the South Shore, generally along Rte. 27A from Lawrence to Bayport.

Saddle Rock Grist Mill

Grist Mill Lane, off Bayview Ave., north
of Northern Blvd. (Rte. 25A),
Saddle Rock (Great Neck)
OPEN: Wed.–Sun., 9 a.m.–5 p.m.,
        April 1–Oct. 31
PHONE: (516) 292–4162

Long Island's many mills were located on
streams and harbors, and were sometimes
powered by tidal waters. The Saddle Rock
Grist Mill was built in 1714 by Henry
Allen, who obtained permission from the
town meeting to set up a mill on
"Madnan's Neck" (now Great Neck), on
an even earlier mill site, on the condition
"that he doth keep a good mill in repair
and grind for the town for the twelft part."
This agreement set the miller's toll at
one-twelfth of the grain ground for his
customers.

The mill has been restored to the period
of the 1850's, when Richard Udall and his
son James were the millers. It still grinds in
accordance with the tides; a tour inter-
prets milling technology. Owned by Nassau County.

Rebhuhn House (9a Myrtle Dr., east of
Bayview Ave., Great Neck Estates). This
brick-and-cypress dwelling, designed by
Frank Lloyd Wright in 1938, has the hall-
marks of the master—window walls, wide
roof overhang, and expressive use of materials. But it shares the romantic attitude
toward nature of the more conservative
period-revival houses built about the same
time in this picturesque suburban development.

Chase Manhattan Bank (22 Grace
Ave., near railroad station, Great Neck).
The design of this bank solves the con-
tradiction inherent in the structure's purpose; it is open and inviting to customers,
yet frankly protective of its contents. The
structure is a glass envelope containing a
concrete strongbox and covered by a waf-
fle concrete roof supported by concrete
piers. The architect, Benjamin Thompson,
was one of the founders of The Architects
Collaborative, perhaps the most influential postwar design group.

Chase Manhattan Bank

Manhasset Valley School

East Shore Rd. and Northern Blvd. (Rte.
25A), Manhasset (Manhasset Valley
area of Whitney Pond Park)
OPEN: Wed.–Sun., 1–5 p.m.
PHONE: (516) 292–4162

"The Little Brown School in the Valley"
was built in 1826 (the date painted by
carpenter Smith Leek on the southeast
corner of the building) to serve the growing school-age population. The typical
shingled frame building served as a one-

room schoolhouse until 1868. It has been restored by the County of Nassau to the period of the mid-1850's, when students used goose quills to write on rough paper made at nearby paper mills.

Community Reformed Church (Plandome Ave., off Northern Blvd., Manhasset). A steep gable, broad tower with a balustrade surrounding the belfry, and deep porch are among the boldly articulated forms that distinguish this church, built in the 1890's.

Manhasset Meeting House (1421 Northern Blvd., at Shelter Rock Rd.). In 1657 the citizens of Flushing refused to accept Peter Stuyvesant's orders to banish Quakers from their midst. In the Flushing Remonstrance, one of the most significant documents in establishing religious toleration in this country, they declared that "we cannot condemn [Quakers] in this case, neither can we stretch out our hands against them, to punish, banish or persecute them." Encouraged by this spirit of neighborliness, Quakers established many settlements on Long Island. The Manhasset Meeting House was built in 1812, a century or so after Quakers had settled in the area. A high wall protects it now from the commercial "Miracle Mile" on Northern Blvd.

Onderdonk House (1471 Northern Blvd., Manhasset). Horatio Gates Onderdonk, a wealthy lawyer and later judge of Kings County, built this fine Greek Revival mansion in 1836. The two-story portico has four massive Doric columns and a triangular pediment. Onderdonk House is now used as a community meeting house.

Willets House

336 Port Washington Blvd. (Rte. 101), Port Washington
*OPEN: Sun., 2–4 p.m.
PHONE: (516) 767–1447; 365–9074

This house, named after the first and last families to own the property, is an ample shingled dwelling. The land was originally granted to Thomas Willets in 1682 by James II; but the earliest section of the house, the low wing to the west, was built around 1735, by John Sands II. In 1839 the Willets family again acquired the homestead, adding the central section with its broad doorway and Greek Revival detailing. It was occupied by the family until 1967. Headquarters of Cow Neck Peninsula Historical Society.

Falaise

Sands Point Park and Preserve, Middleneck Rd. (Rte. 101), Port Washington
*OPEN: Sun.–Wed., May 15–Oct. 31, by appointment only
PHONE: (516) 883–1612

In the 1920's Long Island's Gold Coast was lined with the lavish manors of the rich and/or famous. Capt. Harry F. Guggenheim, the owner of Falaise, was both: a grandson of the peddler-turned-millionaire Meyer Guggenheim, and a well-known aviator in World War I.

Falaise was built in 1923, designed by architect Frederick Sterner to resemble, in its studied informality, the manorial houses of Normandy.

Charles Lindbergh was a frequent guest at Falaise and wrote his book *We* there. In her diary for 1928, Anne Morrow Lindbergh described her fiancé's relaxed attitude at Falaise: "I want to tell you how amazingly at home he is at the swell Guggenheim place (gatehouses and towers and lawns and peacocks), pushing open the great carved door without knocking, picking up his mail casually, introducing me with the most complete poise, strolling into the baronial living room (Madonnas in all the niches, etc.) . . ." The "Madonnas in all the niches" were among the vast collection of sixteenth- and seventeenth-century French and Spanish decorative objects that Guggenheim acquired to furnish the house.

Guggenheim willed Falaise to Nassau County. Also on the vast acreage are Hempstead House, his father's mansion, which dwarfs Falaise in scale, and Castlegould, the early 1900's mansion built for Howard Gould, which will eventually be restored.

Falaise

Christopher Morley Knothole

Christopher Morley Park, Searingtown Rd. (Rte. 101), south of Northern Blvd. (Rte. 25A), North Hills (Roslyn)
OPEN: Thurs.–Sun., 1–5 p.m., April 1–Oct. 31
PHONE: (516) 292–4162

Christopher Morley, essayist, poet, and novelist, celebrated the joys and tribulations of suburban life on Long Island. His home was in Roslyn Estates, which he called "Salamis" in his writings. "I believe it's one of the loveliest places in America but I never write about it by its name because I don't want a lot of people coming here to 'sitt down upon itt' as the old document said of the 1640 settlers at Southampton. You all know what happened to Southampton."

In 1934 he built a studio ("a pine-wood cabin, as aloofly jungled as a Long Island suburb would permit") and called it the Knothole. Inside the humble cabin he installed a "dymaxion bathroom," a one-piece, preassembled unit designed by Buckminster Fuller.

East Williston Railroad Station (off Hillside Ave. [Rte. 25B]). In 1878 the Willis family gave this two-story red-brick station to the Long Island Rail Road; and in exchange the line agreed to stop twice a day. The small depot, impressive for its height, is in fine condition. At one time a family, probably the station agent's, lived in the second story.

When Christopher Morley rode the Long Island Rail Road, he had a feeling that this station "would be a nice place to get off and explore." Following this impulse today, on the south side of Rte. 25B, one finds a number of notable frame dwellings that highlight the community's mid-nineteenth-century aspect.

Entrance Gate, Country Estates Swimming Club (Harbor Hill and Roslyn rds., East Hills). "By the lavish expenditure of money in energetically realizing a comprehensive plan," solemnly reported the *Architectural Record* in 1904, "the architect can keep his client interested by means of quick and spectacular results." The impatient client was Clarence Mackay, radio and telegraph tycoon; the architects were McKim, Mead & White. An enormous complex, called Harbor Hill, was completed in a scant two years. Most of the estate has been replaced by suburban development, but the picturesque French Renaissance gate lodge that guarded the millionaire's playground now encloses a community swim club.

Main Street Historic District, Roslyn

The children of Ellen Ward, a late-nineteenth-century public-spirited citizen of Roslyn, wanted to create a durable memorial to her. Their gift to the town, the robust Ward Clock Tower, still dominates the center of Roslyn, on the grassy triangle at the intersection of Tower and Main sts. The tower, four stories high, its battered granite walls resting on a four-foot-thick foundation, was built in 1895 to the designs of the prominent firm of Lamb & Rich. Its massive curved forms and rich red and brown tones make a strong contrast to the white-painted dwellings, gently

Main Street, Roslyn

pitched roofs, chaste wooden moldings, and neat geometry of the surrounding streets.

Even today, Main St., E. Broadway, and the nearby lanes retain a serene pre–Civil War aspect; more than forty houses date from the period 1820–65. "Roslyn is one of the few places in the world," says Dr. Roger Gerry, a founder of the energetic Roslyn Landmark Society, "that looks better today than it did ten years ago."

Many of the small-scale dwellings that hug the slopes of the harbor are the work of Thomas Wood, a conservative master carpenter of the first half of the nineteenth century. From year to year his designs varied little; only moldings or other small embellishments reflected changing taste and technology.

Main St. is narrow, its widening successfully opposed in recent years. Among the characteristic dwellings that border it are: No. 105, a three-bay clapboard dwelling with superb Greek Revival detailing at the entry; No. 106, built in 1836 for James Smith, the town's most fashionable tailor, and modernized by his son, a blacksmith, by the addition of a shed-roof kitchen and brackets at the eaves; No. 190, the mansarded Warren Wilkey house, built for a well-to-do lawyer around the time of the Civil War; and No. 221, the seventeenth-century Joseph Starkins house, which will open as a museum interpreting Long Island history in 1976.

On E. Broadway, the original Presbyterian Church at No. 35 has been remodeled to a dwelling. The Mott-Magee-Skewes House, with tiny eyebrow windows, was commemorated in "Song for a Little House" by Christopher Morley. The steeply pitched roof and richly carved brackets of No. 95 lend a Gothic flourish to the street.

On Papermill Rd., surrounded by the village park, the early-nineteenth-century home of William H. Valentine has been converted into the municipal building. The simple leaded transom reveals its roots in the Federal period. The reconstructed paper mill itself, now owned by the village, was originally built in 1773, the second mill owned by Hendrick Onderdonk. The first, a gristmill, is at 1347 Northern Blvd; for many years it has been a restaurant. George Washington's diary notes a visit to Roslyn in 1790; he had breakfast at Onderdonk's home (now the Washington Tavern) and remarked that his host "worked a grist, and two paper mills, the last of which he seems to carry on with spirit and to profit."

Trinity Church (Northern Blvd. [Rte. 25A] and Church St., Roslyn). Architects McKim, Mead & White were sensitive to the small scale of neighboring dwellings and the countrified ambience of Roslyn, and in 1917 designed this church in the mood of the medieval English style. A tall bellcote, projecting high above the roof ridge, sounds an aristocratic note; red bricks, laid in header bond, create a rich

and warm surface. The church, parish house, and the connecting cloistered passageway, all designed by the same firm, form a closely unified composition.

Clayton (William Cullen Bryant Nature Preserve) (Northern Blvd. [Rte. 25A] and Mott's Cove Rd., Roslyn Harbor). Ogden Codman, Jr., a maverick architect who refused to join the American Institute of Architects and asked to have his name stricken from the records of MIT, where he studied, designed this large and relatively conventional mansion around 1895. His client was Lloyd Bryce, a writer and editor. In 1917 the house was purchased by Childs Frick, son of Henry Clay Frick, whose home and collection are the basis of the Frick Collection in New York. Frick hired a London architect, Sir Charles Carrick Allom, to remodel the house. The house, surrounded by fine gardens, is now owned by the County of Nassau and will open as an art museum.

Cedar Mere (Bryant Ave., off Northern Blvd., Roslyn Harbor). In 1843, when William Cullen Bryant bought a late-eighteenth-century farmhouse on 40 acres of land overlooking Hempstead Harbor, the community was called "Head of the Harbor." The following year Bryant, editor of the *New York Evening Post* as well as a leading poet, served on a committee that changed the name of the town to Roslyn. The name originated in the song "Roslyn Castle," sung by the Royal American Regiment of Scottish Highlanders stationed here in the Revolution.

Bryant's country home, Cedar Mere, was remodeled to Victorian tastes; a latticed loggia runs across the front of the two-story structure. Frederick Law Olmsted is believed to have designed the grounds, and Calvert Vaux the boathouse as well as the Gothic mill, which later served as a studio.

Bryant lived in Roslyn until his death in 1878, and was the founder of the Roslyn Library, which maintains an excellent collection of his works.

Montrose, renovated in 1869 by Withers & Vaux, and Mayknoll, both on Bryant Ave., date from the same period.

St. Mary's Roman Catholic Church
(Bryant Ave. [Rte. 7], at Summit Ave., Roslyn Harbor). Construction got under way in 1871 for this substantial brick church, which served the small but growing group of Irish Catholics in Roslyn. The name of the architect is not known, but probably the congregation was furnished with ready-made plans by a firm that specialized in church design. It is now painted white, inappropriately for its Italianate style.

Sea Cliff

Prospect and Carpenter aves., Littleworth Lane, and Boulevard Ave; other streets around S. Seacliff Ave.

Along the twisting streets of Sea Cliff, a hilltop village overlooking Hempstead Harbor, are clustered dwellings with every sort of fanciful Victorian detailing—iron crestings, carpenter-Gothic wooden trim, towers, arched openings, and scrolled adornments. Sea Cliff was settled as the site of a Methodist campground in 1871 and attracted year-round residents in the 1880's. The narrow streets in the village were originally paths that led to the tents on the campground.

Sea Cliff Avenue, Sea Cliff

First Presbyterian Church
(corner North Lane and School St., Glen Cove). This rich and free creation, the 1902 design of Harold S. Rolfe, commands a hilltop site on the outskirts of the central business district of Glen Cove. A decisive tower and a portico punctuate the crossing of the gables, which have exposed timbering.

Grace Downs Air Career School
(Crescent Beach Rd., Glen Cove). The former residence of F. W. Woolworth, the five-and-ten magnate, is now a school for working girls. Winfield Hall, a three-story Italian Renaissance mansion designed in

First Presbyterian Church, Glen Cove

1917 by C. P. H. Gilbert, is anything but proletarian. In fact, a critic in the *Architectural Record* commented: "In the future it is improbable that even very rich men will want or can afford a big grandiose formal residence of this kind." The severely classic marble-faced building is undeniably majestic. It is twelve bays wide; a columned portico marks the entrance; an elegant parapet surmounts the roof; and two-story pilasters embellish the façade.

Matinecock Meeting House (Duck Pond [Rte. 30] and Piping Rock rds., Glen Cove). Serene and pacific, the Matinecock Meeting House sits in a clearing on a knoll overlooking a quiet crossroads. A venerable oak tree shades it, and a carriage shed to the rear completes the historic configuration.

The form of the meeting house follows the Quaker practice of simplicity. Its pleasant proportions are no accident, for the dimensions are based on a 12-foot module. The 1725 contract specified: "A house 36 ft. long and 24 ft. wide and 12 ft. in the stud, the work to be done for the sum of 20 pounds nine shillings."

C. W. Post College (Northern Blvd. [Rte. 25A], Greenvale). The formal garden and rolling lawns of the Marjorie Merriweather Post estate are now the campus of C. W. Post College of Long Island University. The Tudor-style house, now the Administration Building, is a fine demonstration that rich invention could be be applied to a period revival. Complex in massing, the structure is playful in its details. Stucco is carefully peeled away to reveal the brick facing, a waterfall trickles down through a wooden arched opening, and carved wooden vines meander along timber framing.

State University of New York at Old Westbury (Store Hill Rd., N. Service Rd. of Long Island Expressway, Exit 40). Like other components in the SUNY system, the Old Westbury campus displays a concern for high standards in architecture.

Close by entrance gate "C" a grouping of utilitarian service buildings, completed in 1971, have been given sophisticated styling in bright-colored steel and glass by architect James Stewart Polshek. About a half-mile farther is Academic Village "A," the first of five clusters planned for the site as part of the master plan developed in 1965 by architects Alexander Kouzmanoff, Victor Christ-Janer, and John Johansen.

The complex is actually a four-level megastructure linked by stairs, ramps, courts, and bridges. Its intricate massing is punctuated by rugged towers, bold openings, and thrusting diagonals. The reflection of noon sunlight on the vast expanse of white concrete is dazzling, and may even seem alien to the placid North Shore ambience. But the analogy to a medieval hill town, where the modern university originated, is remarkably appropriate.

State University of New York,
Old Westbury

Old Westbury Gardens

710 Old Westbury Rd., off Long
Island Expressway (Rte. 495), Exit 39S
*OPEN: Wed.–Sun., 10 a.m.–5 p.m.,
May–Oct.
PHONE: (516) 333–0048

A boxwood garden, a rose garden, a walled Italian garden, a demonstration garden, and a cottage garden surround the Georgian mansion designed for John S. Phipps by London architect George Crawley in 1906. Phipps, son of one of the founders of U.S. Steel, married Margarita Grace, of the shipping family, and promised to build her a country house in the English style to which she was accustomed. The house and gardens are now administered by a foundation, and members of the family still live in smaller homes on the grounds.

Statuary and sculpture are attractive additions to the stately gardens. A lake walk leads to the Temple of Love. Fittingly, the Phipps estate was the setting for part of the film *Love Story*.

Gregory Museum

Heitz Place, off E. Marie St., Hicksville
*OPEN: Mon.–Sat., 9:00 a.m.–
4:30 p.m.; Sun., 1–5 p.m.
PHONE: (516) 822–7505

The 1895 Hicksville Village Hall, a frame structure topped by a bell tower, is now a research museum devoted to earth sciences.

Woodcrest Country Club (Muttontown Rd., Syosset). A curving brick wall marks the entrance to the Woodcrest Country Club, once the country retreat of James A. Burden. The Duke of Windsor stayed here on his visit to America in 1924, and wrote: "All around were fine homes with well-kept lawns and swimming pools. Compared to the creature comforts Americans took for granted, the luxury to which I was accustomed in Europe seemed almost primitive."

Architects Delano & Aldrich modeled the mansion and its parklike setting after the great English estates of the Georgian period, following the trend away from the dramatic and romantic landscaping favored in the late nineteenth century.

Jericho Friends Meeting House (Old Jericho Tnpk., near Hicksville). Walt Whitman called Jericho "a Quaker place, full of stiff farmers." No doubt many of them attended the Jericho Friends Meeting House, built in 1788. Elias Hicks and his wife, Jemima, both influential Quakers, are buried in the adjacent burying ground. In 1827 the usually peaceable Quakers disagreed strongly among themselves. Those who dissented from Preacher Hicks's liberal doctrines, including a ban on products made from slave labor, called themselves "Orthodox" and founded their own meetings. Most of the Long Island meetings remained "Hicksite," and the two groups were not reunited until 1955.

Eastern Military Academy (Avery Rd., off Jericho Tnpk. [Rte. 25], Cold Spring Hills section of Woodbury, at Nassau County line). After financier Otto Kahn died in 1939, his huge French Renaissance mansion, designed by Delano & Aldrich in the early 1920's, became a recreation center for New York City's Department of Sanitation employees. However, Sanita Lodge, as it was called, was soon closed because of neighbors' protests.

Later the lands were sold off to housing developers and the house purchased by the Eastern Military Academy. The vast stone pile guarded by a high wall and towered entry seems appropriately ceremonial. The gatehouse is now a real-estate office.

Planting Fields Arboretum

Planting Fields and Chicken Valley rds., off Wolver Hollow Rd., north of Northern Blvd. (Rte. 25A), Oyster Bay
*OPEN: Daily, 10–5:30 p.m., mid-April–mid-Oct.; daily, 10 a.m.–5 p.m., mid-Oct.–mid-April; greenhouses open daily, 10 a.m.–4 p.m.
PHONE: (516) 922–9200

The Carshalton Gates, a magnificent example of eighteenth-century English wrought-iron work, mark the formal entrance (on Chicken Valley Rd.) to the former estate of William Robertson Coe. Coe, an Englishman who became an American millionaire, built the seventy-five-room Elizabethan Coe Hall between 1919 and 1921. He retained the Indian name—Planting Fields—for the estate, designed by architects Gillette & Walker, and hired the firm of Olmsted Brothers of Boston to do the landscaping.

Justly famous for its extraordinary collections of rhododendrons and azaleas and its fine trees and shrubs, Planting Fields Arboretum's elegant structures, winding roads, and wooded vistas also preserve the memory of the era of great country estates. Maintained by the Long Island State Park Commission.

Raynham Hall

20 W. Main St. (Rte. 14), Oyster Bay
*OPEN: Daily, except Tues., 10 a.m.–noon, 1–5 p.m.; Sun., 1–5 p.m.
PHONE: (516) 922–6808

In the winter of 1778–79, when Long Island had fallen to the British, Lt. Col. John Simcoe, commander of the Loyalist Queen's Rangers, chose Samuel Townsend's house in Oyster Bay as his headquarters. Townsend, a leading patriot, was among the first arrested by the British, but he was later released. His three daughters, fearful that their father might be re-arrested, posed as Loyalists and agreed to entertain the British officers in the vicinity. Among the most charming of the visitors to the headquarters was Maj. John André.

Sally Townsend overheard a conversation between André and Simcoe about plans to take over West Point, and passed along the information to her brother Robert, who was a secret agent in Gen. Washington's Long Island network. Townsend's alias was "Culper, Jr.," but his identity was not revealed until 1939 when a comparison of the spy's and Townsend's handwriting showed them to be the same. The information about West Point resulted in the capture of Maj. André and the thwarting of Benedict Arnold's plans to surrender the fortress.

Sally never married, perhaps grieving for the gallant major who scratched in the pane of his sitting room window the words "The adorable Miss Sarah Townsend," or perhaps alienated forever from Simcoe, another admirer.

The façade of the Townsend home has been restored to its prim eighteenth-century appearance, but the Victorian wing at the rear reveals that the building is really a complex interweaving of different periods. The home was not called Raynham Hall until the early twentieth century. Now maintained by the Friends of Raynham Hall.

Presbyterian Church (E. Main St. [Rte. 17], near Church St., Oyster Bay). This Stick-style church is a typically spirited example of the church-building boom of the 1870's, in which the doctrinally conservative Presbyterians, as if in response to the threat of Darwinism, applied a new vigor to their edifices. The church has exposed diagonal bracing, strongly articulated moldings, and clearly defined functional elements—porte cochere, entry, sanctuary, and tower.

Sagamore Hill

Cove Neck Rd., off E. Main St., Oyster Bay
*OPEN: Daily, and most holidays, 9:30 a.m.–5 p.m.; some seasonal variations
PHONE: (516) 922–4447

Young Theodore Roosevelt made plans in 1884 to build a home near his boyhood summer residence at Oyster Bay. The architectural firm of Lamb & Rich drew up plans for a solid residence to be built on a bluff at Cove Neck, capturing the view of Oyster Bay and Cold Spring Harbor. This comfortable home, called Sagamore Hill after the Indian chief who ruled the area, became Roosevelt's permanent home for the rest of his life and the Summer White House during the years of his presidency, 1901–9.

Roosevelt relied on his architect for the exterior design. "I did not know enough to be sure what I wished in outside matters," he wrote, "but I had perfectly definite views on what I wished in inside matters. . . . I arranged all this, so as to get what I desired in so far as my money permitted, and then Rich put on the outside cover with but little help from me."

The "outside cover" of the vigorous and earthy Shingle-style dwelling is a combination of warm-tone brick, rough-cut granite laid up with rosy mortar, lusty green-painted trim, and strong yellow shingles. In 1905 a spacious North Room was added, the design of Heins & LaFarge, to accommodate TR's trophies and collections. A veranda encircles the house, the railing removed at the spot where Roosevelt addressed political gatherings.

The interior is furnished with the family

Sagamore Hill

possessions, leaving an indelible imprint of the personalities of the residents and the quality of their family life. Administered by the National Park Service as a National Historic Site.

St. John's Church (beyond entrance to Cold Spring Harbor Fish Hatchery, Rte. 25A, Cold Spring Harbor). Snuggly located beside St. John's Lake in the center of a nature sanctuary stands St. John's Church, a small-scale white clapboard church. It was built in 1837 at the lower mill dam on the lake and was remodeled in the 1880's. There are fine stained-glass windows by Louis Comfort Tiffany.

Harbor Road and Main Street (Rte. 25A), Cold Spring Harbor. Following the shoreline of the inner harbor, Harbor Rd. has a large number of late-eighteenth- and early-nineteenth-century buildings. When Cold Spring Harbor was a thriving whaling community in the 1850's, this historic road was called Bedlam St., from the antics of the boisterous seamen. Gristmills, wharves, sailmakers' shops, a hotel, and docks were located along its waterfront.

The historic structures on Main St. have a lively mix of commercial and residential uses, as they did in earlier days. The basic house forms are three-, four-, or five-bay, two-story dwellings on brick foundations. As the Greek Revival succeeded the Colonial period, strong door surrounds,

Main Street, Cold Spring Harbor

marked by side lights, flat moldings, and pilasters, replaced the previously un-adorned door openings. At this period, the houses were frequently built higher; several structures have brick basements a full story above ground. The 1850's and 1860's are represented by several fine buildings; these have gables in the center of the façade decorated with bargeboard.

Whaling Museum

Main St. and Turkey Lane,
Cold Spring Harbor
*OPEN: Sat., Sun., and national
        holidays, 11:30 a.m.–5:30 p.m.,
        all year; weekdays, 11:30 a.m.–
        4 p.m., late June–Labor Day
PHONE: (516) 367-3418

A weathervane in the shape of a whale announces the purpose of this museum— it contains exhibits relating to whaling and the whaler's life, especially as practiced in Cold Spring Harbor. A diorama shows the town around 1850, when the nine vessels of the Cold Spring fleet sailed around the world in search of whale oil and bone.

West Neck Road (north of Main St., east of Cold Spring Harbor). Near town, the dignified homes of the 1870's and 1880's set the tone; angular forms are embellished with spindles and carpenter detailing. Farther north, one-and-a-half-story eighteenth-century dwellings mix with more robust late-Victorian mansions.

Seminary of the Immaculate Conception Conference Center (service entrance, off West Neck Rd., Lloyd Harbor). Off the service road and shaded by broad maple trees, Moran Dr. leads to the original estate house, once the mansion of Roland Conklin. Built in 1905, it was the design of architect Wilson Eyre, who developed his own highly personal mode from the Shingle Style.

The mansion has an expressively carved limestone entry, massive exposed timbers, and overlapping terra-cotta tiles hung on the second story in place of the usual wooden shingles. Farther on, the marvelous towered carriage house–stable is similarly constructed. Much of the original landscaping remains undisturbed.

Joseph Lloyd Manor House (Lloyd Harbor Rd., at Lloyd Lane, Lloyd Neck). Lloyd Neck, a fertile area of about 3,000 acres, called Caumsett by the Indians, was established as a manor in 1685. The Joseph Lloyd Manor House, an impressive Georgian Colonial dwelling, was built in 1766–67 for the grandson of the original landowner.

Like most Long Islanders of wealth, the Lloyd family owned slaves. Jupiter Hammon, the first black poet to have his work published in America, belonged to the Lloyds, living first with Henry Lloyd, Joseph's father, and then at this house. During the Revolution Lloyd Neck was an important command post for the British; Count Rumford, the brilliant scientist turned military man, erected a fort there, and British ships are believed to have rendezvoused with Loyalist supporters in the harbor.

The Lloyd family was forced to flee to Connecticut, where Joseph Lloyd, despondent over the British victory at Charleston, committed suicide in 1780. After the war the Lloyds returned to their home, and the manor house became the property of Joseph's nephew, John Lloyd. Jupiter

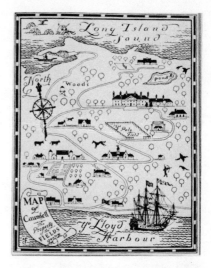

Hammon returned too, and lived the rest of his life there. Now owned by the Society for the Preservation of Long Island Antiquities.

Henry Lloyd Manor House (Lloyd Harbor Rd., outside Caumsett Park, Lloyd Neck). Built in 1711 by Henry Lloyd, the first member of the family to establish residence on Lloyd Neck, the earlier manor house is simpler and smaller. It has a distinctive slanted roof, a side ell, a central chimney, and an unadorned hood over the front entry. The Dutch door, divided horizontally, has a small rectangular four-light transom.

In the 1920's Marshall Field developed a lavish estate called Caumsett here. John Russell Pope designed the grand Georgian Revival mansion, surrounded by cottages, barns, outbuildings, stables, etc. Only the latter buildings can be seen today, along the roads on the perimeter of the complex. Plans to develop Caumsett as a public site have been postponed because of the possible deleterious effect on the surrounding area, but the New York State Division for Historic Preservation is presently restoring the Henry Lloyd Manor House.

Powell–Jarvis House

434 Park Ave., Huntington
*OPEN: Tues.–Fri., 1–4 p.m.;
Sun., 2–5 p.m.
PHONE: (516) 427–3981

The oldest village house in Huntington, the Powell House was built about 1654 and deeded to Quaker Thomas Powell in 1663. Powell was a man of great influence in Huntington and held nearly every public office, except those requiring an oath.

The larger part of the house was built around 1750. It was the birthplace of John B. Jarvis, the engineer who built the Croton Dam and the Delaware Canal.

The Powell House barn, one of the largest barns of its type on Long Island, was moved from Lloyd Harbor in 1972. It was probably built about 1790, and is now used to house a tool collection and as a site for social functions, flea markets, and seminars.

Nearby on Park Ave. are several eighteenth-century structures which preserve a historic configuration. The pre-Revolutionary arsenal is owned by the Town of Huntington and will be restored. The Jarvis–Fleet House (424 Park Ave.) bears the imprint of Capt. William Jarvis' substantial additions after he purchased the property in 1688. The house was later owned by Samuel Fleet, a well-known educator and newspaper publisher. Owned by the Huntington Historical Society.

Old First Presbyterian Church (125 Main St., corner of Sabbathday Path, Huntington). This large shingled church was built in 1784, the third on the site. The previous church was torn down in 1782, on the order of Count Rumford, and the materials used to build a fort. The church bell was sent to New York, where it was to be shipped to England. The parishioners pleaded for its return and won. However, the bell had been so damaged that it had to be recast before it was hung in the newly built church.

A surprising note on the simple country church: a bold, segmentally arched pediment over the central door and carved console brackets on the flanking entries.

Heckscher Museum

Heckscher Park, Prime Ave.,
off Main St., Huntington
OPEN: Tues.–Sat., 10 a.m.–5 p.m.;
Sun., 2–5 p.m.
PHONE: (516) 271–4440

August Heckscher, an industrialist and philanthropist, donated his private collection of European painting and sculpture, from the sixteenth century to modern times, to form the basis of this excellent small museum's permanent collection. There is also a fine collection of American painting, particularly of the Hudson River School, as well as changing exhibits.

The museum was dedicated in 1920; architects Maynicke & Franke designed the svelte neo-Classical building.

In Heckscher Park there is a lake, cobblestone gateposts, a romantic circular gazebo with a conical roof, and a stone cottage, all from the Victorian era when the Prime family owned the property.

Prime House (41 Prime Ave., behind Heckscher Museum, Huntington). In 1859 Ezra Prime, owner of a prosperous thimble factory in Huntington, built a concrete octagon house under the direction of Orson Squire Fowler, the chief promoter of that mode of building. Prime was guided by Fowler's unbounded enthusiasm for concrete, actually a concrete aggregate consisting of coarse stones and lime mortar. This "natural" building material, wrote Fowler, "will be simple, durable, easily applied, everywhere abundant, easily rendered beautiful, comfortable, and in every way complete." The portico is a later addition.

Town Hall (Main St., Huntington). A handsome neo-Georgian building, dignified amid an intensely commercial environment, the Town Hall was designed by Peabody, Wilson & Brown in 1910.

Town Historian's Office (221 Main St., Huntington). Architect Henry Bacon, who designed the Lincoln Memorial in Washington, D.C., created this freely massed brick-and-timber structure in 1891 as the Soldiers' and Sailors' Memorial Building.

David Conklin Farmhouse

2 High St., Huntington
*OPEN: Tues.–Fri., 1–4 p.m.; Sun.,
 2–5 p.m.
PHONE: (516) 427–7045

A farmhouse built about 1760 by David Conklin, whose ancestors came to Long Island in 1639 to build a glass factory, is the headquarters of the Huntington Historical Society. Displays emphasize Colonial Huntington, and rooms are furnished in various periods.

Whitman Village

New York Ave. (Rte. 110) to Lowndes Ave., Railroad St. to Church St., Huntington Station

Whitman Village, completed in 1973, is one of many similar urban-renewal projects which have grown out of Charles Moore's bold experiments in the 1965 Church Street South project in New Haven, Connecticut. Supported by the local municipality's goal of "a multi-functional complex community with stability and suburban beauty utmost in mind," and eschewing the concept of an isolated gleaming tower that ignores existing urban configurations, Moore and his associates used forms and materials of local vernacular architecture and designed the urban-renewal complex at a scale that respects tradition.

A series of four-family houses effects a transition from the Lowndes Ave. neighborhood. A wall of townhouses on the

Whitman Village

east, decorated with supergraphics at the rear, forms a barrier to the noise and ragged commercialism of Rte. 110. These step up along the south-to-north slope of the 14-acre site, climaxed by a community center and a four-story apartment house, and eventually a pedestrian bridge across Rte. 110 to a sister development. The variety of rustic and recreational open spaces answers the diverse needs of the residents.

Walt Whitman Birthplace

246 Walt Whitman Rd. (short street that parallels Rte. 110, between Rte. 25 and the Northern State Pkwy.), West Hills (South Huntington)
OPEN: Daily, 10 a.m.–4 p.m. Closed Christmas and New Year's Day
PHONE: (516) 427–5240

Although Walt Whitman was a poet of the city, memories of his birthplace and his native Long Island haunted and inspired him all his life.

O to go back to the place where I was
born,
To hear the birds sing once more,
To ramble about the house and barn and
over the fields once more,
And through the orchard and along the
old lanes once more.

Whitman was born in 1819 in this West Hills dwelling, built by his father in 1810. His family moved to Brooklyn when he was "still a little one in frocks," but he returned often to Long Island on visits and during school vacations and as a young teacher and printer. He wrote frequently of Long Island, which he called "Paumonok," its Indian name.

The brown-shingled, modest homestead follows a familiar Long Island form: the two-story, three-bay main house is joined by a set-back kitchen ell, both unassuming and seeming to grow naturally from the gentle landscape.

The downstairs rooms are furnished with early-nineteenth-century farmhouse pieces. Upstairs, exhibits and a library are devoted to Whitman's works and memorabilia. Maintained by the New York State Division for Historic Preservation.

Sweet Hollow Road (from Jericho Tnpk. to the Long Island Expressway, West Huntington and Melville). Many of the roads that lead off Sweet Hollow Rd. recapture the pleasant intimacy of the early nineteenth century. Near West Hills County Park, Chichester Rd. is dotted with old frame dwellings, many of them bearing identifying plaques. In Melville, at Sweet Hollow and Old Country rds., is the modest Presbyterian Church, dating from 1829. Clustered around it are many typically conservative farmhouses—shingled, on brick basements.

Estée Lauder (350 S. Service Rd., Long Island Expressway Exit 49, at Rte. 110, Melville). The products of this cosmetics firm promise cool chic, a promise fulfilled by the company's factory and headquarters. The flat landscape has been subtly

Walt Whitman birthplace

Vanderbilt Museum

queathed it to the public on his death in 1944.

Two iron eagles, retrieved from the Grand Central Terminal demolished in 1898, make imposing sentinels at the entrance. The main house is filled with scientific and anthropological specimens collected by Vanderbilt and his family; there is a separate Hall of Fishes, designed in the same style, and a planetarium. Administered by the Suffolk County Museum Commission.

altered to fit the sophisticated, white plastic-sheathed structure. Davis Brody & Associates were the architects.

Vanderbilt Museum and Planetarium

Little Neck Rd., off Rte. 25A, Centerport
*OPEN: Tues.–Sat., 10 a.m.–4 p.m.;
Sun., holidays, noon–5 p.m.;
May 1–Oct. 31
PHONE: (516) 261–5656;
planetarium: (516) 757–7500

The estate of William K. Vanderbilt, Jr., at Centerport, called Eagle's Nest, is, in one observer's words, "very large, very expensive, and very miscellaneous." The serendipitous quality of the mansion, designed in a free Spanish Baroque style by Ronald H. Pearce, is the result of Vanderbilt's own adventurous spirit and far-ranging interests. Mr. Vanderbilt, a descendant of the Commodore, developed the 43-acre estate over the years 1908–34, and be-

Main Street, Northport

Nearly two hundred sailing ships were built in Northport in the nineteenth century, and Main St. bustled. Now the pace is more leisurely, and buildings from the late nineteenth century to the present have joined or replaced earlier structures. The stolid red-brick St. Paul's United Methodist Church, built in 1873, makes a pleasant contrast to the earlier white-shingled First Presbyterian Church, conservatively styled in the Long Island tradition. An insurance office (45 Main St.), whose building dates from 1891, combines the rounded forms of the vogueish neo-Romanesque with the traditional Dutch stepped gables. Bayview Ave., east of Main St., also has many fine mid-nineteenth-century structures.

Eaton's Neck Lighthouse (Lighthouse Rd., off Asharoken Ave.). The waters off Eaton's Neck, a long spit of land extending into Long Island Sound, have been treacherous for shipping since Colonial times. Several tragic shipwrecks preceded the erection of the Eaton's Neck Lighthouse in 1798, the design of John

McComb, Jr. The lighthouse is still in operation and is occasionally open on weekends for tours. Phone: (516) AN1–6868.

Obadiah Smith House

St. Johnland Rd., Kings Park
OPEN: Thurs., Sat., Sun., 2–5 p.m.,
June 1–Dec. 1
PHONE: (516) 724–2027

Nestled in a hillside to protect it from chill winter winds, this two-story farmhouse has a bridge to give access to the hill from the second floor. It was probably built about 1725. Maintained by the Smithtown Historical Society.

First Presbyterian Church (junction of Rtes. 25 and 25A, Village of The Branch, Smithtown). Walt Whitman, who taught school in Smithtown (in a structure now located at 9 Singer Lane, off E. Main St.), found the Village of The Branch "a pleasant one . . . with a Presbyterian tinge of the deepest cerulean." His impression must have been influenced by the striking Presbyterian Church at the village cross-roads. Built in 1827 by George Curtiss, a local builder noted for his woodcarving, the church is a highly original, if somewhat curious, mixture of stylistic elements, displaying virtuoso craftsmanship.

Epenetus Smith Tavern

211 Middle Country Rd. (Rte. 25),
Village of The Branch, Smithtown

The Epenetus Smith Tavern is one of several frame structures, dating from the late eighteenth to the mid-nineteenth century, that line a short stretch of Middle Country Rd. east of the Presbyterian Church, restoring a dignified demeanor to that garish highway. The houses are close to the road on the north side, protected by prim white fences and sturdy black locust trees, used in earlier times for ships' masts.

The tavern was a popular inn, run by father and son, in the Revolutionary period. Later the three-story Hallock Inn (nearby at 263 Middle Country Rd.) became the town's leading hostelry. Walt Whitman took his meals at the Hallock Inn in the winter of 1837–38 when he boarded at another house, which has been moved to Old Bethpage Village. The inn was later used as a library, courthouse, and town hall.

The Homestead (205 Middle Country Rd.), headquarters of the Smithtown Branch Preservation Association, was built early in the eighteenth century and enlarged about 1768. Judge J. Lawrence Smith, a local historian, lived here in the late nineteenth century; his law offices backed on to Judges Lane (a dead-end street accessible from Rte. 25A), which has four early 1800's farmhouses.

First Presbyterian Church, Smithtown

Caleb Smith House

N. Country Rd. (Rte. 25A),
Village of The Branch, Smithtown
OPEN: Thurs., Sat., Sun., 2–5 p.m.,
June 1–Dec. 1
PHONE: (516) 265–6768

Moved from Commack, where it was built
in 1819, the five-bay, frame Caleb Smith
House was presented to the Smithtown
Historical Society in 1955 by Anna
Blydenburgh, a descendant of the original
owners.

St. James Episcopal Church (N. Country Rd. [Rte. 25A], near Highland Ave.).
The village of St. James took its name from
this gleaming white board-and-batten
church, built in 1853. Board-and-batten
construction was praised by A. J. Davis, a
leading tastemaker of that time, for its
"strength and truthfulness." Richard Upjohn, a leading exponent of the Gothic
Revival, was the architect.

St. James Railroad Station (Lake
Ave.). The oldest station still in use by the
Long Island Rail Road has been restored to
its crisp appearance when New York City
Mayor William Gaynor and his cronies
summered here. The board-and-batten
structure was built in 1873 by Calvin
L'Hommedieu.

Mills Pond (N. Country Rd. [Rte. 25A],
west of Mills Pond Rd., Head of the Harbor). Set well back from the rural road, this
high-style clapboard house was built in
1837 from designs by architect Calvin
Pollard, a leading figure in the Greek
Revival style.

St. James Railroad Station

**State University of New York at
Stony Brook** (entrances at N. Country Rd.
[Rte. 25A] and at Nichols Rd. [Rte. 97]).
The quasi-Georgian quadrangles that
were the original Stony Brook campus
have been joined recently by a host of
more innovative buildings, showing the
influence of such modern masters as Le
Corbusier and Louis Kahn. The core of the
campus is the Student Union. Architects
Damaz Pokorny Weigel designed the
brick-and-concrete structure as a hub for
pedestrian circulation as well as for informal student activity.

On the east side of Rte. 97, the Health
Sciences Center tower rises 340 feet
above its hilltop site, the first building in
an expanding megastructure planned to
house seven medical professional and
paraprofessional schools. Gently curved
walls, formed of metal mesh sprayed with
concrete, give an exotic flamboyance to
this building, supported on a massive
cylindrical core. It was designed by Ber-
trand Goldberg Associates.

115

The Museums at Stony Brook

Rte. 25A
*OPEN: Sun.–Thurs., 10 a.m.–5 p.m.;
    April–Nov. (Carriage House);
    April–Dec. (Fine Arts Building)
PHONE: (516) 751–0066

Over 300 horse-drawn vehicles, the collection of Ward Melville, are exhibited in the Carriage House, constructed on the foundations of the Stony Brook Hotel. The variety is enormous: there are gigs, carts, sulkies, chaises, coaches, chariots, landaus, landaulets, broughams, phaetons, game wagons, T-carts, traps, four-in-hand coaches, surreys, buggies, and others.

The Fine Arts Building, added to the complex in 1974, displays a considerable collection of William Sydney Mount's paintings and sketches.

Also on the grounds are a restored 1818 schoolhouse from Nassakeag, a harnessmaker's shop, the last steam locomotive used by the Long Island Rail Road, a printing shop, a blacksmith shop from Setauket, and a barn which displays tools and craft implements.

William Sydney Mount House (Rte. 25A, at Stony Brook Rd., Stony Brook). William Sydney Mount was among the first American artists to take as his subject the life of ordinary people, including the black population, around him. His genre paintings of Long Island, typified by "Eel Spearing at Setauket," painted in 1845, brought new attention to American painting as a distinctive form. Mount refused several offers to study in Europe, because, he said, "originality is not confined to one place or country, which is very consoling to us Yankees."

Mount lived and worked in this large frame house, along with his two brothers, also artists. Built in 1725, and enlarged in later years, the house was the first inn and post office in Stony Brook. Jonas Hawkins, a spy for Gen. Washington, lived in it during the Revolution. The house is now the property of the Museums at Stony Brook (Suffolk Museum) and is open by appointment. Phone: (516) 751–0066.

Stony Brook Grist Mill

Grist Mill Rd., off Main St. (Rte. 25A), Stony Brook
*OPEN: 1–4 p.m., summer months
PHONE: (516) 751–0066

A tidal mill has existed at this spot, opposite the millpond, since 1699, but the current mill probably dates from about 1750. The French millstones in the shingled, double-gabled millhouse and some of the wooden machinery are original.

In the 1870's the miller was so inefficient that the town board authorized any irate customer to bring suit against him, "with the hope that reason or suits will cause the Miller to do right for his good and that of the people." Now owned and operated by the Museums at Stony Brook (Suffolk Museum).

Center for Contemporary and Traditional Crafts (Main St., at Christian Ave., Stony Brook). The Stone Jug, where Mount fiddled for dances and which served as the locale for several of his works, is now part of the Museums at Stony Brook. Open: Sun.–Thurs., 10 a.m.–5 p.m., April–Nov. Phone: (516) 751–0066.

Thompson House

N. Country Rd., Setauket
*OPEN: Fri.–Sun., 1–5 p.m.,
        May through third Sun. in Oct.
PHONE: (516) 941–9444

In this two-story salt-box house, the earliest part of which was built about 1700, Benjamin Thompson, noted Long Island historian, was born in 1784. A wing was added to the clapboard structure in the early eighteenth century. Its austerity reflects puritanical sensibilities. Only the heavy grouped chimneys and the door and window openings break its rigid mass.

The house is owned by the Stony Brook Community Fund and maintained by the Society for the Preservation of Long Island Antiquities (SPLIA), and is furnished in the style of the period.

North of the house is the headquarters of SPLIA and a barn complex, containing a restored eighteenth-century barn from Northport, an octagonal icehouse from Oyster Bay, and a corncrib from Westbury.

Setauket Neighborhood House (Main St.). This long, rambling structure with a friendly porch faces a pleasant pond, giving the surrounding area a strong flavor of the nineteenth century. Now a community center, the building was originally the Elderkin Hotel.

The pond and stone mill at Old Field Rd. and Main St. are part of the Frank Melville Memorial, created by his widow in 1937. The American Corinthian or cornstalk motif on the Setauket Post Office, designed in 1941 by architect Richard Haviland Smythe, was copied from those designed by Benjamin Latrobe for the old Supreme Court building in Washington, D.C.

Caroline Church of Brookhaven, Setauket

Caroline Church of Brookhaven (Village Green, Setauket). An almost primitive vigor and boldness are conveyed by the abstract simplicity of this church. Built in 1729, its name was changed from Christ Church to Caroline Church the next year, in honor of Queen Caroline who donated a silver communion set. A slave gallery was added in 1744. The interior was altered in the nineteenth century but was restored in 1937. Restoration revealed huge hand-hewn oak timbers and wood framing that showed the relationship to ship carpentry, a reminder of Setauket's origins as a shipbuilding center.

A wooden fence encloses the church and graveyard; an open carriage shed, a rare survival of such a structure, still stands close to the church.

Presbyterian Church (Village Green, Setauket). The tall steeple of this appealing church rises in several stages, an elegant finale to its simple volume. Built in 1812 on the site of earlier churches, the church has an adjacent graveyard surrounded by an elegant 1870's cast-iron fence. Buried there are some of Long Island's most illustrious citizens, including William Sydney

Mount and Abraham Woodhull, Gen. Washington's secret agent known as "Culper, Sr."

Emma Clark Memorial Library (Village Green, across from Presbyterian Church, Setauket). The gift of philanthropist Thomas C. Hodgkins in memory of his niece, the Setauket library was built in 1892. Architects Rossiter & Wright followed the Queen Anne style, blending brick, stucco, timber, and stained glass in a picturesque composition.

Sherwood–Jayne House

Old Post Rd., East Setauket
*OPEN: Fri.–Sun., 1–5 p.m.,
    May through third Sun. in Oct.
PHONE: (516) 941–9444

When this salt-box was built by the Jayne family about 1730 and enlarged sixty years later, no doubt they had chickens in the yard and sheep grazing nearby. This rural ambience has been preserved by the Society for the Preservation of Long Island Antiquities, even to the barnyard animals.

Mr. Howard Sherwood, founder of SPLIA, owned and restored the house, adding elements from other houses. He bequeathed the property to SPLIA, and it is furnished with his superb collection of antiques.

John R. Mather House

115 Prospect St., Port Jefferson
*OPEN: Tues., Sat., Sun., 1–4 p.m.,
    March–Nov., and by
    appointment
PHONE: (516) 473–2665; 473–2153

The home of shipbuilder and philanthropist John R. Mather is the headquarters of the Port Jefferson Historical Society and the center of a growing complex of structures relating to the town's history. A toolshed, loom barn, and marine museum are behind the house. The Dedier House, built in the 1850's, has been moved next door and is being restored.

Many dwellings on Prospect and neighboring streets display distinctive carpenter details which are part of the local building idiom. Carved drop pendants, shaped like tears, on the porch supports and the eaves brackets are frequent. The basic boxlike dwellings have embellishments and additions that reflect changes in taste and technology through the nineteenth century. Moldings become more complex and fuller, and clapboard and shingle surfaces give way to richer and more intricate sheathing. Two-story porches are also common.

On Division St., No. 107, a tiny dwelling, has eyebrow windows; and No. 106, a gable-fronted, shingled dwelling, has 6-over-6 lights on the second story and 4-over-4 on the street level, a curious feature seen elsewhere in Port Jefferson. Perhaps the builders tried to keep up with the latest fashion at street level, but stayed close to tradition on the upper story.

E. Broadway and E. Main Street area, Port Jefferson. Along the harbor, where ferries still cross Long Island Sound to Bridgeport, are reminders of Port Jefferson's heyday as a shipbuilding center. Some commercial buildings—offices, warehouses, factories—have been converted to modern uses; one is the office of Tuthill & Young, built in the late 1800's, with round-arched windows on the first floor and rectangular windows on the second.

Rock Hall

199 Broadway, opposite
Lawrence Ave., Lawrence
OPEN: Weekdays, except Tues.,
    10 a.m.–5 p.m.; Sun., noon–
    5 p.m.; April–Nov.
PHONE: (516) 239–1157

A rare example of high-style pre-Revolutionary building in this part of the country, Rock Hall testifies to the contemporary admiration for the English mode, with its carved wood cornice and modillions at the eaves, a curved-roof portico, arched pedimented dormers, and a Chippendale-like balustrade on the roof. But the unpretentious forms and the use of simple wood shingles for sheathing are distinctively American.

The earliest parts of the house were built in 1767, when Josiah Martin, a wealthy planter from Antigua, purchased 600 acres of land in addition to the existing buildings. Martin hired Gerhardus Clowes, a well-known builder, to complete the mansion.

Interior paneling and other architectural elements are fine examples of craftsmanship. The superb collection of furnishings, many on loan from museums, matches the architectural beauty of the exterior.

Thomas Hewlett took ownership in 1824, and the house remained in his family until 1948, when it was donated to the Town of Hempstead. Administered by SPLIA.

Geller House (Ocean Ave. and Tanglewood St., off The Causeway, Lawrence). The sloping roofs of this trend-setting binuclear home converge at the central entry, creating a distinctive butterfly profile, still as fresh as when it was designed in 1944 by Marcel Breuer.

"Isle of Wight" area, Lawrence (Seaview Ave., Albert Place, and nearby streets, off The Causeway). The view across the salt marshes and the bay made this a special place to late-nineteenth-century visitors. They called it the "Isle of Wight," and built comfortable shingled summer homes, many of which remain.

Rockaway Hunting Club (Ocean Ave., Lawrence). Overlooking Brosewere Bay, the rambling, dark-brown-shingled clubhouse and the nearby houses evoke the

Rock Hall

119

period of the 1870's, when men of means found rural Long Island a fine place for riding to hounds, and established the Rockaway Hunting Club.

Trinity–St. John's Church (Broadway, across from Hewlett–Woodmere Public Library, Hewlett). This vigorous Stick-style church, built in 1877, is sheathed in shingle and clapboard with boldly articulated brackets and bargeboards. An earlier church, built in 1836, was converted into the parish house and a covered passageway links it to the later church. A delicate mid-nineteenth-century iron fence faces the churchyard.

Old Grist Mill Historical Museum (corner of Wood and Denton sts., off Rockaway Ave., in park back of Village Hall, East Rockaway). The old Davison millhouse, built of wide clapboards, dates from the early 1800's. It contains exhibits relating to the craft of milling and is open by appointment. Phone: (516) LY9–3356.

Baymen's Cottages, Oceanside (Silver Lane, Rockaway Ave., and Henry St.). Long Island's baymen—both the repository and the source of much of the area's legendry—went out in their open row-

boats in this area, called Christian Hook in the nineteenth century. In those days the bays provided rich supplies of Rockaway oysters, clams, eels, and salt hay, used in New York City for livery stables and insulation. A boisterous crew, the people of the bay world were, according to an 1838 writer, "quite primitive. . . . Neither the weather nor the tides tamed the baymen. . . . Their highest pleasures were found in convivial associations and rough, physical sports found in and about the taverns, which were very numerous."

Salty baymen still carry on some of the traditions, but few of the traditional baymen's cottages—narrow one-and-a-half-story dwellings with an ell at one or both sides or to the rear for storing fishing tackle—still exist. These few—at Nos. 481, 499, 519 Silver Lane, 2815 Rockaway Ave., and on Henry St.—are rare survivals.

Long Beach

Long Beach's glittering reputation in pre-Depression days was largely due to the determined efforts of William Henry Reynolds, a flamboyant real-estate entrepreneur who later commissioned the Chrysler Building in New York City.

To create a fashionable image for Long Beach, Reynolds limited commercialism to the boardwalk and required that buildings be fireproof and uniformly roofed in red tiles. By 1913, more than 200 white and cream stucco-faced concrete mansions surrounded with formal gardens rose above the sand dunes. These residences gave a particular character to the town; many of them survive, particularly around Beech, Penn, and Walnut sts. for a few blocks east and west of Edwards Blvd.

Long Beach Boulevard, Long Beach

Freeport Historical Society Museum and Library

250 S. Main St.
OPEN: Thurs., Sun., 2–5 p.m.
PHONE: (516) MA3–8869

Freeport, where trading vessels in the eighteenth century landed goods without paying duty, became a fashionable yachting and sporting center in the late nineteenth century. This museum of memorabilia chronicles all the changes in village life in the intervening and succeeding years.

St. George's Church (319 Front St. [Rte. 102], off Main St., Hempstead). The weathercock that tops the spire of St. George's was pierced by British musketballs in the Revolution. At that time the cock was on the second church building on this site; the present one dates from 1822. The church is a simple white-shingled structure with a square tower and octagonal belfry.

The Rectory (217 Peninsula Blvd., at Greenwich St.), built in 1793, is a formal shingled structure with a gambrel roof and Palladian windows over the portico.

Methodist Church of Hempstead (Front and Washington sts.). The 160-foot spire of this pleasant Italianate church, built in 1855, soars above its square, three-tiered tower and the flat Hempstead plains.

Hofstra University (1000 Hempstead Tnpk. [Rte. 24], at California Rd., Hempstead). The library, an eleven-story rough-cast reinforced-concrete structure,

St. George's Church, Hempstead

is bold in contour but makes a successful transition from the tall new buildings to the small scale of the original brick-and-limestone structures on the south campus. These, designed in 1936 by Aymar Embury II, were, according to the WPA guidebook writer, "neoclassic in style . . . with the severe plainness of the modern architectural trend."

A svelte glass-and-concrete pedestrian bridge, called a "unispan," connects the original campus with the new student center and dormitories on the north side of Rte. 24. The six dormitories, fourteen-story towers of brick and concrete, form a well-defined urbanistic environment. Pitched-roof penthouses and set-backs on the façade are a somewhat overscaled echo of historic Long Island precedent.

The library, unispan, student center, and dormitories were designed by the architectural firm of Warner Burns Toan Lunde; construction took place from 1965 to 1974.

Doubleday Books (Franklin Ave., between 2nd and 6th sts., Garden City). Designed by architects Kirby & Petit in 1910 to enhance the elegance of its suburban neighborhood, this brick complex was declared to resemble Hampton Court. Doubleday, Page and Company were publishers of *Country Life*, a magazine that reported and encouraged affluent suburban development.

Garden City

Rockaway, Cathedral, and Hilton aves., 9th to 2nd sts.

Alexander Turney Stewart looked at the flat and nearly deserted Hempstead Plain in 1869 and foresaw a "Garden City" blooming there. From a modest start as an immigrant importer of Irish lace, Stewart had by mid-century amassed a fortune in merchandising. His gleaming white-marble wholesale and retail dry-goods emporium was New York's showplace, and his efficient business practices evoked awe and envy.

Stewart worked on plans for the new model community on Long Island with his architect friend John Kellum, who had also designed Stewart's magnificent Fifth

Avenue townhouse and his second store, a grand cast-iron creation, as well as the opulent courthouse commissioned by Boss Tweed in 1861.

A cemetery was moved; a railroad reorganized; and finally a village began to grow in a 500-acre core of the 7,000-acre spread Stewart had acquired. Kellum planned roads 50 feet wide, with a 15-foot strip on either side to be planted with fruit and shade trees. Lot sizes were ample, and dwellings were to be at a uniform 75-foot set-back from the street. Handsome residences, distinguished by their solidity and dignity, were designed by Kellum in a variety of popular styles. After Kellum's death in 1871, his assistant, James L'Hommedieu, carried on. About a dozen of the largest houses built later became known as Apostle Houses. Spacious, man-sarded structures, they were constructed mostly of brick made in Stewart's factory in Farmingdale. About sixty less costly homes for workers, a hotel, stables, a railroad station, and nearly 15 miles of white picket fence were built before Stewart's death in 1876.

The many original dwellings which remain set the prim, Victorian tone that pervades Garden City. On Hilton Ave., near the later railroad station and the library, several of the original commercial blocks remain unchanged.

Garden City Cathedral (Cathedral and 6th aves.). When A. T. Steward died, his devoted widow, Cornelia, determined to erect a memorial worthy of him. Nothing less than a cathedral would do. She persuaded the Episcopal bishop of Long Island to designate the half-built Garden City as the episcopal seat. On June 28, 1877, little more than a year after Stewart's death, the cornerstone of a large

6th Street, Garden City

brownstone church was laid. Completed in 1885, it was adorned, fairy-tale fashion, with flying buttresses, flourishing finials, and carved crockets. Henry G. Harrison was the architect.

As part of the arrangement with the bishop, Cornelia Stewart also provided funds for the construction of the Diocesan House (36 Cathedral Ave.) and St. Paul's School (Rockaway and Stewart aves.), both designed by architect E. H. Harris in an Eastlakian mode in the early 1880's.

Newsday Plant (550 Stewart Ave., Garden City). Harry Guggenheim, member of a highly successful family and a pioneer aviator, was a strong believer in women's rights to a career. When in 1939 he married his third wife, Alicia Patterson, whose father was publisher of the *New York Daily News* and whose grandfather was founder of the *Chicago Tribune*, he felt that she too should try her hand at the newspaper game. So he bought her a newspaper—the struggling *Nassau Daily Journal*. Together they made it over into *Newsday*, one of the most successful and highly respected dailies in the country. The chunky, modernistic Garden City plant was built in 1947, designed by Abbott Wood.

Newsday influenced the present face of Long Island by campaigning vigorously for postwar revision of the building code, thus permitting the construction of Levittown and the influx of thousands of former city-dwellers.

Old Nassau County Courthouse (Franklin Ave. [Rte. 6], between 15th St. and Old Country Rd., Mineola). Nassau County was one of the oldest settled areas in New York State, but it did not become a separate county until 1899. To fit its new status, a county courthouse was built the next year, the design of architect William Tubby. Theodore Roosevelt, then governor of New York State, laid the cornerstone for the Renaissance-flavor, poured-concrete structure.

Roosevelt Field Shopping Center (Garden City). The whole world waited anxiously on May 20, 1927, when Charles Lindbergh took off on the first solo transatlantic airplane flight from Roosevelt Field, the airfield then on the site of this shopping center. A later pioneer was the Roosevelt Field commercial development, planned in the early 1950's by Skidmore, Owings & Merrill and I. M. Pei Associates as a suburban shopping center, integrated into major traffic arteries.

The Franklin National Bank, on Stewart Ave., was designed by Pei a few years later; it is a precise steel-framed structure, sheathed in mesh and anodized gold panels. Nearby (1035 Stewart Ave.) is the stepped-back façade of the red-brick Hempstead Bank, designed in 1971 by Long Island architects Bentel & Bentel.

Endo Laboratories, Inc. (Stewart Ave. and Endo Blvd., Garden City). Paul Rudolph was the architect of this

Endo Laboratories   123

modern-day cousin to the battlemented medieval castle. Rudolph's preference for complex massing was encouraged by the building's purposes, which demanded a highly specialized plan and intricate horizontal–vertical relationships. The facility was begun in 1962.

Nassau County Historical Museum

Eisenhower Park, off Hempstead Tnpk. (Rte. 24), East Meadow
OPEN: Daily, 9 a.m.–5 p.m., to Nassau County residents only
PHONE: (516) 292–4162

This attractive brick-and-timber Tudor Revival house, formerly the estate of the Lannin family, is now part of the Nassau County Museum system. It presents displays of history from the early Dutch and English settlers to postwar suburban expansion.

Jones Beach State Park

Meadowbrook State and Wantagh State pkwys.

Jones Beach sprang full-blown from the head of Robert Moses. It was the first spectacular achievement of a long career devoted to bringing parks and parkways to the people of New York, whether they wanted them or not.

In 1926 Moses was the first president of the Long Island State Park Commission and, according to his biographer–critic Robert Caro, he sketched out on an envelope, to an incredulous audience of architects and engineers, his unprecedented conception of a public recreational complex. Within a few years, Moses had accomplished everything he planned. He hired a young designer, H. A. Magoon, to translate his grandiose ideas into working drawings, and challenged the ingenuity of architect Arthur Gilmore and his engineering staff who had to construct buildings, parkways, and parking lots on a barrier beach. He also shrewdly outwitted his political opponents to gain control of the land and the money to complete the project.

Architecturally, Jones Beach reflects the vision of 1920's modernism. Bathhouses, restaurants, parking lots, pedestrian walkways and underpasses, and the massive soaring water tower which serves as a visual symbol and traffic hub are conceived as part of a grandiloquent ensemble. Massive, blocky forms are executed in concrete, Ohio sandstone, and Barbizon brick; rugged sculptured silhouettes are adorned with modernistic carved ornamentation. The design is coordinated down to the smallest detail—signs, benches, even the waste receptacles. Forty years after its construction, much of the integrity of the original has been preserved; Jones Beach has become a living landmark to a controversial modern-day prophet.

Wantagh Railroad Station (Wantagh Ave., south of Waterbury Dr.). This clapboard railroad station, with pierced decorations at the eaves and on the roof of the platform, has been moved to a residential street. Also within the fenced site are a section of rail and an old train. Open by appointment with the Wantagh Preservation Society. Phone: (516) 785–2436.

Broadway (Rte. 110), Amityville (from Wanser Place south to Merrick Rd.). This well-preserved streetscape has a wealth of fine old buildings. Number 100 seems to have been constructed directly from a mid-nineteenth-century builder's plan book. Number 74, now an office, is a superb example of the early Dutch type of eighteenth-century house. Typically, it has two doorways, the result of lateral additions to an original structure. The carpenter who crafted the ornate woodworking of No. 56 in the 1870's translated his enthusiasm for the new woodworking tools into his creation. At 137 Merrick Rd., west of the intersection with Rte. 110, is the low, frame Carman House. This one-and-a-half-story dwelling with gingerbread trim is one of the few early-nineteenth-century survivals on this historic road.

Broadway, Amityville

Across the street (175 Broadway) is St. Mary's Episcopal Church, a small Shingle-style church of simple charm.

Lauder Museum (Amityville Historical Society)

170 Broadway, Amityville
OPEN: Tues.–Fri., Sun., 2–5 p.m., March–Dec.
PHONE: (516) 598–1468

At the turn of the century many towns, even those as placid as Amityville, had several impressive bank buildings. One of these, a brick-and-granite structure built in 1909, is now the headquarters of the Amityville Historical Society, and displays artifacts and handicrafts. Paired Ionic columns set off its formal portico, and a carved cartouche flourishes above the cornice.

Old Bethpage Village

Round Swamp Rd. (Rte. 110), Old Bethpage. North of Bethpage State Park and Farmingdale. Exit 48 of Long Island Expressway, Exit 39 of Northern State Pkwy., or Old Country Rd.
*OPEN: Daily, 10 a.m.–5 p.m.; winter months, 10 a.m.–4 p.m. Closed Christmas, Thanksgiving, and New Year's Day
PHONE: (516) 420–5280

A dirt road that twists through an expanse of low fields links more than two dozen farm structures and dwellings saved from demolition elsewhere on Long Island and brought to Old Bethpage Village. Such a village never existed, but the simulated community is typical of the rural atmosphere of the pre–Civil War era.

Two roads widen at their intersection and create the center of the village. At one corner is the Layton General Store, an

Kirby House

several agricultural complexes. The Powell farmhouses and outbuildings were built over several generations from the mid-eighteenth to the mid-nineteenth century; this complex is the only one original to the site, which is land bought by Thomas Powell from the Indians in 1695.

A one-room circuit church, the Manetto Hills Methodist Church, was built in 1857. Its styling reflects earlier Greek Revival taste, adapted to the slow pace and simplicity of mid-nineteenth-century Long Island life.

1860's dwelling and store with a welcoming loggia. Nearby is the utilitarian Luyster store, on a rubblestone foundation and framed with heavy timbers.

The mid-eighteenth-century Schenk House is among the more widely spaced structures along the rural road. Originally from Manhasset, it illustrates Dutch practices common in the western end of the island. The nearby Dutch barn, broad and low, is a fine example of the intricate Dutch technique of framing heavy timbers.

Similar to the Schenk House in age, but larger in scale and reflecting English carpenter technology, is the shingled, two-story, gambrel-roofed Lawrence House. The existence of Dutch and English types, side by side, is a particular characteristic of Long Island architecture. Isolated from the fast changes of sophisticated centers, Long Island builders preferred to remain true to tradition.

The Kirby House illustrates a type dominant in the 1825–50 period in Nassau County. The clapboarded frame dwelling was once the home of Richard Kirby, a Hempstead tailor. Fashionable Greek Revival details enliven the modest residence.

Set on the fringes of the community are

Old Village Hall Museum

215 S. Wellwood Ave., Lindenhurst
OPEN: Mon., Wed., 2–4 p.m.; Fri.,
    7–9 p.m.; June–Sept.
    Wed., Sat., 2–4 p.m., Oct.–
    May. First Sun. of each month,
    winter only
PHONE: (516) 884–4385

The Lindenhurst Historical Society has furnished several rooms of this house and has arranged displays depicting Lindenhurst's origins as a planned industrial community in the 1870's.

Depot and Freight House (S. Broadway and S. 3rd St., Lindenhurst). Lindenhurst's 1901 depot has been replaced, but the old structure was moved, along with a short section of track, to a residential area near the new station. Open Wed., Sat., and first Sun. of each month, 2–4 p.m.

Babylon (Deer Park Ave., Main St., and surrounding streets). A fine collection of mid-nineteenth-century frame and brick structures has remained intact. The 1870's brick commercial block at the northeast corner of Main St. and Deer Park Ave. is imposing because of its three-story height and stylishly molded window caps. The Italianate First Presbyterian Church (Main St., east of intersection with Deer Park Ave.) and the adjacent carpenter-Gothic church office are enclosed by a wooden fence with square posts surmounted by carved wooden urns. The United Methodist Church, small-scale dwellings on Deer Park Ave., Totten Place, and James St., and Danny Boyle's Babylon Hotel (northwest corner of Main and Cooper sts.) date from the mid-1800's.

Sea View

Sagtikos Manor

Rte. 27A, near Bradish Lane,
Brightwaters section of Bay Shore
*OPEN: Wed., Thurs., Sun., 1–4 p.m.,
    or by appointment, July–Aug.
PHONE: (516) 665–0093

Since the earliest parts of Sagtikos Manor were built about 1697 for Stephanus Van Cortlandt, a New York City businessman and its first native-born mayor, the structure has been enlarged and remodeled continuously. The manor house today contains some forty-two rooms and bears little resemblance to the Colonial dwelling.

Through the years the house has been owned by prominent Long Island families—the Carlls, the Gardiners, and the Thompsons. It is now owned by Robert David Lion Gardiner of Gardiner's Island, and is the headquarters of the Sagtikos Historical Society. The room where George Washington really did sleep, as the guest of Judge Isaac Thompson, on his tour of Long Island in 1790 has been preserved. The manor house displays furnishings of the Gardiner family.

Fire Island

The isolated residential communities nestled on the shores of Fire Island, a narrow coastal barrier of shifting sand, can be reached only by ferry. Perhaps because of this isolation, each community has developed a special character, determined more by architectural peculiarities than by variety of landscape.

A ferry from Bay Shore provides access to two diverse communities. Seaview has modest vacation homes, built in the time-honored vernacular of wood and shingle, pitched roofs, and unadorned construction. Within these parameters, playful contemporary vacation homes vie for a view of the ocean and originality of

Point O' Woods   127

design. The dwellings designed by Horace Gifford are recognizable by their pinwheel configurations and wooden cylindrical shapes. Andrew Geller's designs, also fresh and inventive, make use of more familiar profiles.

A short walk east along the beach leads to Point O' Woods, an exclusive community which originated in the late nineteenth century as a Chautauqua assembly. Large late-Victorian shingled houses, "old-fashioned" in appearance but in reality—with their ample porches and broken silhouettes—close relatives of the contemporary idiom, elbow each other on the now-eroding sand dunes.

St. Mark's Episcopal Church (Main St. [Rte. 27A], Islip). William Kissam Vanderbilt, Sr., was the benefactor of this Stick-style church, designed in 1878–80 by Richard Morris Hunt, one of the family's favorite architects. Hunt's eclectic approach dictated the use of a variety of decorative devices—exposed framing, extravagant carvings, shingles, and varied surfaces—which were combined with sure skill. The sophistication of this country church is an agreeable contrast to the vernacular styling of the Shingle-style Methodist Church and the Italianate Presbyterian Church just a short distance west on Main St.

Brentwood

According to an observer of social mores in this community, "The arrangements of marriage were, of course, left entirely to the men and women themselves. They could be married formally or otherwise, live in the same or separate houses, and have their relationship known or unknown to the rest of the village. . . . It was not considered polite to inquire who might be the father of a new-born child, or who the husband or wife of any individual might be." The time: 1850. The community: Modern Times, founded by Josiah Warren, a reformer and anarchist. The utopian Modern Times lasted about ten years; in its place grew the more conventional community of Brentwood.

A few architectural survivals remain from the earlier era. Among them are the grid plan; Christ Church (Third Ave.), a tiny board-and-batten church with a steeply pitched roof and vigorous decoration; and Christ Church Rectory (1769 Brentwood Rd., off Third Ave.), a simple two-story, octagonal structure with a pitched roof. Across the street from the rectory is the News and Sentinel Company, with mid-nineteenth-century carpenter trim on its central gable and dormers.

Bayard Cutting Arboretum

Montauk Highway (Rte. 27A),
Great River
*OPEN: Wed.–Sun., holidays,
10 a.m.–5:30 p.m.
PHONE: (516) JU1–1002

William Bayard Cutting, a railroad execu-

St. Mark's Church, Islip

Mill, South Side Sportsmen's Club

tive, began to develop 690 acres of woodland next to the Connetquot River in 1887, along the lines of the plan laid out for him by Frederick Law Olmsted. He hired architect Charles Haight, who specialized in city clubs and offices for the very rich, to design a suitable mansion for the lavishly landscaped setting. Westbrook is impressive, a freely massed Shingle-style structure with Tudor detailing.

Today the property belongs to the Long Island State Park Commission. Westbrook has refreshment facilities, and the grounds have been developed as five nature walks.

South Side Sportsmen's Club (Sunrise Highway, Connetquot State Park, Oakdale).

Connetquot State Park now occupies the site of the South Side Sportsmen's Club, founded in 1864. But the spot was a favorite one for hunters and fishermen as early as 1836, when New York City Mayor Philip Hone recorded in his diary that "we went to Snedecors after dinner, where we found the house so full that, if we had not taken the precaution to write in advance for beds, we might have lain on the floor." Snedecor's Tavern is now the northerly end of the clubhouse, a

much-added-to building. Diverse structures from other periods remain— masculine, utilitarian masses with weathered shingled surfaces. The earliest is a mill that was old even in Hone's time. The mill, which used three primitive tub wheels, is currently being restored by the New York State Division for Historic Preservation.

Dowling College (Montauk Highway [Rte. 27A] and Idlehour Blvd., Oakdale).

Idlehour, the country estate of William Kissam Vanderbilt, Sr., was designed about 1900 by architect Richard Howland Hunt. Though intended as a simple country retreat, the lavish brick-and-limestone mansion had flamboyantly curved gables and a grandiose palm court. The expansive plan was determined by the necessity to separate bachelor guests from married couples. Elaborate as it was, Idlehour was more modest than many such estates. The quality of a home was the goal; and, the *Architectural Record* pronounced, "Despite the money spent on it, this is what it is."

Until a recent fire, the mansion was used by Dowling College for classrooms and administration, and it will be restored. The powerhouse is now used as a per-

Gatehouse, Idlehour   129

forming arts center, the icehouse for the president's residence, and the carriage house as a gymnasium.

A fanciful Tudor-styled gatehouse (corner of Idlehour Blvd.), designed a few years before the house by the architect's father, Richard Morris Hunt, is now a beauty salon.

St. John's Episcopal Church (Montauk Highway and Locust Ave., Oakdale). Originally named the Charlotte Church, in honor of George III's queen, St. John's is a diminutive country church with forthright vigor. Built in 1769, it follows the Georgian formula of a rectangular mass preceded by a square tower, but its New World sensibilities are reflected in its stark geometry and its unadorned shingled surfaces. The door surrounds and heavy pediment probably date from 1843, when the church was enlarged.

Edwards Homestead (Sayville Historical Society Museum)

39 Edwards St., at Collins Ave., Sayville
OPEN: Wed., Sat., 2–5 p.m., June– Labor Day; first Sun. of each month, 2–5 p.m., winter months

This forthright country homestead belonged to seven generations of the Edwards family and is now the museum of the Sayville Historical Society. Built in 1784, it is shingled on a low brick foundation. Its original three-bay plan was expanded in the 1840's with a two-bay addition. Only the detailing around the door relieves the simplicity of its design. There are several outbuildings on the property.

St. John's Episcopal Church, Oakdale

Congregational United Church of Christ

(Middle Rd. [Rte. 65], near Collins Ave., Sayville). Shingles set in curving patterns contribute to the sense of vitality imparted by this broad-fronted and towered Shingle-style church, built in 1888 by Deacon Robert Nunns.

Suffolk County News

(23 Candle Ave., just south of Main St., Sayville). Handsome Greek Revival styling distinguishes this newspaper office. Its four columns have fine carved Ionic capitals.

Middle Road, Bayport.

The progression of nineteenth-century Long Island architecture, from formal Greek Revival to vigorous Victorian, is on proud display along Middle Rd. and the west side of Ocean Ave. A particularly interesting example is the Edwards–Bush House (Middle Rd., near East Lane), built in the 1850's by a sea captain who brought the wood for three houses from Barbados. Fluted columns with unfolding acanthus leaves support a bracketed pediment, adding an Italianate flourish to a Greek form. The second-story porch has a fine iron balcony, and the windows have old stained and etched glass.

Seafaring vessels no longer come home to harbor in Great South Bay, bearing products from all over the world. But Middle Rd. and streets like it preserve the memory of that era in Long Island's history.

Edwards–Bush House

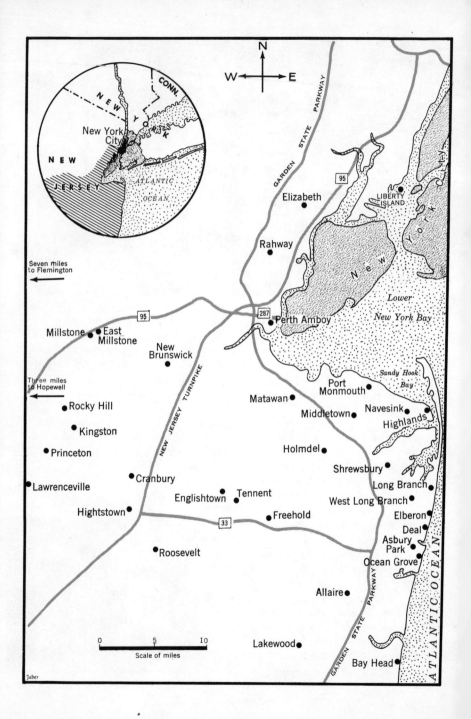

N
W ← → E

CONN.

NEW YORK

New York City

NEW JERSEY

ATLANTIC OCEAN

Seven miles to Flemington

Three miles to Hopewell

Elizabeth

LIBERTY ISLAND

Rahway

New York

95

287

Perth Amboy

Lower New York Bay

Millstone · · East Millstone

New Brunswick

NEW JERSEY TURNPIKE

Sandy Hook Bay

Rocky Hill

Port Monmouth

Matawan

Navesink

Middletown

Highlands

Kingston

Holmdel

Princeton

Shrewsbury

Cranbury

Long Branch

Lawrenceville

Englishtown

Tennent

West Long Branch

Hightstown

33

Freehold

Elberon

Deal

Roosevelt

Asbury Park

Ocean Grove

Allaire

ATLANTIC OCEAN

GARDEN STATE PARKWAY

0   5   10
Scale of miles

Lakewood

Bay Head

Jaber

5 | Central New Jersey

Giovanni da Verrazano sighted the Jersey shore in 1524; Henry Hudson landed in 1609; and ever since, settlers and visitors alike have been attracted to the bountiful seashore and fertile inland plains.

During the Revolution this area was the scene of bitter fighting and clever intrigue; the mills, inns, and farmhouses that remain from the period have been part of a tumultuous past.

In the second half of the nineteenth century, lured by the ocean breezes, New Yorkers and Philadelphians flocked to the Jersey shore. The summer resorts that flourished then, varied though they were, gave the region a distinctive architectural flavor which still persists.

Many communities developed along the main land routes between New York and Philadelphia and in the Millstone Valley, along the Delaware and Raritan Canal. The extraordinary combination of wealth and intellectual activity that existed in Princeton from its earliest days is reflected in its architectural richness.

The sites are arranged in a generally circular pattern, but follow no particular road. The route starts in Jersey City and Elizabeth and moves south to Lakewood, usually quite close to the shore. Then the route zigzags along country roads north and west through Princeton to Flemington, travels through the Millstone Valley, and ends at New Brunswick.

Pilgrim Pathway, Ocean Grove

Statue of Liberty

Liberty Island, Hudson River (ferry from
Battery Park, Manhattan)
OPEN: Daily, 9 a.m.–5 p.m.
PHONE: (212) 732–1286

The Statue of Liberty is one of the last of
the overscaled public monuments in a
tradition that began with the Colossus of
Rhodes. Dedicated in 1886, it was intended as much to glorify Napoleon's
Second Empire as to praise the Centenary
of the American Revolution, its avowed
purpose. Although at the time some
wished "its size smaller and its name more
modest," "Liberty Enlightening the World"
is one of the most powerful mass symbols
ever devised. For nearly a century visitors
and immigrants to America have been
thrilled by the heroic stance of the figure
welcoming them to New York. Actually,
the "mighty woman with a torch" is
welcoming them to New Jersey, for Liberty
Island is geographically in that state.

The enormous statue, 153 feet high,
was designed by French sculptor Frederic
Auguste Bartholdi. Its copper form
sheathes a wrought-iron armature whose
technology was important for the development of skyscraper construction;
Gustav Eiffel was the designer. The Classically styled granite pedestal on which it
rests follows the plan of architect Richard
Morris Hunt, the first American to study
architecture at the French École des Beaux
Arts.

The American Museum of Immigration
is located in the base of the statue. Administered by the National Park Service.

Holland Tunnel. In November 1927,
20,000 people walked through the Holland Tunnel at its official opening; thereaf-
ter, it was closed to pedestrians and became the first long tunnel built especially
for heavy motor traffic. Originally called
the Hudson River Vehicular Tunnel, it was
renamed in honor of its chief engineer,
Clifford M. Holland, who devised the
forced-air ventilation system that solved
the problem of large quantities of exhaust
fumes and whose fanatic devotion to his
job cost him his life. The Lincoln Tunnel,
opened ten years later, followed the same
principles of construction.

Jersey City

Jersey City evokes only a confused, amor-
phous image, according to city planner Kevin Lynch's now-classic study, *The
Image of the City*. Natives think of Jersey
City as "a place on the edge of something
else," says Lynch; but for the observer
looking for intimate spaces, welcoming
scale, and architectural novelty, it has
much to offer.

Hamilton Park (off Jersey Ave., at 9th
St., Jersey City). This distinguished ensemble shares a dignified uniformity with the
great Georgian squares of London. The
expansive open space, formally laid out, is
defined by three-story brick townhouses at
its perimeter. The tile-encrusted St. Michael's Roman Catholic Church, built in
1876, is an imposing element.

Jersey Ave., leading from Hamilton
Park, is lined with brick townhouses. The
street façade between 6th and 8th sts. is
particularly notable for rich cast-iron stair
and balcony railings. The North Baptist

Jersey Avenue, Jersey City

Its restrained forms, characteristic of the early Gothic Revival, recall the churches of rural England, popularly admired for their "simplicity" and "truthfulness." The stone church is sensitively proportioned; a single wooden door in the main gable end is hung with magnificent foliated straphinges and surmounted by a carved trefoil motif.

City Hall (Mercer and Grove sts., Jersey City). City Hall, lavishly encrusted with limestone and granite columns, friezes, cornices, and pediments, was scorned as an "architectural aberration" in an 1895 article in the *Architectural Record*. "This is not the brutality of a blundering beginning," scolded the author, "but the hopelessness of a completed degeneration." Today we can be more tolerant of

Church (Jersey Ave. and 4th St.), built in 1885, is monumental in size, a pleasant shift in scale. Romanesque in form, it is embellished by decorative pressed-brick motifs.

Grace (Van Vorst) Church (Erie and 2nd sts., Jersey City). Now surrounded by prim rowhouses (good candidates for preservation efforts), this church was built in 1850–53 to the design of New York City architect Detlef Lienau. Additions and alterations were made in 1864 and 1879.

New Jersey Title Guarantee & Trust

its exuberance. At least the building, designed by architect Lewis H. Broome, was never bland.

Frank "Boss" Hague, one of the most powerful political figures in New Jersey, began his career in City Hall—as a janitor.

A few blocks east of City Hall are the former offices of the New Jersey Title Guarantee & Trust Company (83 Mont-

Architect's rendering of Grace Church, Jersey City

135

gomery St.). Now a four-story apartment building, it was completed in 1888 and embellished with a stylish Art Deco portal in 1931. It is faced with handsome cast-terra-cotta ornaments and yellow brick.

Ionic House (83 Wayne St., Jersey City). The popular name for this impressive frame mansion is apt; five massive Ionic columns support a flat pediment across the façade. This was one of two similar mansions built in the 1830's by a New York City physician.

Seven rowhouses, between Ionic House and the corner of Barrow St., are emblazoned with brightly colored ceramic tiles. In the 1870's decorating furniture and mantles with tiles was in vogue, but such use on a building's exterior was a New Jersey specialty. Jersey City potters were production and stylistic leaders in ceramics through much of the nineteenth century.

Hudson County Courthouse (Newark Ave., between Baldwin and Pavonia aves., Jersey City). "Precedent Makes Law: If You Stand Well, Stand Still" is the motto carved on the frieze of the Hudson County Courthouse. Such sentiment seems a bitter irony today. Made obsolete by the erection of a new courthouse building, the grandiose granite-faced structure has been vacant for nearly a decade. Decay is gradually eroding its Classical dignity, and its eventual fate is uncertain.

Hugh Roberts, a Jersey City native, was architect of the opulent structure, completed in 1910. The lavish interiors, faced with multicolored marble, were praised in the official description as "reminiscent of one of the baths of imperial Rome." Such civic pride is less in evidence today.

Quinn Funeral Home

Quinn Funeral Home (298 Academy St., Jersey City). Tucked away on a narrow street off Bergen Sq., a key intersection in Jersey City, this nineteenth-century brownstone farmhouse is now a funeral home of cheerful demeanor. Both the main section and kitchen wing are fronted by porches and decorated with rich wooden trim. As a dwelling, the structure was called the Apple Tree House, named for the site where Gen. Washington and Gen. Lafayette dined and planned military strategy.

Old Bergen Church (Bergen and Highland aves., Jersey City). The pristine forms of the Greek Revival appear here in the somber tones of New Jersey brownstone. The church, built in 1841, retains some fine Classical embellishments.

Singer Company (southeast end of Trumbull St., on Newark Bay, Elizabeth). "The sewing machine," declared Mahatma Gandhi, "is one of the few useful things ever invented." Isaac M. Singer was the inventor, in 1851; by 1873 the new machine had caught on so well that his small factories in New York were combined into one large factory in Elizabeth, with access to both rail and ship transportation. "The Great Factory" is still manufacturing sewing machines; it is a huge, three-story, mansard-roofed brick building.

Belcher–Ogden Mansion

1046 E. Jersey St., Elizabeth
OPEN: Wed., 9:30 a.m.–noon,
      Sept.–May

Jonathan Belcher, royal governor of New Jersey from 1751 to 1757, lived in this fine brick house during his administration. Belcher, a Harvard man, gave the College of New Jersey its charter, but refused to have the first building erected on the present Princeton campus named after him, preferring instead to call it Nassau Hall.

The house had probably been built at the beginning of the eighteenth century by John Ogden, Jr.; in 1797 Col. Aaron Ogden, a descendant, bought it. He later became governor of New Jersey, and the house became, for the second time, an official mansion.

English bond brickwork (rows of brick headers alternating with rows of brick stretchers) side by side with Flemish bond brickwork (glazed headers alternating with unglazed stretchers) reveals the several additions during the early years. More refined detailing of later additions are the quarter-round attic windows and the cove cornice on the front and rear façades.

The interior, notable for its rich woodworking, has been furnished according to an inventory left by Jonathan Belcher in 1757; one room has been restored to the

period of Gov. Aaron Ogden. Maintained by the Elizabethtown Historical Foundation.

Bonnell House (1045 E. Jersey St., Elizabeth). This one-and-a-half-story clapboard structure on a high brick basement, with steps leading up to a porticoed entrance, dates from the 1680's, but its appearance is of the mid-eighteenth century. Nathaniel Bonnell, a Huguenot, was one of the early settlers of Elizabethtown (now Elizabeth), named, so it is believed, after Sir George Carteret's virtuous wife. Headquarters of the New Jersey Society of the Sons of the American Revolution.

Boxwood Hall (Boudinot Mansion)

1073 E. Jersey St., Elizabeth
OPEN: Tues.–Sat., 10 a.m.–noon,
      1–5 p.m.; Sun., 2–5 p.m.
      Closed Thanksgiving, Christmas, and New Year's Day
PHONE: (201) 352–3557

Samuel Woodruff, mayor of Elizabethtown, built this gracious frame-and-shingle dwelling in 1750 on the same street as Gov. Belcher's mansion. In 1772 the

Boxwood Hall

house was purchased by Elias Boudinot, one of New Jersey's leading patriots. Boudinot was married to Hannah Stockton, of a wealthy Princeton family, and the rich architectural detailing of the northwest parlor reflected the couple's social and economic status. Boudinot served as president of the Continental Congress and signed the treaty of peace with Great Britain at war's end.

Boudinot entertained Gen. Washington on his way to New York for his inauguration, and was appointed superintendent of the United States Mint in Philadelphia in 1795. Gen. Jonathan Dayton, a signer of the Constitution and the next owner of the house, was host to Marquis de Lafayette on his return trip to America in 1824.

Boxwood Hall was restored as a WPA project and opened to the public in 1943. Maintained by the New Jersey Historic Sites Section of the Department of Environmental Protection.

Christ Church (E. Jersey St. and W. Scott Place, Elizabeth). The placid dignity of architect Richard Upjohn's Christ Church is expressive of the religious convictions of its designer. The stone chapel, with bell gable, was completed in 1854; the rectory dates from 1871.

First Presbyterian Church (Broad St., south of Caldwell Place, Elizabeth). Near the busy intersection of Broad and E. Jersey sts. are several notable churches. This fine late-Georgian brick church was built between 1784 and 1789. Reflecting the period, the square tower is directly over the front gable, which is embellished with wood-trimmed oculi. The adjacent large burying ground has a rich collection of early gravestones, including many cut

and signed in the mid-eighteenth century by New Jersey stonecutter E. Price.

Union County Courthouse (Elizabeth Ave. and Broad St., Elizabeth). An austerely Classical City Beautiful monument, the courthouse was built in 1903 to the designs of Ackerman & Ross; the fourteen-story annex, designed by Oakley & Son, was added in 1925–31.

Elizabeth Public Library (Broad St. and Rahway Ave., across from the courthouse). A 1905 New Jersey law enabled municipalities to collect taxes for library construction. But by the time this fine Renaissance Revival library was completed in 1912, there was a deficit of more than $200,000—made up by Andrew Carnegie, who similarly endowed many libraries. Edward L. Lilton and E. G. Poggi were the architects.

Merchants' and Drovers' Tavern

Corner of St. Georges and Westfield aves., Rahway
OPEN: First Sun. of each month,
        2–5 p.m.; and by appointment
PHONE: (201) 548–4979

This spacious, three-and-a-half-story clapboard inn, built about 1735, was an important stagecoach stop on the New York–Philadelphia route. George Washington paid a visit on his first inaugural journey in 1789. The smaller Terrell Tavern is also on the property. Maintained by the Rahway Historical Society.

The Westminster

149 Kearny Ave., Perth Amboy

William Franklin, the illegitimate son of Benjamin Franklin and the last royal governor of New Jersey, lived in the oldest portion of this splendid salmon-toned brick building. At that time it was known as Proprietary House, but no drawing of its appearance then has survived. Gov. Franklin remained loyal to the King but tried to effect a reconciliation with his father, who adamantly refused, declaring, "I am deserted by my only son."

The house was rebuilt in the early nineteenth century after two fires and became the Brighton House, a hotel which prospered during Perth Amboy's heyday as a resort in the 1860's. Its appearance today, revealing a serious need of repair, dates from that construction. There is a high cut-brownstone basement with a walk-in entrance; four stories rise to a gambrel roof. Fine Federal details include a leaded fanlight over the first-story entrance and deep splayed window lintels with carved projecting keystones.

Called The Westminster since the late nineteenth century, when it briefly served as a home for disabled Presbyterian clergymen, the structure is now owned by the State of New Jersey.

Kearny Cottage

Hayes Park, southeast end of
Catalpa Ave., Perth Amboy
OPEN: Tues.–Thurs., 2–5 p.m.;
and by appointment
PHONE: (201) 826–1826

This two-story frame cottage was built in the 1780's by the Kearny family, leading citizens of Perth Amboy, and moved to this site in 1938. Owned by the City of Perth Amboy and maintained by the Kearny Cottage Historical Society.

City Hall (Market Sq., off High St., Perth Amboy). Facing historic Market Sq. is the City Hall, with lushly carved pilasters flanking the entry. Adjacent is the small, gable-fronted brick structure, built in 1867, that contains the records of the General Proprietors of the Eastern Division of New Jersey. This organization, a survival of the Colonial land-grant system, still holds shares and meets to distribute any new lands discovered in its portion of the state.

St. Peter's Episcopal Church (Gordon St., at Rector St., Perth Amboy). A fine cast-iron fence, with octagonal posts supporting a web of intertwined foliate railings, surrounds this gabled Gothic brick church, built in 1853.

Main Street, Matawan. "The picturesque village of Matawan," wrote New Jersey historian W. Jay Mills in 1902, "is

Main Street, Matawan   139

noted for its old trees, old churches, and old dwellings." Several of the churches are gone now, but the old trees and dwellings still dignify the busy roadway. A subtle shift in scale can be seen from the cozy one-and-a-half-story late-eighteenth- and early-nineteenth-century dwellings to the aloof towered mansions of the post–Civil War period. Doorways, too, record changing tastes: contrasting forms include the delicacy of Federal leaded fanlights, the strong geometric side lights around doors of Greek Revival dwellings, and the curvy moldings on the door surrounds of Italianate mansions.

Burrowes Mansion (94 Main St., Matawan). John Burrowes, a major in the New Jersey militia and son of a merchant called the "Corn King," lived in this two-and-a-half-story frame house with round-butt shingles during the Revolution. The oldest section of the house had been built in 1723 by John Bowne, Jr., son of one of Monmouth County's earliest settlers. Burrowes was a particular target of British vengeance and escaped from the house while his wife defied the Tories and was seriously wounded. Maintained by the Matawan Historical Society.

Shoal Harbor Marine Museum (Spy House)

End of Wilson Ave., near shore of
Raritan Bay, Port Monmouth
OPEN: Sat.–Sun., 2:30–5 p.m.; winter
    months by appointment
PHONE: (201) 291–0559

During the Revolution the British incorrectly believed that the owners of this house, then the only one situated on the dunes, were spying on their ships. The real spy, Col. John Stilwell, was actually stationed with his telescope on a hill high above the beach.

Construction of the earliest part of the ample, three-section homestead began in 1663, when Thomas Whitlock, with a party of settlers, moved from Long Island. In the late eighteenth century the home was converted into a tavern to serve travelers on the Philadelphia–Elizabethtown stagecoach line. It remained an inn for two centuries.

The museum displays artifacts and exhibits of the fishing and shipping trades. Three other old buildings have been relocated on the property to serve as the Penelope Stout Museum of the Crafts of Man. Maintained by the Middletown Township Historical Society.

Navesink Twin Lights Museum

Highland Ave., off Ocean Ave.
(Rte. 36), Highlands
OPEN: Daily 1–5 p.m.,
    Memorial Day–Labor Day

This part of the highlands was the highest point on the Atlantic coast—195 feet above sea level—and the obvious choice for the construction of a lighthouse. A beacon was erected in 1764 on this promontory, overlooking the confluence of the Navesink and Shrewsbury rivers and the waters of Sandy Hook Bay. It not only welcomed sailors but warned citizens that the French, then at war with the British, were entering the harbor.

In 1828 a double lighthouse was

140

erected in its place, replaced in 1862 by the present crenellated red-sandstone structures, linked by rusticated stone walls. The gabled central pavilion forms a bold façade to the central section. Each of the towers—one octagonal, the other square—is 50 feet high. Radar replaced the function of the lighthouse towers in World War II.

The northern tower of the Twin Lights is open to visitors who want to climb to the top for a fine view; a marine museum displays exhibits about the area on the ground floor of the connecting building. Maintained by the Navesink Twin Lights Historical Society.

All Saints Memorial Church in the Highlands of Navesink (Navesink Ave. [Rte. 8B]). This Gothic Revival church was built in 1864 by the master of the style, architect Richard Upjohn. More romantic in quality than his earlier designs, this "exquisite little English Gothic church" looked to an 1879 visitor who recorded his impressions in *Harpers New Monthly Magazine* "as if some genii had borne it over the sea and dropped it on the sunny side of the hill." The church was built of local "puddingstone," and trimmed with red sandstone; the rectory, parish house, stable, and sheds complete the complex.

Baptist Church (Kings Highway, east of Hartshorne Place, Middletown). A pair of Ionic columns punctuate the smooth matchboarding of this small church, built in 1832 on a historic road. Middletown was a Baptist settlement, and the first congregation was organized in 1688.

Christ Church (Kings Highway and Church St., Middletown). A tiny church

only three bays deep, this 1853 structure has an elegant portico, arched windows, and a pointed-arch transom over the entry. William Leeds, a landowner believed to have been a cohort of Capt. Kidd, was saved from his wicked ways by Rev. George Keith, a minister sent from London in 1701 to Middletown, where the people were "perhaps the most ignorant and wicked in the world." Leeds left most of his estate to this congregation and the Christ Episcopal Church in Shrewsbury. A monument honoring his benefactions stands in the churchyard.

Marlpit Hall

Marlpit Hall

137 Kings Highway, Middletown
OPEN: Tues., Thurs., Sat., 11 a.m.–
5 p.m.; Sun., 2–5 p.m.
Closed January
PHONE: (201) 671–3237

Broad, deep, and low, the proportions of this one-and-a-half-story shingle structure follow the Dutch Colonial taste. The smaller, kitchen wing was built in 1684, the more ample main section in 1712. The heavy door is carved and paneled; bull's-eye glass is set in the top panels.

Marlpit Hall was for many years the home of the Taylor family, Englishmen who operated a tannery in Middletown. Many of the family furnishings have been retained. Owned by the Monmouth County Historical Association.

Bell Telephone Laboratories (Crawfords Corner-Everett Rd., off Roberts Rd., Holmdel). Pioneering in the use of reflecting glass as a sheathing material, architect Eero Saarinen, in collaboration with Kevin Roche, built in 1962 what was then called "the biggest mirror ever made by man." Saarinen himself described his plans for the research facility rather more modestly. "The right character," he said, "is rather formal . . . not just any ordinary office building." As originally built, two six-story blocks—now enlarged to four—each with an elevator tower, were wrapped within glass corridors. Landscape architects Sasaki, Walker Associates created the setting.

Bell Telephone Laboratories

Holmes –Hendrickson House

Longstreet Rd., east of Rte. 4, Holmdel
OPEN: Tues., Thurs., Sat., Sun.,
    1– 5 p.m., May–Oct.
PHONE: (201) 462–1466

This house was built for Jonathan Holmes, whose grandfather was one of the original English patentees in the area in the 1660's. It may have been a gift on his marriage to his Dutch bride Teuntje Hendricks. Like that marriage, the house united several traditions: details such as the beaded clapboard and exposed chimney base are of English origin, while the basic plan of the dwelling and the flared eaves reflect the Dutch tradition.

Garret Hendrickson, a nephew of the original owner, was a member of the militia in the Revolution. A group of British refugees raided the house and took him prisoner, along with other residents of the area. He later escaped, and the "atro-

cious villains" who had plundered the area were captured.

The house was on property purchased by the Bell Telephone Laboratories in 1929; it was moved to its present site in 1959. Restoration was simplified because plumbing, central heating, and electricity had never been installed, and no major architectural changes had been made in modern times. Maintained by the Monmouth County Historical Association.

Nearby on Longstreet Rd. and other historic roads remain many farm complexes which preserve the eighteenth- and nineteenth-century configuration of the landscape.

Allen House

Broad St. and Sycamore Ave.,
Shrewsbury
OPEN: Tues., Thurs., Sat., 10 a.m.–
4 p.m.; Sun., 11 a.m.–3 p.m.
Closed mid-Dec. to mid-Jan.
PHONE: (201) 462–1466

In this gambrel-roofed structure, a tavern known in the eighteenth century as the Sign of the Blue Ball, the embittered passions of the Revolution resulted in bloodshed. A British spy was killed by the Continental soldiers. A young man, hiding to escape military service, died; his skeleton was discovered years later. Three unarmed Virginians were killed by Tories; the rest of the party of twelve was taken to prison in New York City. The homestead was built prior to 1700 by Judah Allen. Maintained by the Monmouth County Historical Association.

Friends Meeting House (Broad St. and Sycamore Ave., Shrewsbury). The plain forms of the Quaker meeting-house style are evident in this structure, built in 1816. Separate doors for men and women are a typical feature. An old burying ground is adjacent.

Christ Episcopal Church (Broad St., and Sycamore Ave., Shrewsbury). Built in 1769 on the site of two earlier churches, the church is a rectangular structure with an octagonal belfry and a Georgian tower in three stages. Zealous patriots fired their guns at the crown that surmounts the weathervane; it survived, with some visible bullet holes.

Presbyterian Church at Shrewsbury (Sycamore Ave., just east of Broad St.). This small Greek Revival church, built in 1821 and extremely simplified in form, has a matchboard façade with a tall paneled door. Across the street is a four-bay clapboard house built in 1789 by Benjamin White.

Ocean Avenue, towns of Sea Bright and Monmouth Beach. Walt Whitman declared in 1879, "It is the seaside region that gives stamp to Jersey." Along this stretch of ocean front are distinctive massive, shingled homes dating from the late nineteenth century, when the Jersey shore attracted wealthy summer residents. Typically they have broken, irregular silhouettes and open loggias. Each community had a special appeal: Sea Bright, called by an 1889 guidebook "one of the gayest resorts on the coast," boasted a popular Lawn Tennis and Cricket Club; Monmouth Beach was an enclave of musicians.

Monmouth College (Cedar and Norwood aves., West Long Branch). Founded in the Depression year of 1933, Monmouth College was to gain what the wealthy were losing—expensive land and elegant estates. Woodrow Wilson Hall, the main building on campus (Norwood Ave. entrance), was built in 1930 by Hubert T. Parson, then president of F. W. Woolworth Company, on the site of Shadow Lawn, Woodrow Wilson's mansion, which had been destroyed by fire three years earlier. In the lower level of the mansion, which is patterned on Versailles, is the College Chapel, with woodwork and leaded-glass windows imported from a sixteenth-century Tudor abbey.

The Department of Business Administration is housed in the Cottage in the Woods, the original guesthouse for Shadow Lawn. The garage and courtyard area of Shadow Lawn have been remodeled to provide facilities for the arts curriculum, retaining the flavor of their original use.

Now the Teacher Education Building (Norwood Ave.), the Daniel Guggenheim Mansion was designed by Carrère & Hastings in 1890. The tall clapboard villa was somewhat haughty in appearance, with smartly curving eaves and lavishly decorated interiors. Socially "promiscuous" families, chided a critic in the *Architectural Record* in 1903, were "more interested in show than in substance."

Carrère & Hastings also designed Murry Guggenheim's formal mansion in 1903, in the Renaissance style which became the firm's trademark. The architects were praised this time for having achieved "the mixture of dignity, distinction, courtesy and gayety characteristic of the better French 18th century house and manners," while the owners were reminded that "houses such as these should, of necessity, be an instruction in good form to their

inhabitants." The Murry and Leonie Guggenheim Memorial Library now occupies the mansion, and the coachhouse is now the home of the Fine Arts Department.

The Reservation (1–9 New Ocean Ave. [Rte. 36], Long Branch). In the late nineteenth century, Long Branch was rivaled only by Newport as a fashionable summer resort. In 1900 Nate Salsbury, the creator of Buffalo Bill's Wild West Show, introduced the vigor of the Old West into this refined atmosphere when he constructed The Reservation, a compound of nine massive Shingle-style summer homes. A road called The Trail passes through the center of the development, situated on a flat seaside expanse of land. Each of the three-story houses was named after an Indian tribe represented in the Wild West show—Cheyenne Lodge, Arapahoe Lodge, and so on. Six of the houses remain, still with a fine view of the ocean.

Long Branch Historical Museum ("Church of the Presidents")

1260 Ocean Ave. (Rte. 36), near
Takanassees Bridge, Elberon
OPEN: By appointment
PHONE: (201) 222–9879

L. B. Brown founded the southernmost subdivision of Long Branch in the 1870's and named it Elberon, a contraction of his own name. President Ulysses S. Grant brought fame and prosperity to the area when he established a summer residence here. Besides Grant, five other American presidents—Garfield, Hayes, Harrison, McKinley, and Wilson—attended summer church services in this unsophisticated country chapel, founded in 1879 as a branch of fashionable St. James Episcopal Church in Long Branch. An enormous square tower dominates the smaller-scale portico and front section. The chapel now is a museum displaying memorabilia of the presidents. Headquarters of the Long Branch Historical Society.

Across the street, near the site where President Garfield was brought to die after he was shot, is Sea/Mer (1245 Ocean Ave.), a formal chateauesque mansion with a steeply pitched roof and formal gardens.

Moses Taylor House (1083 Ocean Ave., near Park Ave., Elberon). Built for multimillionaire Moses Taylor in 1877, this clapboard-and-shingle seaside home has a commanding presence on the flat, open landscape. Architect Charles McKim respected the vernacular architectural tradition of nearby communities in his choice of forms—intersecting gables, open loggias, and articulated wooden members—but the sophisticated massing and open plan are a giant step from the more modest vacation homes.

Elberon Memorial Church (Park Ave., off Ocean Ave.). On a low foundation, the massive wooden structure seems to hug the ground. Intersecting volumes and planes are set off by weathered shingle surfaces, gabled buttresses, carved wooden framing members, louvered belfry, articulated portico, and fantastic foliate strap-hinges on the doors. The church was completed in 1887.

Stella Maris (981 Ocean Ave., Elberon). This vigorous Stick-style mansion has open loggias which overlook the sea.

Taylor House

Now a vacation and retreat house, the structure was originally built in 1868 for James B. Brown, a New York banker. One year later it was purchased by George W. Childs, the Philadelphia newspaper publisher who persuaded President Grant to accept the offer of a summer house donated by a group of wealthy Elberon residents. That house, now destroyed, was on the present property of the convent. From 1894 until 1938 Adolph Lewisohn, copper magnate and philanthropist, summered here.

Ocean Avenue, Deal Esplanade section, Deal. Named for Deal, England, this summer resort cultivated an air of formality and seclusion. Tightly massed and extravagantly scaled mansions, often with tiled roofs and entrance pylons guarded by stone lions, are surrounded by crisply clipped shrubbery.

Ocean Avenue, Deal

The carrousel at Asbury Park

Asbury Park

Founded in 1870 by James A. Bradley, who had an "intense and lifelong hatred of the liquor traffic," Asbury Park was Bradley's attempt to prove that a seaside resort could be a financial success without the evil attractions of rum, casino gambling, and horseracing that brought hordes to nearby Long Branch. Asbury Park, separated by Wesley Lake from the Methodist community of Ocean Grove, did thrive, building its reputation on such genteel amusements as strolling along the Boardwalk and observing the annual Baby Parade, begun in 1890.

In the flamboyant building boom of the 1920's, Asbury Park gained some of its distinctive landmarks: in 1928, the Convention Hall (Ocean Ave. and 5th St.), a brick-and-concrete complex decorated with gaudy green-and-yellow glazed terra cotta in the forms of dolphins, wreaths, and shells; and in 1929, the Casino (Asbury and Ocean aves.), a theater, a vast steel-framed amusement arcade, and a carrousel megastructure. Constructed for functional efficiency, but frivolous in appearance, the carrousel is sheathed in sheet copper punched into ornate forms, such as gorgon heads and winged pegasuses.

Ocean Grove

Methodists who desired "rest and great salvation" in an atmosphere where Bible study, quiet living, and abstinence from liquor were the rule found many hospitable communities along the Jersey shore in the late nineteenth century. Only Ocean Grove, however, has retained not just its appearance of that time but its purpose as well. Bible meetings are held regularly, and on Sundays the automobile is banned from the streets.

The Auditorium (Pilgrim Pkwy.) is the heart of the community. A masterpiece of vernacular architecture, it was built in 1894 and can hold more than 9,000 people. It is a vast gabled-and-towered structure framed by massive wooden trusses.

Pilgrim Pkwy., leading toward the Boardwalk and the ocean, is lined with a parade of boardinghouses and hotels. Gable fronts, balconies, and lacy carpenter detailing embellish the angular wooden forms.

In Auditorium Park, on the other side of the Auditorium, are the Tabernacle, a low, one-story octagonal wooden structure with pointed-arch windows; the Young People's Temple, built in 1897, another vast structure whose austere form is enlivened by bright red doors; and Beersheba, a lacy carpenter-Gothic well-cover.

In what was formerly The Grove are rows of tents rented to vacationers by the Ocean Grove Camp Meeting Association.

Centennial Cottage

Central Ave. and McClintock St.,
Ocean Grove
*OPEN: Mon.–Sat., 10 a.m.–noon,
2–4 p.m.

An especially pleasing Ocean Grove house is Centennial Cottage, moved from its original site and restored with period furnishings from the 1870's. It is typical of many similar dwellings on nearby streets. Eaves, balconies, and loggias supported on wooden posts project well forward from the façade of the house. Vigorously framed, and embellished with jigsawed carpenter trim, these airy enclosures gaily break up the tight cubic volumes of closely spaced dwellings.

Centennial Cottage

Deserted Village of Allaire

Allaire State Park (entrance on Rte. 524,
off Rte. 34)
*OPEN: Daily, 10 a.m.–5 p.m.,
April–Oct.; weekends only,
10 a.m.–4:30 p.m., March
PHONE: (201) 938–2105; 938–2371

At the northern edge of the New Jersey Pine Barrens, enterprising men in the early nineteenth century started to exploit the iron ore in the bogs. One of them, James P. Allaire, purchased the Howell Furnace in 1822 and developed it into a self-sufficient community of more than 500 people, with ironworks, dwellings, church, company store, bakery, blacksmith shop, and other buildings.

Allaire operated the Howell ironworks until about 1846, when the bog-iron industry declined rapidly as a result of the development of anthracite coal and coke for smelting ore and the discovery of richer and more profitable iron-ore deposits elsewhere. The village deteriorated until by 1889, when Gustav Kobbé, a traveler and journalist, visited it, he saw "the most extensive and picturesque ruins . . . and the only stack still standing among the Pines."

But a great many buildings survived, and recent restoration has recreated much of their original appearance. In the park setting, the two- and three-story brick buildings evoke the feeling of community life, if not the bustle of a manufacturing center. The tall brick beehive furnace stack (now protected by a wooden roof) is all that remains of the ironworks; but many of the shops, built in the 1820's and 1830's, are used to demonstrate crafts.

Deserted Village of Allaire

The frame farmhouse that was once the manager's dwelling has been furnished with antiques. The first brick building erected in the village, in 1827, a diminutive combination foreman's cottage and post office, is restored as a post office. The only surviving example of workmen's rowhouses is now an orientation center. Christ Church, a frame structure originally built in 1831, was later enlarged; the steeple had to be placed at the rear of the church instead of over the front entrance because the building would not support its weight. The bell was cast at the Howell forge.

The Pine Creek Railroad, a narrow gauge, live-steam railroad of the type used to open up the West, operates on a short stretch of track near the Deserted Village. The train runs on weekends only in the spring and fall and daily during the summer.

Bay Head (Rte. 35). This tightly developed late-Victorian seaside community was established by Princetonians as a summer enclave about 1879. Seaside villas, boardinghouses, and hotels with weathered shingles in shades of brown and gray politely vie with each other for room on small lots.

Georgian Court College (main entrance at 7th St. and Lakewood Ave., Lakewood). At the turn of the century Lake Carasaljo (named for ironmaster Joseph Brick's daughters Carrie, Sally, and Josephine) was the center of Lakewood's lavish estates for the crème de la crème—Astors, Vanderbilts, Goulds, and Rockefellers. Georgian Court, at the northern end of the lake, was designed by Bruce Price and built in 1898–1900 for George Gould. The formal mansion, now the center of a Catholic college for women, is based on Price's original interpretation of Renaissance forms. It is set in a landscaped grove of oak and pine trees, whose fragrance was the lure to the area.

Main Street (Rte. 537), Freehold. Once the Kings Highway and the old Burlington Trail, Main St. in Freehold has been traveled since Colonial days by settlers and soldiers. As is true of many county seats, Freehold's buildings have been more substantial than in other, less important towns and have been well preserved. The neat façades of similarly scaled wooden dwellings, decorated with skill and imagination by local artisans, evoke the decades of the mid-nineteenth century.

Especially notable is the First Baptist Church (W. Main St. and Manalapan Ave.), a fine late Gothic Revival church dating from 1846 with a dramatic ogee-arched window in the central gable and bold wooden tracery. Others are the clapboarded United Methodist Church (W. Main St. and Hull Ave.), decorated with applied wooden tracery; and the First Presbyterian Church (W. Main St.), dedicated in 1873, a more ample brownstone structure with turrets and towers.

Monmouth County Historical Association

70 Court St., north of Main St., Freehold
OPEN: Museum: Tues.–Sat., 10 a.m.–
5 p.m.; Sun., 2–5 p.m.
Closed July 15–31 and
Dec. 15–31
PHONE: (201) 462–1466

Clinton's Headquarters

Architect J. Hallam Conover designed this fine neo-Georgian building in 1931. The museum contains an outstanding collection of American furniture, decorative arts, and local artifacts; the library maintains an extensive collection of local and state historical materials.

The building faces the large grassy triangle formed by Court and Monument sts., which is rimmed by prim late-nineteenth-century gable-fronted dwellings and sturdy copper beech trees. On Monument St., as elsewhere in Freehold, the porches are often punctuated at one end by a rounded flourish covered by a flaring dome-shaped roof.

Clinton's Headquarters

150 W. Main St. (Rte. 537), Freehold
OPEN: By appointment
PHONE: (201) 462–1466

Sir Henry Clinton took over this house, the home of William and Elizabeth Covenhoven, for thirty-six hours in June 1778; and by the time the British left, according to Mrs. Covenhoven's affidavit, "her house was stripped of her bed, bedding, the cloaths of her whole family, and every thing of any value." Even worse, the elderly owner had been subjected to rude treatment, "obliged to sleep on a cellar door in her milk room for two nights, and when she applied for only a coverlet it was refused her."

Clinton chose this house for his headquarters because it was the most substantial in the neighborhood. The first house on the property had been built around 1706; the tiny structure covered by a steeply pitched roof and sheathed with boards is the original section. When William Covenhoven acquired the property in 1723, he made a substantial addition to the simple farmhouse. Of particular interest are the paneled double-leaf door, flanked by fluted pilasters, and the modillions beneath the eaves.

William Covenhoven's 1790 inventory was a guide for the restoration and furnishings. Maintained by the Monmouth County Historical Association.

Broad Street, Freehold. The Reformed Church is a lively mid-nineteenth-century design with crockets and wooden corbelling at the cornice of the square tower. Distinguished dwellings line Broad St.; the Italianate mansion at No. 3 is notable for the cadence of its carved, paired brackets.

149

St. Peter's Church, Freehold

St. Peter's Church (33 Throckmorton St., Freehold). During the Battle of Monmouth, this white-shingled, two-story church was used by the British as a hospital; at other times the Americans used it as a barracks and ammunition station. It was built about 1770 by Quakers who had converted to the Church of England and moved to Freehold. The Gothic moldings around the pointed-arch door openings and lancet windows date from a mid-nineteenth-century alteration.

Old Tennent Church (Rte. 3, off Rte. 522, Freehold). A simple oblong structure, with gracefully flaring eaves, the Old Tennent Church was built in 1751 and reflects the simplicity preferred by its founders, a group of Scottish Presbyterians who organized the congregation in 1692. It was later named after the Tennent brothers, both pastors. The church, set back from the country road, is surrounded by gravestones, many of men who fell in the Battle of Monmouth, fought near the hill on which the church stands.

Cobb House (Rte. 522, between Freehold and Englishtown). This tall, three-story clapboard mansion was built in 1870 and was used as the summer home of Archibald Cox, pastor of the nearby Old Tennent Church. It is now the headquarters of the Monmouth Battlefield Historical Society and is open Sun., 2–4 p.m.

Village Inn (Main and Water sts., Englishtown). As was characteristic of the eighteenth century, this inn was built low to the ground and close to the street with its covered sidewalk. It was built in 1732 and was host to Gen. Washington and his aides on the eve of the Battle of Monmouth, June 27, 1778. After the battle, in which Gen. Charles Lee inexplicably retreated, the Americans again took refuge in the inn. There Washington granted Lee's request for a court-martial to establish his guilt or innocence. The inn, owned by the Borough of Englishtown and maintained by the Monmouth Battlefield Historical Society, has been converted into apartments.

Roosevelt

In 1936, needle-trade workers in Philadelphia and New York City were offered a chance to escape the city slums and to participate in a bold new experiment in cooperative living, a community called Jersey Homesteads, sponsored by the U.S. Resettlement Administration. The pioneers encountered much hostility from local residents, who believed that the venture was "Soviet inspired."

The garment factory that was to be the cooperative's economic base soon failed, and the cultivation of garden plots to augment income proved unfeasible. But, when the community was opened to all comers, it attracted many intellectuals and

artists. Ben Shahn came to paint a mural in the School and Community Building in 1937, and stayed to become a permanent resident and ardent spokesman for the community, renamed Roosevelt after FDR's death.

The physical plan of the cooperative was as progressive as its purpose. The one-story, one- or two-family structures were sensitively sited along curving lanes. Garden plots at the rear of each dwelling extended into communally owned wooded spaces, creating a sense of privacy.

The designs reflected the sophisticated functionalism of Bauhaus-trained architect Alfred Kastner and his young assistant, Louis Kahn. Although outwardly similar, floor plans were modified to achieve maximum efficiency and optimal view and orientation. "For hours at a time, Ben and I would watch Alfred and Louis working with models," recalls Bernarda Shahn. "It was supporting walls that determined the house, and they would twist them this way and that to get the design to work."

Kastner's unembellished, flat-roofed, concrete-and-cinderblock "boxes" have proved to be remarkably adaptable. From the street they look much the same as they did in the 1930's, but from the rear and side can be seen the ample additions and swimming pools that are the tangible symbols of better times.

House at Roosevelt

Peddie School (S. Main St. [Rte. 539], Hightstown). The first building on the campus of the Peddie School, founded in 1864 as a private school for boys, was Wilson Hall, designed in 1866–69 by P. S. Davison of Philadelphia. The first plans for the building were already under construction when D. M. Wilson, president of the Board, saw another set of plans. He immediately ordered the new design to be substituted, and within a few weeks the walls of the first had been torn down and the new building—a fine Victorian Gothic mass with a mansard roof —was under way.

Surrounding streets are lined with many fine homes of the post-1850's. A clapboard octagon (239 S. Main St.) was a gift to the school in 1894.

Stockton Street (Rte. 571), Hightstown. Between Oak Lane and the town center, an orderly array of Victorian homes, evenly spaced and set back from the street, display a dazzling variety of details—molded brackets, scalloped shingles, and carpenter woodwork. The Sarah B. Smith House (137 Stockton St.) is one of many eighteenth-century dwellings later embellished with elaborate iron grillwork. The United Methodist Church, of neo-Romanesque design, is a striking contrast.

Main Street (Rte. 539), Cranbury

Following the long tradition of foreign visitors who have recorded their impressions of America, James Morris, a British writer, noted in 1953: "All around [Brainerd] Lake stand the comfortable houses of Cranbury. . . . They are generally trim, clean and newly painted, their smartness enhanced rather than spoiled by a few yellowing renegades with peeling paintwork." Main St., from Station Rd. to Bunker Hill Rd., presents a charming village streetscape. Uniformly scaled dwellings from different periods, set close to the road, are amiable neighbors. There is a profusion of porches, distinctively decorated. Portions of the sidewalks of Main St. are paved in brick, a stylish and expensive form of pavement popular in the early eighteenth century. Cranbury Brook, which flows into the lake in the center of town, adds to the pastoral quality.

The First Presbyterian Church (N. Main St.) was built in 1839, probably by Charles Steadman, who designed many buildings in Princeton. It has two massive columns and fine Greek Revival details. Across the street is the Cranbury Inn, a large frame structure built in 1780 as a dwelling and converted into a tavern in 1808.

Cranbury Inn

The Museum (Cranbury Historical and Preservation Society)

4 Park Place, off Main St., Cranbury
OPEN: Sat.–Sun., 2–5 p.m.; and by appointment
PHONE: (609) 395–0657; 395–0757

The original two rooms of this small frame house were built about 1834 by Dr. Garrett P. Voorhees; the Snedeker family enlarged it to its present size in the 1850's. Now it has been restored and furnished with a collection of local antiques, along with a display of memorabilia from Cranbury's past.

Main Street, Lawrenceville (Rte. 206, south of Princeton). Narrow, tree-shaded, and peaceful, Main St. has resisted commercial development; residences from the late eighteenth and the nineteenth century form an appealing catalogue of American building tastes. Many of them were part of the Lawrenceville School, founded in 1810 as the Maidenhead Academy. Lawrenceville's prosperity as an agricultural center is reflected in large impressive homes, such as the Richard Montgomery Green House (2549 Main St.), a two-story stone mansion built in the late eighteenth century, and the charming two-story clapboard Greek Revival Romney House (2579 Main St.), probably built by Charles Steadman.

Some of the early houses are brick, but most are built of clapboard or locally quarried stone, handsomely laid in random courses. The fine doorways and elegant details testify to the availability in the area of skilled craftsmen.

The Old Davis House (2868 Main St.), a Federal-style house built in 1830, was Thornton Wilder's residence when he was a French teacher and assistant housemaster at the Lawrenceville School in the late 1920's. It was here that he wrote *The Bridge of San Luis Rey*, his first successful novel. The dwelling is now privately owned.

Lawrenceville School (Main St.). Imbued with enthusiasm for the spirit of late-Victorian educational reform in England, Lawrenceville headmaster James MacKenzie translated those ideas into the building plans for a new campus, begun in the 1880's. Departing from the axial plan which characterized American educational institutions, Frederick Law Olmsted designed landscaping in the Romantic tradition. Over 300 varieties of trees and shrubs were used to mold the terrain into intimate configurations. Olmsted also designed sophisticated drainage and sewerage systems. Although much of the original shrubbery has perished, the quality of the original landscaping can still be felt.

The architectural firm of Peabody & Stearns designed four domestically scaled brick-and-timber residences, designed to accommodate, in relatively cozy fashion, two dozen youngsters and a resident housemaster. Asymmetrically massed, they are grouped in an informal semicircle.

Memorial Hall, also designed by Peabody & Stearns, skillfully employs widely popular motifs of the period—a heavy Romanesque arched entrance, a frieze of windows separated by stubby columns, and brownstone trim carved in intricate grotesques.

In the 1920's the firm of Delano &

Cleve Hall, Lawrenceville

Aldrich designed a number of red-brick and limestone classroom buildings that hark back to the vocabulary of the Federal period and to Jefferson's organizing principles at the University of Virginia.

Princeton

In 1910 Montgomery Schuyler, dean of American architectural critics, advised the "lover of architecture" to "go to Princeton." Good advice then; better still today, for few communities have inherited such an extraordinary legacy and guarded it more devotedly through the years. There are literally hundreds of structures of outstanding merit, from all periods, in the green valley between the Stony Brook and Millstone River.

The many fine eighteenth-century homes have created an ambience of rare dignity in this wealthy and sophisticated exurb. Edmund Wilson, a Princeton graduate, scorned New Jersey as "uniformly blighted," but recalled with nostalgia the town of Princeton, "where clear windows and polished knockers are still bright on Colonial houses . . . [and where] the eternal lowlands haze becomes charming, the languor a kind of freedom."

The parallel development of the town and the college has contributed to the special qualities of reflection and continuity that pervade Princeton. As educator Stringfellow Barr sees it, the institutions of learning give Princeton "not only a lived-in quality but also a thought-in presence."

The highlights of Princeton's architecture described here are but a sampling of the rich fare accessible to the visitor. The selection covers, first, sites in the town of Princeton; second, the front campus of the university; and third, other parts of the university.

Friends Meeting House (Quaker Rd., off Princeton Pike [Rte. 583], Princeton). Quaker families from New York, New Jersey, and Long Island settled near the Stony Brook in the 1690's. This meeting house, the third on the site, was constructed in 1760. It is modestly proportioned and without embellishments, but distinguished by a fine sense of scale and rhythm. It was probably the handiwork of William Worth, a local craftsman, who showed his skill in the careful coursing of the golden-toned fieldstone and in the construction of segmental brick arches above the window openings.

Through the early part of the eighteenth century, the Quakers prospered and remained in a majority in the small farming community. The clustered dwellings east of Quaker Rd. on Stockton St. (Rte. 206) preserve the scale and relationships of that period. Typically, Princeton dwellings were enlarged vertically rather than laterally, creating a distinctive local silhouette.

The Barracks (32 Edgehill St., off Stockton St., Princeton). In 1696 Quaker Richard Stockton bought a 5,500-acre spread from William Penn. The eleven-room home, "plain, but neatly furnished," earned its present name when it was taken over by the British, who quartered troops there during the Revolution.

Morven (Stockton St., east of Library Place, Princeton). Richard Stockton, signer of the Declaration of Independence, built Morven to reflect the culture and life style of the English country gentleman. Eschewing local fieldstone, beloved by earlier builders, he chose brick as a building material. In spite of the formality of the mansion—with its symmetrical façade, high basement, and side chimneys—it was the center of a working farm, planted with every consideration for "taste and elegance."

During the Revolution the British took over Morven, and "suffering and woe held terrible rule," according to Benson Lossing's *Field Book of the Revolution*. Morven is now the official residence of the governor of New Jersey, and is open Tues. afternoons by appointment. Phone: (609) 924–3980.

Princeton Battle Monument (intersection of Nassau, Mercer, and Stockton sts.). Dedicated in 1922, this massive limestone monument to Washington's victory at Princeton is carved dramatically in high relief. The central figure is Washington leading his troops, urged on by Liberty. Thomas Hastings was the architectural designer. The sculptor was Frederic W. MacMonnies, whose essays in monumental sculpture include the figures above the fountains at the New York Public Library.

Drumthwacket (344 Stockton St. [Rte. 206], Princeton). Built in the mid-1830's for Charles Olden, a New Orleans clothing manufacturer who later became governor of New Jersey, this extraordinary Greek Revival mansion had a finesse and sophistication that far outstripped its contemporaries. Six monumental Ionic columns support a flat entablature, and the proportions have a stately dignity. Moses Taylor Pyne, Princeton alumnus and trustee who settled here in 1896, added the side wings (a neo-Georgian anachronism) and the elaborate formal landscaping.

Alexander Street, Princeton (off Nassau St. [Rte. 206]). Charles Steadman, a progressive builder and businessman who moved to Princeton in the 1820's, made a significant and lasting contribution to the town's development, bringing elegance and sophistication to the thriving village.

Alexander St. is one of his achievements, opened in 1832 as part of a link with the Delaware and Raritan Canal, then under construction. Steadman bought up much of the land on both sides of the street, and built and sold comfortable homes to prosperous artisans and tradesmen. The endless interplay among differences in decorative wooden detail and similarities in scale and form creates one of the most fascinating ensembles in Princeton.

Thomson Hall (50 Stockton St.), built in the 1820's and later mansarded, and the brick mansion at 2 Bayard St., with a fine Ionic-columned porch, are two other examples of Steadman's work for Princeton's elite. Both houses were built for members of the Stockton family.

Alexander Street, Princeton

Bainbridge House

158 Nassau St., across from
Washington Rd.
OPEN: Tues.–Fri., 10 a.m.–4 p.m.;
        Sat., 1–4 p.m.; Sun., 2–4 p.m.
PHONE: (609) 921–6748

As Morven resembled the dwelling of a Georgian squire, so Bainbridge House was the equivalent townhouse. The frame dwelling, veneered on its façade with rosy brick, had several other sophisticated details: a molded water-table, decisively setting the structure on the ground; a formal, pedimented entrance marking the center of the façade, which leads to a wide central hall; splayed wooden lintels with ornamental keystones; and modillions at the eaves.

Bainbridge House was built by Job Stockton in 1766; for a short time it also served as the home of Loyalist physician Absalom Bainbridge. His son, Commodore William Bainbridge, commander of "Old Ironsides," was born in the house. It is now owned by Princeton University and leased to the Historical Society of Princeton, which has several furnished period rooms in addition to display and library space.

Offices of Alumni Council (Maclean House) (Nassau St., Princeton). Built in

Offices of Alumni Council

1756 by Philadelphia craftsman Robert Smith, this five-bay brick dwelling served as the home of every Princeton president until 1878. For fifty years it was the only building besides Nassau Hall on the campus. The taut lines of the Georgian-style house are set off by splayed wooden lintels with projecting keystones and a sensitively proportioned door surround. The roof was raised and the portico added in 1869.

First Presbyterian Church (61 Nassau St., Princeton). Beginning in 1766, ministers of this church were also presidents of the College of New Jersey. Woodrow Wilson was the first president who was not a Presbyterian minister.

This church, the third on the site, was designed in 1836 by Charles Steadman. No doubt he worked with a builder's handbook. The successful architect John Haviland had published *The Builder's Assistant* in 1821, the first American book to illustrate the Greek orders of columns and entablatures. But Steadman's use of Greek decorative motifs was spare; the simplified capitals of the Ionic columns and the pilasters on the façade of the church charm by their simplicity, not by their richness. Steadman's real skill as a builder is seen more clearly in his sure handling of the relationships among the smooth planes of the walls (actually stuccoed brick), the deep void of the entry, and the mass implied by the broad gable.

Nassau Hall (Princeton University campus, Princeton). The entrance to the front campus of Princeton University is marked by the FitzRandolph Gateway (Nassau St.), a grandiose wrought-iron gateway between stone pillars surmounted by

eagles. It was designed by McKim, Mead & White in 1905.

No stronger visual image expresses the close relationship of town and gown than the quiet dominance of Nassau Hall at the south end of the front campus.

The College of New Jersey, founded in 1747, was induced to move to Princeton in 1752 by an offer of land and the newly built Nassau Hall, "the largest stone building in the Colonies." The stone walls survived the Revolution and an 1802 fire, probably set by rebellious students, and were incorporated into the remodeling undertaken by Benjamin Latrobe. The brilliant architect–engineer experimented with the use of cast-iron for the roof, supposedly fire- and weatherproof.

The present appearance of Nassau Hall is basically the result of the 1855 remodeling by architect John Notman. He created an arched entry of lofty proportions, accented it with a graceful gable, and added impressive stair towers at either end (now lacking their original Italianate cupolas). Romantic as a stylist, Notman was practical as a builder: for fireproof construction, the architect purchased 2' x 2' iron beams "of the size and weight of the best iron-rails for railroads."

Stanhope Hall, a dignified survival from

Latrobe's plan for a symmetrical campus, remains from that period, west of Nassau Hall. Orange Key, which conducts regularly scheduled guided tours of the front campus, has offices in Stanhope Hall. Henry Moore's bronze "Oval with Points" one of fifteen pieces of outstanding modern sculpture donated to the University in memory of a World War II officer, stands between Stanhope and West College.

Alexander Hall

Alexander Hall (west of Nassau Hall, Princeton). The robust mass of Alexander Hall is punctuated by four vigorous towers with conical roofs. An enthusiastic late-Richardsonian statement, the auditorium building was designed by William Appleton Potter and completed in 1892. Built of contrasting tan and brown sandstone, it has thick piers and low arches. On the southern façade, a richly carved frieze by J. Massey Rhind depicts notable figures in the arts and sciences.

Chancellor Green (east of Nassau Hall, Princeton). When Chancellor Green, an expressive Venetian Gothic structure, was designed in 1871 by William Appleton Potter, it was Princeton's first separate library building. President James McCosh was shocked to find the library, in a room in Nassau Hall, "insufficiently supplied with books and open only once a week and for one hour."

Pyne Hall, which replaced Chancellor Green as the library in 1896, was the first example of English Gothic architecture on the campus; Potter was again the architect. Chancellor Green is now a student center.

Prospect (off Washington Rd., Princeton). John Notman, in the 1830's a pioneer in Romantic landscape and architectural design, was the architect of Prospect, built in 1849. It was during this period that Tuscan villas replaced Greek temple dwellings as the most fashionable style.

Used since 1879 as the home of Princeton's presidents, Prospect is now a faculty club. The 1971 addition to the rear, overlooking the gardens, is a dining facility designed by architect Warren Platner. Like the older section, though dignified, it is playful in spirit; the glass enclosure gaily breaks away from the mass of the heavy masonry structure.

Prospect Avenue Eating Clubs (Princeton). The elegant period-revival houses along "the Street" symbolize the social hierarchy that until recent years characterized undergraduate life at Princeton. Not to receive a "bid" from the right club during "Bicker," the selection week, was bad enough; even worse was to receive a "hat bid," based on the random selection from the names of all those who indicated a desire to join a club but were not chosen by any.

Holder Hall and dining halls (corner of University Place and Nassau St., Prince-

Holder Hall

ton). Princeton President Woodrow Wilson, outlining a building campaign to alumni in 1902, declared: "By the very simple device of building our new buildings in the Tudor Gothic style we seem to have added to Princeton the age of Oxford and of Cambridge." As supervising architect of the college, responsible for developing the master plan, Wilson chose Ralph Adams Cram, noted for his exposition of the Gothic style. Cram worked with a number of architectural firms on this grouping, constructed between 1910 and 1916.

The spine of the complex is the cathedrallike Sage Dining Hall. At one side is the soaring Holder Memorial Tower, "seeming to symbolize the aspirations of a seat of learning," which serves as a strong visual accent for the double quadrangle of low dormitories. A sophisticated counterpoint is the horizontality of the limestone moldings and coursings and of the roof parapets.

Graduate College (College Rd., east of Alexander St., Princeton). A graduate college was an important part of Woodrow Wilson's plan for a democratic university, "in the Nation's service." He wanted it built on the existing campus, but he was ultimately defeated by Dean West, who secured the promise of "very large additional sums" to build a separate (and in Wilson's view "undemocratic") graduate campus. Wilson resigned soon after, and the graduate college was built on a hilly site about a quarter of a mile away and across the railroad tracks.

A grand tower in commemoration of Grover Cleveland, masters' rooms, dining facilities, and dormitories were completed in 1913. These were designed by the Boston firm of Goodhue, Cram & Ferguson, all in the same Gothic style admired by Wilson and Cram.

Princeton Theological Seminary (Mercer and Alexander sts.). Student riots and undisciplined behavior were a common feature of the early years of the College of New Jersey. After a particularly severe riot in 1807, it became necessary to form a separate institution, the Theological Seminary, to fulfill the college's purpose of training Presbyterian ministers of the revivalistic New Light Wing. The seminary, founded in 1811, has maintained a close relationship with the college and, in terms of its architecture, echoes the main campus.

From the Federal period, Alexander Hall, built in 1817 by John McComb, Jr., reflects the influence of the earlier Nassau Hall. Miller Chapel, built in 1833 by Charles Steadman, is a gem of Greek Revival sensibility. Stuart Hall, built in 1876 from the designs of William Appleton Potter, is a fine example of Venetian

Stuart Hall

Gothic architecture. Springdale (86 Mercer St.), a sprawling Gothic Revival mansion, is now the home of the seminary's president.

Institute for Advanced Study (off Mercer St., Princeton). Albert Einstein, Abraham Flexner, and Robert Oppenheimer have been among the members of this institute, founded in 1930 "for the pursuit of advanced learning and exploration in fields of pure science."

The original structures of this "penthouse on the ivory tower" were placid neo-Georgian structures; later additions have been more innovative. The Dining Hall Commons and Academic Building, built in 1971 by Geddes, Brecher, Qualls & Cunningham, enclose a cloistered gar-

Institute for Advanced Study

den at their center. The façade of the emphatic Academic Building is layered and scaled by the windowed grid of office spaces; exterior stairways, à la Corbusier, are playful sculptural elements.

A student-housing complex was built in 1958; these flat-roofed, brick and concrete-block units designed by Marcel Breuer were intended to provide an atmosphere of semi-retreat. Sited around open courts, variety and private spaces are created through ingenious setbacks and projections of wall surfaces.

Queenston (intersection of Nassau and Harrison sts. and surrounding area, Princeton). In the early 1800's, Queenston was a busy crossroads on the journey from New Brunswick to Trenton. Now at the eastern border of downtown Princeton, it shares the prosperity of the larger community. The three-story brick house at 306 Nassau St. was built in the middle of the eighteenth century; like many structures in active communities, constant renewal has prolonged its life while preserving tantalizing glimpses of its historic appearance. The façades of 342 and 344 Nassau St., painted-brick dwellings on the north side of the street, tell of similarly eventful histories.

Kingston (Rte. 27, north of Princeton). Moving anthracite from the Pennsylvania coalfields to the manufacturing centers of New York was accomplished after 1834 by mule-drawn barges on the Delaware and Raritan Canal. Constructed between Bordentown on the Delaware River and New Brunswick on the Raritan, the canal and its sister company, the Camden & Amboy Railroad, effectively prevented any competition on this lucrative route.

The canal, which carried no passenger traffic, was operated into the 1930's.

The canal itself is now used for recreation under the auspices of the State of New Jersey; many of the original bridgetenders' and lock-tenders' houses remain in the once-bustling canal towns, such as Kingston, Griggtown, Millstone, and East Millstone.

In Kingston, a small, two-story masonry lock-tender's house and a wood frame tollhouse next to it are located along the canal. The Kingston Mill, a large, three-

Kingston Mill

story mansarded mill built in the 1880's, on the site of earlier mills, has a commanding position in a park near the canal and the Millstone River. A stone bridge over the river was built in 1798 to replace the one destroyed by Washington's troops to escape the pursuing British. The mill is at one end of Lake Carnegie, formed in 1906 by damming the Millstone River to provide boating facilities at Princeton.

The Kingston Presbyterian Church, built in 1852, is a Victorian interpretation of a classic Dutch form, with rich detailing in the square belltower and belfry. The plastered stone is painted buff.

Rockingham (Washington's Headquarters)

Rte. 518, Rocky Hill
*OPEN: Tues.–Sat., 10 a.m.–noon,
1–5 p.m.; Sun., 2–5 p.m.
Closed Thanksgiving,
Christmas, and New Year's Day
PHONE: (609) 921–8835

In 1783 George Washington revisited Princeton at the request of the Continental Congress, then sitting in Nassau Hall to await the signing of the peace treaty. The widow of Judge John Berrien rented her spacious home to the Washingtons, and here Washington entertained many illustrious visitors and wrote his farewell orders to the army.

The house had been built about 1734 or possibly earlier by a Connecticut carpenter, John Harrison, Sr., but Berrien made additions when he purchased it in 1764. He called his fine home Rockingham. Berrien drowned himself in the Millstone River in 1772, after inviting several important men to dine with him and witness his will and—unbeknownst to them—his suicide.

The two-story farmhouse has beaded clapboards, paneled shutters, and 9-over-6 windows. A double-tiered pil-

lared porch spans the façade, which now faces away from the road but was the front of the house before it was moved to its present site. Many furnishings are from Washington's period. Maintained by the New Jersey Historic Sites Section of the Department of Environmental Protection.

Rocky Hill First Reformed Church (Rte. 518). This especially charming little board-and-batten church has a very simplified, pointed window with diamond panes in the belfry. It was built in 1856 by Henry W. Laird, a carpenter who had worked with John Notman on rebuilding Nassau Hall in Princeton.

Hopewell Museum

28 E. Broad St. (Rte. 518)
OPEN: Mon., Wed., Sat., 2–5 p.m.

This three-story stone mansion, built in 1877, was one of the many fine homes that lined Hopewell's main street. It now houses a community museum with a good collection of antiques and artifacts of local history. Downstairs, one parlor is furnished in the Colonial period and a second according to Victorian tastes. Many

other elegant homes have been converted to antique shops. Maintained by the Hopewell Historical Society.

Old School Baptist Church (W. Broad St. [Rte. 518], Hopewell). Gable to the street, this simple two-story brick building with twin doors in the gable entrance is adjacent to an old graveyard where many leading figures of the Revolutionary period lie buried.

Hopewell Railroad Station (foot of Blackwell Ave., off Broad St.). Its original elegance nearly intact, the station has ornate gables on the long side, decorated with openwork, and dormers in the mansard roof. Like many of the stations built in the late 1800's, this one expresses the aspirations of the town, if not its actual prosperity.

Hunterdon County Courthouse (Main and Church sts., Flemington). A solid symbol of judicial power, the courthouse was built in 1828, in an early and extremely simplified version of the Greek Revival style. The building committee visited courthouses in neighboring counties and approved a plan drawn up by a Mr. Saxon. Four Doric columns support the pediment, and an octagonal cupola bears a weathervane.

Across the street, the vigorous pace of

Union Hotel

the 1870's can be sensed in the exuberant scale of the three-story, mansarded Union Hotel. Porches and a pillared loggia enclose welcoming semipublic spaces, where busy barristers and others on county business could meet informally. Urban planners today find it difficult to duplicate this kind of satisfying visual and social focus for a town center. However, the writer of the New Jersey WPA guide failed to appreciate this building as one of the real achievements of the American vernacular tradition. "A lumbering Hudson River bracketed structure of nondescript date," he scoffed, terming it "sparrow-grass architecture."

Main Street, Flemington. The rich visual mix of downtown Flemington's nineteenth-century architecture is perhaps disorderly, but it displays dynamic contrasts in form, scale, and texture. Decisive notes are the Hall of Records, a substantial late-Victorian building; the Flemington Borough Hall, a two-story Gothic structure, originally a lyceum; and, across from the courthouse, the brick-and-granite Hunterdon County National Bank, built in 1859.

Doric House

114 Main St., Flemington
OPEN: Thurs., 1–3 p.m.; Sat., 1–4 p.m.
PHONE: (201) 782–1091

Serene among the stimulating mix of Main St.'s architecture are several extraordinary Greek Revival buildings by Mahlon Fisher, a local designer, builder, and craftsman. Doric House is Fisher's own home, maintained by the Hunterdon County Historical Society.

Doric House

Hillsborough Reformed Church (intersection of Rtes. 514 and 533, Millstone). This handsome shingled church was built in 1828. Triple windows highlight the triple entry.

Bachman–Wilson House (1423 Main St., Millstone). The traditionally styled architecture on Main St. has a proud modern neighbor, a flat-roofed cypress and concrete-block dwelling designed by Frank Lloyd Wright in 1954. The bold planes of overhanging eaves and projecting balconies give a strong horizontal emphasis. An addition on the north dates from 1970.

Millstone Forge (River Rd.). On this winding street, with several restored structures, is the Millstone Forge, built of brick and shingle and believed to date from the late seventeenth century. It is now a museum of the smithy's craft.

Other legacies of Fisher's skill are the Wurts Law Office (59 Main St., near the courthouse), a small pillared structure whose frieze is lovingly embellished with carved wreaths; and the Reading–Large House (119 Main St.), a fine mansion with two-story Ionic-columned portico built in 1847. Its law office in the rear has served lawyers of the Large family for several generations. The John G. Reading double house at 151–153 Main St., another example of Fisher's work, was built about 1845.

Fleming Castle (5 Bonnell St., Flemington). Not a castle at all, but a simple, two-story clapboard-and-fieldstone house, this was the original home and inn of Samuel Fleming, for whom Flemington is named. The house was built in 1756. Open by appointment with the Daughters of the American Revolution. Phone: (201) 782-7185.

Canal-tender's dwelling (Rte. 522, banks of canal, East Millstone). This simple plastered-stone dwelling was one of many that were built along the banks of the Delaware and Raritan Canal. Many have been converted to private residences; this one will open as a museum. Near it is an old barn where barge-pulling mules were stabled.

Canal-tender's dwelling

163

Bishop House

Across the lawn is the former Franklin Inn, an unadorned clapboard structure of impressive scale, built in the eighteenth century and little altered. It now houses an antiques shop.

Queen's Campus, Rutgers University (Somerset St., New Brunswick). The grace and dignity of conservative styling characterize the architecture of Queen's Campus, the original site of Queen's College. The college had been founded in 1766 to train ministers for the Dutch Reformed Church. The Queen's Building by John McComb, Jr., was completed in 1825. Now used for administrative offices, it was the college's first permanent residence. The brownstone building, three stories high, with a central arched entry at ground level and a low-pitched pediment setting off the central pavilion, harks back to the later Colonial tradition of American college architecture.

Geology Hall and Kirkpatrick Chapel, flanking Old Queen's, were designed by Henry J. Hardenburgh. He was a descendant of Rev. Jacob Hardenburgh, the Dutch minister who was one of the founders of the college. Geology Hall was built in 1870; it was believed that this would honor the college's centennial, but it was later learned that the date of the original charter was 1766. The brownstone Kirk-

patrick Chapel, another sober exercise in Gothic design, was completed in 1872. Hardenburgh was later known for more flamboyant designs, including the Dakota apartments and the Plaza Hotel in New York City.

East of the chapel is the Daniel C. Schrank Observatory (George St.). The delicately scaled structure consists of two octagonal sections of cream-colored brick, linked by a passageway. It was designed by Willard Smith in 1866; he found his inspiration in the Tower of the Winds in Athens.

Along Somerset St., opposite the campus, is the towered and pinnacled brownstone St. Peter's Church, and several wooden dwellings and stores with dignified Greek Revival detailing.

Bishop House (College Ave., near Bishop St., New Brunswick). Gracing the center of the Rutgers University Bishop Campus, this handsome Tuscan mansion was built in 1852 as a residence for James Bishop, an active local politician. It is now a faculty residence.

Gardner A. Sage Library, New Brunswick Theological Seminary (21 Seminary Place, off College Ave.). In designing a library for a theological seminary in 1873, architect Detlef Lienau conceived it as a chapel. The tall, basilica-shaped red-brick building is sober, befitting its purpose. The interior is also chapellike; a large central nave is lit by clerestory windows, and side aisles serve as reading alcoves.

Guest House (58 Livingston Ave., at Morris St., New Brunswick). Henry Guest, a whaler and tanner, built this simple two-and-a-half-story house of local stone around 1760. Thomas Paine is believed to have taken refuge here from the pursuing British in the Revolutionary War. The house was moved to this site and is now an annex to the New Brunswick Public Library. Open by appointment. Phone: (201) 249–3344.

Buccleuch Mansion

Buccleuch Park, College Ave. and George St. (Rte. 172), New Brunswick
OPEN: Sat.–Sun., 3–5 p.m., May–Oct.
PHONE: (201) 356–1457

An expansive gambrel-roofed dwelling with a pitched roof wing, Buccleuch Man-

sion has a fine site on a grassy knoll overlooking the Raritan River. In its early history it was the home of military men, both English and American. The earliest, central, part was built in 1734 by Col. Anthony White and was known as White House Farm.

During the war a British officer took over the house, and the famed Enniskillen Guards were quartered here. The American Col. Charles Stewart bought the house after the war; and the kitchen wing was added about 1800. In 1820 it passed to Col. Joseph Warren Scott, who renamed the house Buccleuch Mansion, in honor of a kinsman.

The mansion is the result of a rich agglomeration of additions and renovations. Both the main section and the wing have central gables rising from the eaves, a Federal fanlight in one and an arched Italianate window in the other. The fine Greek Revival entry includes a paneled door with geometrically leaded transom and side lights and elaborately carved surrounds.

The interior decoration reflects various periods as well. Owned by the City of New Brunswick.

Buccleuch Mansion

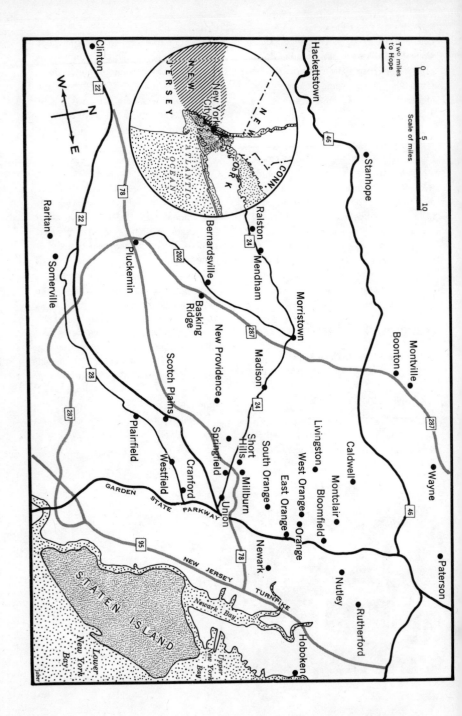

6 | New Jersey:
From Hoboken to Hope

The traveler emerges from the Lincoln Tunnel in New Jersey to a densely developed area which has been significant as a gateway since the nation's earliest history. The commercial and heavily industrialized core of Newark is surrounded by concentric rings of contiguous suburbs, small towns once favored by the wealthy as their "Jersey retreats," and, finally, fertile fields dotted with substantial farmhouses and pleasant village crossroads.

This section first describes the perhaps unexpected pleasures of Hoboken and Newark and then moves outward in three routes. The first, from Cranford to Clinton, generally follows the Old York Rd. (Rte. 22) and Rte. 28. The second follows the old Morris Tnpk. (Rte. 24) from Union to Chester, with a side trip at Morristown south on Rte. 202. The third trip, from South Orange to Hope, covers communities on both sides of the Garden State Pkwy. north to Paterson and then Rte. 46 west toward Hope.

Clinton Historical Museum

Brownstone Revival, Hoboken

Bloomfield, Garden, and Hudson sts.,
from 2nd to 13th sts.

For successive waves of ethnic groups
—Germans, Irish, Italians, blacks, Yugo-
slavs, Puerto Ricans—Hoboken has
provided comfortable homes in a neat grid
of three- and four-story townhouses,
pleasantly relieved by a few open squares
and a glorious view of the New York City
skyline. In the past few years the special
character of Hoboken's townhouses and
the mid-nineteenth-century streetscapes
have attracted writers, artists, and profes-
sionals.

Their spontaneous preservation efforts,
domino-fashion, are rapidly altering Hoboken's "unfashionable" image. Land-
mark-preservation laws, which might
alienate some owners, are not generally
considered to be necessary. "It makes
more sense," says one preservationist, "to
point out to an owner that the original
shutters are cheaper than Venetian blinds,
that repointing brick is more economical
in the long run than covering a façade
with permastone, and that saving fences
and fireplaces can add to resale value."

An enlightened Model Cities program
sees the future of Hoboken in the preservation of its historic texture. One project is
the modernization of blocks of five-story
cold-water tenements (in the area around
12th and 13th sts., on Willow, Washington, and Park sts.), retaining the façades
which relate comfortably to neighboring

Erie–Lackawanna Terminal

three- and four-story rowhouses. In an
equally ingenious project, the 1906 concrete Keuffel & Esser pencil factory
(Adams and 3rd sts.) has been renovated
for low- and middle-income housing.

Erie–Lackawanna Terminal (Hudson
River waterfront, at the foot of Hudson
Place, Hoboken). In 1907 the grandiose
copper-plated forms of this terminal had
an appropriately impressive name—the
Delaware, Lackawanna & Western Railroad Terminal and Ferry in Hoboken.
Now the terminal serves only train and
tube passengers and is called, more hum-
bly, the Erie–Lackawanna Terminal. Even
that status is tenuous, as the bankrupt
railroad's disposition of its valuable real
estate remains in doubt.

Architect Kenneth Murchison and engineer Lincoln Bush designed the structure, which is built entirely over water,
with steel-and-concrete footings to secure
the massive complex in the unstable terrain. Writer Edward Abbey nostalgically
recalled the terminal as looking like "a
square fruitcake coated with green mold.
It was enormous, a cavernous interior with
a capacity for a dozen trains, the boats,
the shops and offices and waiting rooms,
the multitudes of hustling men."

Stevens Institute (east end of 6th St., Hoboken). Col. John Stevens of Hoboken had a dream: as early as 1812, he envisioned all the states of the Union as "one family intimately connected" by railroads. Even though Stevens was a successful steamboat owner, his contemporaries scorned his plan, for at the time there was not a single operating railroad in the world. But Stevens pursued his idea persistently and built the country's first railroad locomotive, his "Steam Waggon," operating it on 630 feet of circular track near his home in Hoboken. He died in 1838, before the great period of railroad expansion proved his vision.

His sons, however, participated in that development, as well as in yachting, which brought further fame to Hoboken. Edwin Stevens' success was quite visible, for in 1850 he hired A. J. Davis, the leading architect of the day, to build him a fine castle on a promontory in the Hudson. Ironically, it was torn down in 1959 to make way for the expansion of the Stevens Institute of Technology, which he had endowed in 1870. Only the gatehouse of Stevens Castle remains, with crenellated towers and stepped gable, built of irregularly cut greenish stone and romantically contrasting with the New York City skyline which is its backdrop.

Facing Hudson Park is the original structure built by Edwin Stevens in 1870, an impressive cut-granite building trimmed with brownstone and carved foliate motifs. Nearby Hudson St. is lined with fine mansions, originally the homes of late-nineteenth-century transportation magnates and wealthy merchants. The subdued St. Matthaus Kirche, a mid-Victorian brick-and-brownstone structure, testifies to the strong German influence in Hoboken in the nineteenth century.

Trinity Episcopal Church, Hoboken

Church Square Park (Park Ave., between 4th and 5th sts., Hoboken). Our Lady of Grace Church, a grandiose Venetian Gothic brick building with limestone trim, designed in 1875 by Francis G. Himpler, dominates the east side of this pleasant open space. The Stevens Academy building (across the park on 5th St. and Willow Ave.) was built in 1860; the monumentality appropriate to its Italianate style is lessened by its cool yellow paint. Three streets at right angles to Garden St. (between 5th and 7th sts.) form a charming mews; it is said that these tiny, pitched-roof, brick dwellings were the homes of workmen employed by the Stevens family.

Trinity Episcopal Church (701 Washington St., Hoboken). Richard Upjohn was the architect of this restrained granite church, built in 1848 on the model of an English Gothic country church. The little church and rectory are fine examples of his style.

Washington St., a main shopping thoroughfare, retains much of its mid-nineteenth-century character in scale,

mass, and details. Alterations at street level, though disturbing, also emphasize the continuing vitality of the area.

Hoboken Engine Company No. 2 (Washington and 13th sts.). A solid neo-Romanesque building of yellow brick, this firehouse was built in 1890. It was set back from the building line, so the story goes, so that firemen leaning against the wall could spit without hitting pedestrians.

Pulaski Skyway (Rte. 1, between Hoboken and Newark). Giant concrete piers dramatically rise as high as 145 feet above the Hackensack and Passaic rivers and the marshy peninsula that separates Hoboken and Jersey City from Newark. The piers carry the heavy steel superstructure of the Pulaski Skyway, three and a half miles long, built in the early 1930's and hailed for its ingenious solution of carrying traffic over, rather than through, an intensively developed area.

Newark

Of all the cities in what Van Wyck Brooks called "the unloved state of New Jersey," probably none is more unloved at the present time than Newark. On the decline since World War II, Newark's image was further tarnished by the riots of 1967 and 1968. Emigration of business, commerce, and, most of all, its middle class has transformed central Newark into a city of the poor. Vast clearance projects, derided by local leaders as "urban removal," have uprooted its population and drained the city of much of its vitality.

Despite recent scars, downtown Newark has physical and visual qualities

that may yet witness the city's rebirth. As Mayor Kenneth Gibson has prophesied, "Wherever American cities are headed, Newark will get there first."

An impressive array of religious, civic, commercial, and educational buildings are clustered in downtown Newark, the area crossed by Broad St.; its narrower cross axis, Market St.; with High St. as its western terminus. The following structures make up a brief tour of Newark, starting at its heart.

Pennsylvania Station (Raymond Plaza W., Market and Ferry sts., Newark). The traveler arriving in Newark by train or tubes disembarks in a monumental station, designed in 1935 by McKim, Mead & White, who updated their Classical formula with svelte and stylish Art Deco details. Two arched entrances, framed by convex molding, break the limestone-and-granite façade. Windows are framed with stainless-steel mullions and stylishly abstracted foliate motifs.

The central interior space dwarfs human scale. Its high blue ceiling is decorated with elaborate hanging globes; large wall plaques celebrate Newark's transportation history. A modern glass-covered passageway connects the terminal to the Gateway project.

Gateway Towers and Gateway Motel (McCarter Highway, between Raymond and Market sts., Newark). The Gateway Urban Renewal complex, designed by Victor Gruen Associates and completed in 1971, was conceived as the center of a rejuvenated Newark. Critics, however, point out resentfully that one can arrive at Penn Station, enter the complex through the connecting ramp, do business, dine, shop, be entertained, and get a good

night's sleep—all without ever setting foot on Newark's streets.

Nevertheless, as an urban ensemble, the project has considerable appeal. The well-proportioned tower, thirty stories high, rises on steel-and-concrete piers above pedestrian and shopping plazas.

Kinney Building (southeast corner of Broad and Market sts., Newark). Limestone sheaths the steel shell of this lean thirteen-story structure at the crossing of Newark's busiest streets. A two-story colonnade and an ornate copper cornice crown the severely simplified façade of this Classically styled building, designed by Cass Gilbert and completed in 1913, the same year as his Gothic-inspired Woolworth Towers in New York City.

"Old First" Presbyterian Church (820 Broad St., south of Market St., near Edison Place, Newark). The balanced and harmonious design of "Old First" is a dignified contrast to its grandiose next-door neighbor, the First National State Bank. A gem of Georgian sensibility, "Old First" is built of sandstone, light-chocolate-brown in hue. Begun in 1787, the sophisticated design includes round

and elliptical openings in the tower, quoins at the corners, and masterful woodworking details. Until the mid-nineteenth century, the church was a symbol of the control exercised by leading Presbyterian families over the affairs of Newark.

Newark has an extraordinary collection of fine churches, twenty of them included in the National Register of Historic Places.

Grace Church (956 Broad St., at Walnut St., Newark). Richard Upjohn, a leading church architect of the 1840's and 1850's, set the stage for the wholesale American adoption of the English Gothic Revival style. Soon, turrets and towers, in somber tones, replaced the gleaming white temples of the previous decades. The medieval English parish church became the accepted model for the "most Christian architecture." This architectural revival went hand in hand with ecclesiology, a reform movement in liturgy and church practice within the Protestant Episcopal church.

Grace Church, completed in 1848, was one of Upjohn's most eagerly awaited designs. The trustees paid him the then-extravagant fee of $11,000. The structure is built of irregularly laid cut brownstone, with a side tower topped by a belfry and spire.

South Park Presbyterian Church (1035 Broad St., at Clinton Ave., Newark). This small twin-towered church, built of creamy-brown Nova Scotia sandstone, was designed in 1853 by architect John Welch, a Scotsman who came to Newark in 1849. Welch stayed close to the Greek mode, still much loved by Americans at the time.

South Park Presbyterian Church, Newark

Gibraltar Building (153 Halsey St., off W. Kinney St., Newark). Newark has long been noted as an insurance center; the recent overscaled buildings dwarf the Gibraltar Building, designed by Cass Gilbert in 1927. Exposed steel is used for window mullions and for spandrels. In contrast to this is the richly traceried parapet marking the tenth-story setback and the elaborate steel cresting that surmounts the steeply pitched attic.

Essex County Courthouse (Market St., at Springfield Ave., Newark). Cass Gilbert designed this white marble courthouse in 1906, masterfully embellishing Renaissance forms with florid details. Life-size figures top the double-columned Corinthian façade.

In front of the courthouse is Gutzon Borglum's seated bronze statue of Abraham Lincoln, created in 1911. Borglum designed the statue to be accessible to the public; he envisioned children climbing up to sit on Lincoln's lap, and so they do.

Behind the courthouse is the Essex County Hall of Records (High St. and 13th Ave.), designed in 1927 by Guilbert & Betelle.

Essex County College (Market St., Newark). A "megastructure" to serve an open-enrollment community college, the new facility of Essex County College is scheduled to open late in 1975. Grad Partnership of Newark is the architect of this intricately massed complex. Solar bronze-tinted glass complements the buff-colored brick and concrete. An interior multileveled street will serve as a central forum and link the various sections of the college.

American Red Cross–Essex County Chapter (710 High St., between Spruce and Longworth sts., Newark). Brewing became a major industry in Newark as early as the 1850's. Among those who entered the industry was Christian Feigenspan, whose descendants built this fine orange-brick Italian Renaissance mansion in 1906.

Eberhardt Hall (367 High St., Newark). Overlooking downtown Newark and flanked by the modern construction of Rutgers University, this elaborately massed, Flemish Gothic, red-brick and brownstone structure is part of the Newark College of Engineering. It was designed in 1856 by John Welch as the Newark Orphan Asylum. North of the college on High St. is a civilized fraternity row of ornate Victorian dwellings.

Colonnade Park Apartments (two towers at 7th and Clinton sts., and a third overlooking Branch Brook Park, Newark). Sheathed in anodized aluminum with glass-curtain walls rising on concrete piers over a two-story glass lobby, the three twenty-two-story apartment towers were designed in 1960 by Mies van der Rohe and resemble his Seagram Building in New York City, which he had completed two years earlier, and the large Lafayette Park renewal project in Detroit.

Herbert Greenwald, the developer, died before the towers were officially opened, so the amenities he planned—landscaping, shops, and services—were never carried out. It was hoped that Mies's concept, the ultimate in refinement, would serve as a prototype for mass housing in the area, but this has not happened.

House of Prayer Church and Rectory
(Broad and State sts., Newark). The House of Prayer Church was designed in 1850 by Frank Wills, chief architect of the New York Ecclesiological Society. The church is built of brownstone, with a tall tower and spire, and windows with Gothic arches.

The rectory is the Plume House, two and a half stories in the Dutch Colonial style. Possibly the oldest house in Newark, it was owned by Mistress Ann Plume, who gained a reputation for stout-hearted patriotism in the Revolutionary War when she captured a Hessian soldier and locked him in the icehouse until the Continental soldiers came to arrest him. The church was built on the site of her dairy.

Newark Museum

43–49 Washington St.
OPEN: Mon.–Sat., noon–5 p.m.;
    Sun., holidays, 1–5 p.m.
PHONE: (201) 733–6600

Founded in 1909, the Newark Museum was one of librarian John Cotton Dana's great contributions to the cultural life of Newark, and, like the Newark Public Library, exemplified his concern for the needs of the people. Jarvis Hunt was the architect of this severely Classical limestone structure, completed in 1926. The building was located on the site of the home of Marcus Ward, a prominent civic leader; the carriage house of the Ward estate is presently being restored.

In 1938 the museum acquired the adjoining John Ballantine house, an 1870's dwelling owned by the scion of the beer-brewing family. The Ballantine house now serves as the administrative headquarters of the museum and is linked to the main building by a passageway.

The museum garden contains the Newark Fire Museum with exhibits of old-time fire-fighting apparatus (open Mon., Wed., Fri., noon–3 p.m.; Tues., Thurs., Sat., noon–4:30 p.m.; Sun., 1–4:30 p.m.) and Newark's oldest schoolhouse, built in 1784 and moved to the grounds in 1938.

A junior museum and a planetarium are regular attractions; special events and exhibitions are held in the main building.

National Newark Building (744 Broad St., Newark). In the 1920's and 1930's Newark was New Jersey's center of business and finance, as it had been its center of trade in the nineteenth century. When the thirty-five-story National Newark

Colonnade Park Apartments   173

Building, designed by John and Wilson Ely, was opened in 1931, it was the tallest building in the state. Built of cream-colored brick and stone, its Moderne styling and distinctive setbacks make it a skyscraper classic.

Howard Savings Bank (768 Broad St., Newark). In the burst of Classical fanfare sounded by the 1893 Columbian Exposition, architect George B. Post designed a number of banks around the country. This one, completed in 1899, is of granite, its pediment supported by Ionic columns.

New Jersey Bell Telephone Company (540 Broad St., Newark). Voorhees, Gmelin & Walker were the architects of this polished twenty-story modernistic office building completed by 1929. Colossal carved terra-cotta figures enliven the skyscraper's smooth surfaces. The decorative metalwork is especially attractive.

First Baptist Peddie Memorial Church (Broad and Fulton sts., Newark). Designed in 1888 by W. Halsey Wood, this imposing brownstone church, Richardsonian in inspiration, was a gift from wealthy industrialist Mayor Thomas B. Peddie.

New Jersey Historical Society

230 Broadway, near Taylor St., Newark
OPEN: Tues.–Sat., 10 a.m.–4:30 p.m.
PHONE: (201) 483–3939

This neo-Georgian structure houses extensive collections of historical materials, as well as paintings and documents. The Antill–Ross parlor from a New Brunswick mansion of the 1740's has been preserved here.

Cranford Hotel

Cranford Historical Society

124 N. Union Ave.
OPEN: Sat., 9 a.m.–12:30 p.m.;
Sun., 2–5 p.m.
PHONE: (201) 276–0082

At the hub of town, across from the municipal center and the impressive late-nineteenth-century shingled First Presbyterian Church, stands this pleasant, small-scale frame cottage. Mid-nineteenth-century gingerbread fancifies the modest dwelling.

It now serves as the headquarters for the Cranford Historical Society and offers displays of the development of Crane's Ford on the Rahway River, a mill site, to Craneville, a farming community, to Cranford, a suburban village. The Rahway River winds its way through Cranford, giving it its late-nineteenth-century nickname of "the Venice of New Jersey." Many fine Victorian homes still stand along the riverbanks.

Cranford Hotel (South St., at the railroad station). The Elizabeth & Somerville Railroad stopped at Cranville, now Cranford, as early as 1838, but it carried little passenger traffic until the suburban growth of the post–Civil War period. The Cranford Hotel, an imposing three-story brick-masonry mass, with a fancy two-story wooden balcony across the façade, dates from that period.

Miller–Cory House

614 Mountain Ave., Westfield
*OPEN: Sun., 2–5 p.m.
PHONE: (201) 237–1776

This charming farmhouse, dating from the 1740's, has been restored and surrounded with Colonial gardens. In December 1776 a company of Jersey militia managed to recapture 400 cattle from British foragers and drove the herd up Mountain Ave. For the first time in New Jersey, British troops fled from the Americans.

Presbyterian Church (on the Green, Broad St. [Rte. 509] and Mountain Ave., Westfield). This dignified white frame

Miller–Cory House

Presbyterian Church, Westfield

church stands at the top of an expansive sloping Green, a reminder of the New England origins of many of New Jersey's early settlers. The church was built in 1861, on the site of an earlier church, and has rare bead-and-reel molding.

Stage House Village (Park Ave., at Front St. [Rte. 28], Scotch Plains). Eighteenth-century travelers traversed the Old York Rd. between New York and Philadelphia, a two-day journey on the Swift Sure Stage Line. Taverns along the route served meals and put up overnight guests. The Stage House Inn, parts of which were built in 1737, was one such tavern; even after the railroads replaced the stagecoaches, it continued to serve the traveling public and does so still.

The inn has become the center of a small collection of rescued buildings moved here in 1961 and converted to shops. In a courtyard are the Tempe House, one of the oldest houses in Scotch Plains; the Buell Barn, dating from 1760; and the Poff House, from 1810. The parking attendant takes shelter in a tiny white structure that originally served as the "Necessary House," or outhouse, for the home Duncan Phyfe designed for his daughter. (The impressive Greek Revival house still stands, altered, on New Market Rd. in nearby Dunellen.)

Scotch Plains Baptist Church (corner of Park Ave. and Grand St.). This church, built in 1870, is a fine example of local American Gothic. Cream-colored and red bricks are set off by fanciful wooden trim. The gable-fronted structure has a multicolored slate roof and is surrounded by a wrought-iron fence. The parsonage on the opposite corner (347 Park Ave.) is a brownstone house in the Dutch Colonial style.

Plainfield

At the end of the nineteenth century, Plainfield was a "full-blown Wall Street suburb," according to Van Wyck Brooks, the author and critic who described his youth in Plainfield in *Scenes and Portraits*. Plainfield was the home not only of "wildcat speculators," but of "quiet solid men of money, unobtrusive often to the point of being mousy." These millionaires built "vast red sandstone houses . . . like so many Kenilworth castles, with turrets, verandahs, balconies and porte-cocheres, with arches, fountains, coach-houses, kennels and stables and with sons who had an air of owning all creation and whose thoughts and talk were entirely about yachting and coaching."

A stubborn survival from this period is the neo-Romanesque gatehouse (901 E. Front St. [Rte. 28]) of the estate of John Taylor Johnson. He was first president of the New Jersey Central Railroad, president of the Metropolitan Museum of Art in New York City, and foreman of the jury that convicted Boss Tweed. The gatehouse, now a residence, is a delightful anachronism amid Georgian-styled garden-apartment complexes.

Friends Meeting House (Watchung Ave. [Rte. 531], at North Ave., Plainfield). Built in 1788, the Friends Meeting House adopts the austerity decreed by Quaker philosophy. Typically, two doors penetrate the long wall, and a porch runs across the gable end. The town's name originated in the place-name of the first Quaker Meeting, John Laing's "Plainfield" plantation.

Crescent Avenue and First, Second, and Third places, Plainfield. Fine Victorian ensembles, developed about the time Plainfield incorporated, in 1869, lend the Crescent Ave. area an ambience of rare dignity. Similarly scaled and styled dwellings are enlivened by subtle differences in carpenter detailing.

Board of Education Administration Building (W. 5th St. and Madison Ave.) and Seventh Day Baptist Church (W. 5th St. and Central Ave., Plainfield). Standing back-to-back are two structures built by the same congregation, each reflecting its own era. The present Board of Education building was the original church, an Italianate clapboard structure with a spirited tower, built in 1867 by Joseph Hubbard. Moved to its present site in 1892, it became a school five years later.

The structure that replaced the first church was far more monumental, a gorgeous flight of late-Victorian fantasy. The climax of the elaborately massed brick, tile, and terra-cotta structure is the attenuated bell tower, decorated with terra-cotta figures of twelve trumpeting apostles.

Martine House (950 Cedar Brook Rd., at Brook Lane, off Watchung Ave., Plainfield). A large part of this spacious clapboard, two-wing house belongs to the original structure, erected in 1717. In the 1840's Fdmund Clarence Stedman spent his boyhood years here with his widowed mother and grandfather. His grandfather, a stern and devout man, locked young Edmund in a closet for his statement in Sunday School that the chief end of man was "to get all the money you can and keep all you get." Stedman didn't recant, and pursued his financial goals by becoming a successful banker and stockbroker after his years as correspondent for the *New York World* in the Civil War. He was also a prolific poet.

Drake House

602 W. Front St. (Rte. 28),
at Plainfield Ave., Plainfield
OPEN: Mon., Wed., Sat., 2–5 p.m.,
and by appointment
PHONE: (201) 755–5831

The outlines of an eighteenth-century farmhouse can be clearly seen beneath the 1860's embellishments: a steep roof and an iron-crested tower, projecting bays, and fanciful stickwork on the dormers. In the Revolutionary period the farmhouse belonged to Rev. Nathaniel Drake; it had been built in 1745 by his father. Rev. Drake was an outspoken supporter of the Revolution, and four of his sons served in the Continental Army. When Gen.

Washington was planning the battle for the Watchungs in June 1777, he conferred with his aides here. The house, now maintained by the Historical Society of Plainfield and North Plainfield, commemorates that association in exhibits and Colonial furnishings.

Drake House

Old Dutch Parsonage

65 Washington Place, off Middagh and
Somerset (Rte. 567) sts., Somerville
*OPEN: Tues.–Sat., 10 a.m.–noon,
1–5 p.m.; Sun., 2–5 p.m.
PHONE: (201) 725–1015

The first resident of this two-story brick dwelling, built in 1751, was Rev. John Frelinghuysen, a minister for the Dutch Reformed Church who was instrumental in establishing the first theological seminary in America. The seminary became Queen's College, the antecedent of Rutgers University.

When Frelinghuysen died, his widow, Dinah, married another good domine, Rev. John Hardenburgh of the First Reformed Church in Raritan. He became the first president of Queens College, and was a strong supporter of the American cause during the Revolution (as were most of the Dutch Reformed clergy).

The close relationship between this mansion and its English country cousin is evident in many features: small window openings in relation to wall surface, 12-over-12 windows, brownstone quoins, and Flemish bond brickwork.

Maintained by the New Jersey Historic Sites Section of the Department of Environmental Protection.

Wallace House

38 Washington Place, Somerville
*OPEN: Tues.–Sat., 10 a.m.–noon,
       1–5 p.m.; Sun., 2–5 p.m.
       Closed Christmas, Thanks-
       giving, and New Year's Day
PHONE: (201) 725–1015

The winter of 1777–78 was mild, and little military action occurred in New Jersey. While the armies were waiting for spring in the Middlebrook Encampment, George and Martha Washington lived in this newly built house, rented for $1,000. The large frame section is adjoined by a small kitchen wing. The rooms are furnished with pieces of the mid-eighteenth to nineteenth century.

The back of the house (with an asymetrical arrangement of windows) faces the street and is now used as the main entrance.

Borough Hall (Somerset and Main sts., Somerville). This graceful mid-nine-teenth-century Gothic Revival structure, once the home of prominent Somerville citizens, has housed the municipal offices since 1958. The police force occupies the former carriage house. A major addition was completed in 1939; it is now the Somerville Public Library.

Somerset County Courthouse (Courthouse Sq., Somerville). In the form of a Greek cross, this three-story courthouse is built of brilliant white marble. It is crowned with a colonnaded dome, supporting the figure of justice holding the familiar sword and scales. Formal porticoes adorn each face, supported by elegantly proportioned Ionic columns. Inside, the rotunda is highlighted with a stained-glass skylight. The courthouse, the design of Gordon, Tracy & Swartout, was dedicated in 1909.

The serene façade has sheltered some sensational trials, including the highly publicized Hall-Mills double-murder case of the 1920's.

Frelinghuysen House

Somerset St. (Rte. 567) and
Wyckoff Ave., Raritan
*OPEN: By appointment
PHONE: (201) 725–3951;
       725–0413 (library)

This two-story gambrel-roofed brick residence was built about 1810 by Gen. John Frelinghuysen; a wooden addition housed

Somerset County Courthouse

slaves. The house was a tavern and, for a time, a prison. The library is open to the public. Now owned and maintained by the Borough of Raritan.

St. Paul's Presbyterian Church (Rtes. 202 and 206, off Rte. 78, Pluckemin). Pluckemin, described in the 1939 WPA guide to New Jersey as "another little village that ends just as its houses seem to be getting into the swing of being a community," boasts a fine Greek Revival church, with robust Ionic columns in its recessed porch. It was built in 1839 on the site of St. Paul's Lutheran Church, whose cornerstone is embedded in the portico of the successor.

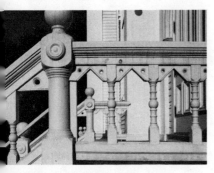

Presbyterian Church, Clinton

Center Street, Clinton. Proud Victorian homeowners planted trees along the main street leading to the heart of town; today the dignified frame dwellings that line Center St. have ample shade. The Presbyterian Church (91 Center St.), richly carved and embellished, was the work of a fine folk artist. Similar carpenter virtuosity and sophisticated design can be seen in a number of nineteenth-century wooden structures in downtown Clinton.

Clinton Historical Museum (Old Red Mill)

56 Main St.
*OPEN: Mon.–Fri., 1–5 p.m.;
    Sat., Sun., noon–6 p.m.
    Closed Nov.–March
PHONE: (201) 735–4101

This lovely spot is graced by two mills, one on either side of the Raritan River. The Old Red Mill, now the Clinton Historical Museum, was built in 1763 and enlarged in 1820. It was first a gristmill; later its products included lime and linseed oil. The waterwheel still turns, but the interior of the three-and-a-half-story frame building has been converted into exhibition space for displays of nineteenth-century crafts and farm and household equipment.

The former miller's residence, on Main St., a proud square dwelling with rich carpenter details, is now the Trimmer Funeral Home.

Hunterdon Art Center (Old Stone Mill)

7 Center. St., Clinton
*OPEN: Tues.–Sun., 1–5 p.m.
    Closed holidays
PHONE: (201) 735–8415

The older of the twin mills is the stone mill, built in 1756. Known as Hunt's Mill, it was purchased by the Hunterdon Art Center, which presents changing exhibits and musical performances.

Clinton House (Main St.). This two-story frame inn was built in the 1830's and was a popular stagecoach stop on the Easton road. It is now a restaurant.

Town Hall, Clinton

Town Hall (Old Rte. 22 and Leigh St., Clinton). An urbane Victorian mansion, once the home of the prosperous Leigh family, has contained municipal offices since 1959.

Union to Chester

Caldwell Parsonage

909 Caldwell Ave., Union
OPEN: 2nd and 4th Sun. of each
month, and by appointment
PHONE: (201) 688–5370

This white clapboard building, now the Union Historical Society Museum, was Rev. John Caldwell's temporary parsonage during the Battle of Springfield. Caldwell, pastor of the First Presbyterian Church in Elizabeth, was called the "fighting parson" by the Continental troops; the Tories derisively dubbed him the "high priest of the Revolution." Caldwell's wife, Hannah, was shot in this house by a British soldier; Caldwell himself was later murdered by an American, James Morgan. The house was rebuilt in 1780.

Connecticut Farms Presbyterian Church (892 Stuyvesant Ave., Union). The first church in the village then called Connecticut Farms was burned by the British in the seventeen-day raid on Springfield. This church, on a bluff overlooking the village, took its place in 1783. The brownstone-and-brick building has a wooden tower and belfry rising above its gable.

St. Stephen's Church (Main [Rte. 527] and Church sts., Millburn). The humble material of this small board-and-batten church is transformed by the sophistication of its execution. Perfectly proportioned, it has paired ogee-arched window openings in the nave and quatrefoil clerestory openings. The Rectory (135 Main St.), with highly original trim, makes a suitable companion.

Racquets Club (162–74 Hobart Ave., Short Hills). In the "ideal village" of Short Hills, conceived in the 1870's by merchant–artist–inventor Stewart Hartshorn, successful businessmen returned from the exertions of money-making to "inviting retreats," their richly inventive stone, brick, and shingled suburban mansions. The social center was the casino, designed by Society's favorite firm, McKim, Mead & White, and built in

Casino, Short Hills, in 1884

The Mall, Short Hills

1882–83, following by several years its first great casino at Newport.

A contemporary writer, struck by the whimsey of the gabled structure with its idiosyncratic tower, archly noted: "As we turn from the station a quaint looking building with a quainter tower appears from behind the trees, and we find that it is a building dedicated to the Muses." Today it is dedicated to tennis.

The Mall, Short Hills (Canoe Brook and Country rds., Morris and Essex [Rte. 24] tnpks.). The sensitive design and site plan of this high-fashion shopping center place it well above the ordinary. An attractive covered walk runs next to the plate-glass shop windows on the upper parking level. Below, a pedestrian mall lined with smaller shops hums with pleasant bustle. Skidmore, Owings & Merrill controlled all the design features. Softly tinted gray brick was used throughout, and a modular construction system ensured a harmonious scale. The project was completed in 1962.

First Presbyterian Church of Springfield (corner of Morris Ave. [Rte. 82] and Church Mall). On the site of an earlier church, a lovely new Federal structure with a fine belfry was erected in 1791. A marker commemorates the zeal of the Revolutionary War parson James Caldwell, who came here from Elizabeth to be in the thick of the fighting. When the Americans ran out of gun wadding, Caldwell supplied the soldiers with Watts hymnals and encouraged them to "Give 'em Watts, boys—give 'em Watts!"

Cannonball House

126 Morris Ave., Springfield
*OPEN: Sun., 2–4 p.m.
PHONE: (201) 376–0039

This five-bay shingle house, decorated with modillions and dentils at the eaves, was one of four that survived a devastating raid by the British in June 1780. In the battle the Americans forced the better-equipped British troops to retreat. The Cannonball House, so named because of a cannonball that pierced its west side, was built about 1741 and was known as the Hutchings Homestead. It may have been spared because it was used as a hospital by the British. It is now a museum maintained by the Springfield Historical Society.

Summit Playhouse (10 New England Ave., off Springfield Ave.). A one-story brick-and-stone structure with a rounded tower and arched doorway, this community theater was built in 1891 as the Summit Library. It became a playhouse in 1918.

"Salt Box" Historical Society Museum

1351 Springfield Ave. (Rte. 512), New Providence
OPEN: Sun., 2–4 p.m.
PHONE: (201) 464–4751

The original one-and-a-half-story section

of this salt-box was built about 1759 as the parsonage of the Presbyterian Church; a second, two-story section was added in the mid-nineteenth century, giving the structure a split-level appearance. The Presbyterian Church (1307 Springfield Ave., at Passaic St.) was designed in 1834 by architect Amos Wilcox.

E. Main Street Historic District, Chatham

Rte. 24

Chatham's early settlers were attracted by the mill sites along the Passaic River; after the Revolution, the Morris Tnpk., New Jersey's first, passed through the town, stimulating trade and development. Today the active commercial center on E. Main St., from the Passaic River to University Ave., presents a miniature review of the growth and development of small-town architecture from the 1770's to the late nineteenth century.

Chatham Potters (32 Watchung Ave., off Fairmont Ave., south of Main St., Chatham). The Bonnells were the most prominent family in early Chatham, which was in fact called Bonnell Town. This house, built about 1750 by Nathaniel Bonnell IV, a miller, was occupied by the family until 1916.

Madison Borough Hall (Kings Rd., opposite the railroad station). Mrs. Marcellus Hartley Dodge, daughter of William Rockefeller, donated this building, costing a million dollars, to the Borough of Madison in 1935. Designed by New Jersey architect B. Spencer Newman, it is a granite building with a cupola on top. The doors are solid bronze and the interior is finished in multihued marble. After a thorough inspection, the WPA New Jersey guidebook writer noted in awe that "the rest rooms for policemen and firemen rival those of exclusive clubs."

Museum of Early Trades and Crafts

Main St. (Rte. 24) and Green Village Rd., Madison
OPEN: Mon.–Sat., 10 a.m.–5 p.m.; Sun., 2–5 p.m. July 1–Labor Day: Tues.–Sat., 10 a.m.– 4 p.m. Closed on all major holidays
PHONE: (201) 377–2982

In 1900 Mr. and Mrs. D. Willis James, of the Morristown millionaire set, presented Madison with a gift—a library building. The building was small but very special—a towered Gothic miniature built of pink limestone quarried nearby at Boonton. Tiffany medallions were inset into the leaded-glass windows. Appropriate to the spirit of the times, the interior was meticulously handcrafted.

In 1970 this distinguished building became the home of the Museum of Early Trades and Crafts, which presents changing displays and demonstrations of early American technology.

Drew University

36 Madison Ave. (Rte. 24), Madison

A mood of quiet contemplation envelops the handsome campus of Drew University, in keeping with its origin as a

Methodist theological siminary in 1866. Paradoxically, the school was founded by Daniel Drew, the unscrupulous railroad tycoon.

Mead Hall, now the administration building, was the home of William Gibbons, member of another ambitious family. His father, with whom he was associated in business, was Thomas Gibbons, a wealthy plantation owner from Savannah, Georgia, who moved to New Jersey about 1800. The elder Gibbons entered the steamboat business at a time when states granted monopoly rights to various transportation companies. To break the monopoly of his arch-enemy, Col. Aaron Ogden of Elizabethtown, Gibbons hired Cornelius Vanderbilt as a captain. Vanderbilt was already a successful sailing master but he took this subordinate position to learn about steamboats, which he foresaw as the wave of the future. Gibbons took his case against the monopoly to the Supreme Court, and in 1824 Chief Justice Marshall, in the historic case of *Gibbons v. Ogden*, ruled that Congress had the power to regulate interstate commerce.

William Gibbons built Mead Hall in 1834. A gracious portico with two-story Corinthian columns embellishes the symmetrical red-brick building. An addition in the same style, the Rose Memorial Library, was built in 1939.

Some of the outbuildings of Gibbons' vast estate have been converted to university use. Asbury Hall, an elegant carriage house, is now a dormitory. Embury Hall, a yellow-brick granary, now houses offices and apartments.

Other buildings were added to the campus in the 1880's. Among them is the collegiate-Gothic Seminary Hall, built in 1887 by architects W. B. Bigelow and F. E. Wallis. Modern construction maintains the dignified atmosphere of the earlier buildings.

Twombly Hall

Florham–Madison Campus of Fairleigh Dickinson University, Rte. 24, Madison

When Florence Vanderbilt, granddaughter of Commodore Cornelius Vanderbilt, married Hamilton McKeown Twombly in 1877, the young couple started married life in royal style: a combined fortune of $70 million, a fashionable wedding in New York for 2,000 close friends, a 70-room mansion on Fifth Avenue, a Newport summer place, and a country house on 900 acres in Morris County for the off-season.

Florham, the 100-room country seat named after the couple's first names, is a grandiose brick-and-limestone creation designed by Stanford White and completed in 1897. Modeled after one wing of Hampton Court, it faced a similarly styled Orangerie, now the library, across a broad lawn.

Twombly Hall

The spectacular mansion, now called Twombly Hall, has been the administration building of the Florham–Madison campus of Fairleigh Dickinson University since 1958.

Morristown Green (center of town; Bank, South, and Morris sts.). Morristown has flourished in two widely separated periods in America's history. It was George Washington's headquarters for two critical winters of the Revolution, earning the town the title of "Military Capital of the Revolution." In contrast, at the turn of the twentieth century, Morristown was a gathering place for the social elite. As *World Magazine* described the "City of Millionaires" in 1905, "In one little circle, within a radius of three miles, [there are] more men of millions than can be found elsewhere in many times the area the country over."

Today Morristown is a thriving suburb, but survivals from its past are vivid reminders of its rich heritage. The Green has been, since the earliest days, the hub of the town; and the sites described here radiate from this point.

St. Peter's Church, Morristown, in 1887

Morris County Courthouse (Washington St. [Rte. 24], between Court St. and Western Ave., Morristown). Architects Lewis Carter of Chatham and Joseph Lindsley of Morristown designed this two-story brick-and-sandstone structure in 1827. Lindsley later became sheriff and occupied part of the courthouse. A new wing, designed by Edward A. Berg, was added in 1956.

Lanterman Funeral Home (126 South St., Morristown). In 1894 the exclusive Morristown Club was transferred to this house on fashionable South St. Tired businessmen stopped here after a hard day's work on Wall Street; ladies, of course, were not invited. The move to South St. reportedly brought decorum and such dignified activities as cards, pool, billiards, and squash to the membership, which previously had engaged in chasing greased pigs in the clubhouse.

Woman's Club of Morristown (51 South St. [Rte. 24]). Dr. Lewis Condict, an active physician and politician, built this five-bay, Federal-style clapboard house in 1797. Fine detailing includes transom and side lights.

St. Peter's Church (South St. and Miller Rd., Morristown). A spirit of invention underlies the design of this imposing limestone structure, with its battlemented tower supported by stepped buttresses. It was designed by McKim, Mead & White in 1887.

Otto Kahn, the brilliant financier and patron of the arts, was a parishioner. Despite his fiscal credentials, he was a controversial figure in society in Morristown, for he had been born a Jew. Half of the "best" people in Morristown accepted him anyway; the other half ignored him.

The gabled brownstone parish house designed in the 1920's by Bertram Goodhue, has a striking iron weathervane.

Morristown Municipal Building (South St., between Pine and Elm sts.). Surely few municipalities can boast of offices as lavish as this marble monument, once the home and private museum of Theodore Vail, president of the American Telephone and Telegraph Company. Built to resemble the palazzo of a Renaissance prince, it was designed in 1918 by William Welles Bosworth. Vail bequeathed the building to the city, along with an endowment of $200,000.

Macculloch Hall

45 Macculloch Ave., off Miller Rd.,
Morristown
OPEN: By appointment
PHONE: (201) 538–2404

George Perrat Macculloch, an enterprising Scottish engineer, built this formal brick home in 1810. It has a pedimented portico with four columns, and the interior is beautifully furnished with period pieces. Macculloch was the designer of the Morris Canal, opened in 1831 (see Waterloo Village).

Thomas Nast Home (Villa Fontana) (Macculloch Ave. and Miller Rd., Morristown). Among the many fine structures in the Macculloch Ave. Historic District (which includes Miller Rd. and Maple Ave.) is the former residence of Thomas Nast, the political cartoonist whose biting commentaries on Tammany Hall helped bring about Boss Tweed's downfall. Nast lived in this house from 1873 until 1902 and was an active participant in Morristown's social life.

Villa Fontana is a singularly appealing Victorian mansion with a flaring mansard roof and lavish Classical details. It has been altered since Nast's ownership.

Schuyler–Hamilton House

5 Olyphant Place, off Morris St.
(Rte. 510), east of Green St., Morristown
OPEN: Tues., Sun., 2–5 p.m.,
and by appointment
PHONE: (201) 267–4039

The sagging fortunes of the Continental Army and the ravages of winter did not deter the spirit of romance at Morristown in 1780. Alexander Hamilton, then twenty-three years old and Washington's brilliant and charming aide, courted and won the hand of Elizabeth Schuyler, daughter of Gen. Philip Schuyler of Albany, who was visiting her aunt in this house.

Betsy was everything Hamilton wanted in a wife, as he had specified in a letter to a friend a year earlier. He wanted a wife who was young, beautiful, shapely, sensible, well bred, and chaste, but "as to fortune, the larger stock of that the better." Hamilton, illegitimate and poor, found his alliance with the powerful Schuyler clan of great help in his career.

The simple two-story Colonial house was purchased in 1923 and restored by the Morristown Chapter of the DAR.

Acorn Hall

Acorn Hall

68 Morris St., at intersection with
Rte. 55, Morristown
*OPEN: Thurs., 11 a.m.–3 p.m., and by
appointment
PHONE: (201) 267–3465

The headquarters of the Morristown Historical Society since 1970, Acorn Hall is a splendidly decorated Victorian mansion with a central tower, designed in 1853 by Ira Lindsley for Dr. Schermerhorn of New York. An embroidery of scrollwork—circles, S-shapes, and lattices—decorates the porch and the parapet above.

Morris Museum of Arts and Sciences

Normandy Heights and Columbia rds.,
Morristown
OPEN: Mon.–Sat., 10 a.m.–5 p.m.;
Sun., 2–5 p.m. July 1–Labor
Day: Tues.–Sat., a.m.–
4 p.m. Closed on major
holidays
PHONE: (201) 538–0454

The former home of Peter Frelinghuysen, this fine neo-Georgian structure by

McKim, Mead & White was completed in 1912. It is now the home of an active community museum.

Morristown National Historic Park

Headquarters at 230 Morris St. (Ford Mansion), 1 mile east of Morristown Green
*OPEN: Ford Mansion and museum:
daily, 10 a.m.–5 p.m.; Wick
House: daily, 11 a.m.–5 p.m.;
Feb.–Nov. Park roads in Jockey
Hollow open 9 a.m.–sunset.
Closed Thanksgiving,
Christmas, and New Year's Day
PHONE: (201) 539–2016

When the land and historic buildings of Morristown's revolutionary history were offered as a gift to the federal government in 1933, some congressmen were reluctant to accept. One complained that no battles had ever been fought at Morristown, another thought the maintenance would be too costly, and a third wanted to link the bill with one to take over the Florida Everglades. Finally, a sense of history prevailed, and the bill was passed.

Gen. Washington and the Continental Army set up winter quarters at Morristown

Washington's Headquarters, Morristown

Factory, Speedwell Village

daughter Tempe (short for Temperance) saved a horse from being commandeered by two mutinous soldiers by riding it straight into the house and hiding it while the soldiers searched the barns and woods in vain.

Speedwell Village

333 Speedwell Ave. (Rte. 202), 1 mile northwest of Morristown Green, Morristown
*OPEN: Fri.–Sat., 10 a.m.–4 p.m.;
           Sun., 2–5 p.m., April 1–Nov. 1
PHONE: (201) 540–0211

in January 1777 and again in December 1779, two of the most critical and discouraging winters of the war. The Washingtons stayed with the widowed Mrs. Ford, in the fine home built in 1774 by her husband, Col. Jacob Ford, Jr., a wealthy iron and powder manufacturer. The mansion is a superb American translation of the English Georgian style, especially distinguished by masterly craftsmanship in wood. The smooth matchboard facing on the façade is set off by the rich detailing of the Palladian doorway.

At Jockey Hollow, four miles south of Morristown and also part of the historic park, the American soldiers endured severe deprivations during the winter of 1779–80, the coldest of the century. Washington wrote that his soldiers went "five or six days without bread" and at one time "ate every kind of horse food but hay." Log huts and a Revolutionary hospital have been reconstructed, and nature trails are marked out.

The Wick House and Farm (Tempe Wick Rd., off Jockey Hollow Rd.) was the home of Capt. Henry Wick of the New Jersey Militia and served as headquarters for Maj. Gen. Arthur St. Clair. A frame-and-shingle farmhouse with a steeply pitched roof, the Wick House was built about 1750. According to legend, Wick's

To whom did Samuel F. B. Morse send his famous 1844 telegraphic message, "What hath God wrought?" To Alfred Vail, his assistant who had been working with him since 1837. Although Vail was responsible for the mechanical perfection of Morse's equipment, he lost interest in the project and profited little from the invention.

Vail's father, Stephen, was the owner of the Speedwell Iron Works in Morristown, which operated from 1814 to 1873, primarily as a foundry and machine shop. In 1837 he approved a contract between his son and Morse and agreed to finance the undertaking.

Morse, Vail, and a third associate, Leonard D. Gale, set up a laboratory on the second floor of the Speedwell factory, the first floor of which was a gristmill. Here Morse and Vail made the first public demonstration of the electromagnetic telegraph on January 10, 1838. The message transmitted at that time was "A patient waiter is no loser," perhaps a reference to Stephen Vail's financial contribution. Although Alfred Vail worked with Morse for several years after this occasion, he eventually retired to Morristown, where he spent most of his time compiling a family genealogy.

Speedwell Village also contains Stephen Vail's home and outbuildings of the ironworks. Several other late-eighteenth- and early-nineteenth-century homes, barns, and sheds have been moved to the park as well. Speedwell Village hopes not only to preserve the Vail family farm but to become a safe haven for threatened buildings.

Speedwell Road, Morristown. The delightful Gothic Revival villa of rough-cut stone, across Rte. 202 from the Vail home, was once the residence of George Vail, Alfred's younger brother. Next to it, in a public park by the riverside, the ruins of Stephen Vail's forge have been stabilized.

Borough Hall (Rte. 202, Bernardsville). In 1844 John Bunn built a stone mill complex, a combination grist- and sawmill, cider mill, and distillery that produced applejack. A very large wooden waterwheel was powered by the nearby stream and turned the four millstones. His family continued to operate the mill until 1913. In more recent years, the mill has become municipal headquarters for the Borough of Bernardsville.

Bernardsville Railroad Station (Rte. 202). In 1905 the Lackawanna Railroad urged its customers to come to New Jersey's Suburban Summerland, promising a delightful climate, "the air dry and bracing . . . at night laden with the delicious odor of pine and hemlock." Those who accepted the invitation disembarked at the same railroad station in use today—a smart pink-stone building with a wide overhang and eyebrow dormers.

Bernardsville Library (Rte. 202). Legends as romantic and stirring as those in the books on its shelves are told about the Bernardsville Library. Parts of the gable-fronted frame building date to 1730; in the Revolutionary War it was a tavern operated by Capt. John Parker, patronized by Washington's officers traveling between Morristown and Pluckemin.

Parker's daughter Phyllis fell in love with a young doctor, new in town, who was a spy for the British. His true purpose was discovered and he was tried and hanged as a traitor. His body was brought back to the tavern in a sealed wooden box. Later that night the guests heard the sounds of hammering and rending of boards. Crazed Phyllis was discovered beside the body of her lover. Naturally, her ghost returns to haunt the premises.

Gill–St. Bernard's School (Claremont Rd., north of Bernardsville). A pair of stone pillars, carved with the legend "Stronghold," flank the driveway leading to a formal two-story Renaissance-styled stone mansion. An arched loggia, stone balustrade, decorative rondels, and sculptured capstones are among its lavish adornments.

Stronghold is now a private school, but it was once the home of J. Fairfield Dryden, U.S. Senator and first president of the Prudential Insurance Company, and one of the several millionaires who lived in the "Mountain Colony" in the hills of Bernardsville at the turn of the century. George B. Post, the eclectic architect who designed Stronghold as well as many other Colony homes, was among the first to discover the charms of the area. The estates of the wealthy were hidden behind high shrubs and reached by winding lanes.

188

Gill–St. Bernard's School

In the separate little world created by the Mountain Colony people, servants lived by the rule, as one put it, "that They might become familiar with you, but that never, under any circumstances, did you become familiar with Them."

By the 1920's, when income tax had been levied, the Colony was declining; the Depression dealt it a fatal blow. The Gill School took over the Dryden estate in 1934.

Basking Ridge Presbyterian Church (foot of Maple Ave., at E. Oak St.). This brick church was built in 1839 and dominates the pleasant village of Basking Ridge. The congregation, like many others that took pride in the heritage of individual freedom, built it in the Greek Revival style. A 500-year-old oak tree spreads its branches protectively over the gravestones in the adjacent burial ground.

Township Hall (W. Oak St., Basking Ridge). Municipal offices now occupy this gable-fronted brick building that looks almost as it did when it was built in 1809 to house the classical school founded by Rev. Robert Finley. In an advertisement in 1827 seeking prospective students, Finley enumerated the advantages of Basking Ridge: "Its inhabitants are distinguished for their exemplary morals, hospitality and intelligence, and it is believed that there are fewer temptations to vice here than in most places."

The academy served as a public school from 1853 to 1903 and became Township Hall in 1924.

Mendham (Rte. 24, west of Morristown). In the eighteenth century Mendham boasted two inns at its crossroads (Rte. 24 and Hilltop Rd.)—the Black Horse Inn and Phoenix House. The latter now houses municipal offices. Many of the venerable buildings in the center of town have been converted to antiques shops and boutiques, creating an air of studied charm. The First Presbyterian Church (top of Hilltop Rd., at Talmadge Rd.) stands serenely above it all. It was built on its lofty site in 1860, its burial ground adjacent.

First Presbyterian Church, Mendham

John Ralston's General Store

Rte. 24, at Roxiticus Rd., Ralston,
west of Mendham
OPEN: Sun., 2–5 p.m., June–Nov.

John Ralston built this small frame shop in 1775; his tasteful home, built four years earlier, is behind the store. Hand-hewn oak was used for the frame; horizontal planks across the front are protected by the wide overhang. From 1792 until 1941 the building also served as a post office; it was acquired by the Ralston Historical Association in 1941.

Roxiticus Road, Mendham Township (south of Rte. 24). The devotion of the area's residents to horses is evident here—in the enormous gambrel-roofed barn complexes, riding rings, and horse paddocks that delineate the rolling valleys.

Chester (Rte. 24). Chester was promoted by the Lackawanna Railroad in the early 1900's as a town of "fertile farms, quaint houses and old-fashioned ways," a description that still seems apt. Loggias run across shopfronts and wooden platforms are reached by a run of two or three steps. The three-story brick Chester Inn was built

Chester Inn

in 1812. The clapboard Turkey Farm Inn has a gambrel roof. The Centennial Building (18–25 Main St.), built in 1876, encompasses six shops with a porch across the front and scrollwork decorations. East of the Chester Inn is the small-scale and sensitively designed Community Presbyterian Church.

South Orange to Hope

Carriage House, Seton Hall University.

Seton Hall University (S. Orange Ave. [Rte. 510], South Orange). Seton Hall College was founded as a Catholic school in 1856 in Madison, New Jersey. But that location seemed too isolated for even its handful of students, and four years later it moved to South Orange, closer to Newark.

From its Victorian period there are several fine survivals. President's Hall is a stately 1870's Venetian Gothic structure; an aristocratic tower marks the center of its expansive façade. An 1887 carriage house designed by architect John Baker, which initially served the adjacent estate of New York banker Eugene V. Kelley, has recently been restored and remodeled to serve as an arts center. A romantic brick tower sets off the gabled façade. Originally, horses were lodged in mahogany stalls, each marked by a brass nameplate.

South Orange Methodist Church (Prospect St. and S. Orange Ave.). Among the dignified buildings in the town center is this elaborately massed church with an open belfry. Built in 1901, it combines limestone, dark-red shingles, and a red tile roof to rich effect. Close by, the Trinity Presbyterian Church, dating from 1881, is more sober but also handsome. The attractive rough-textured, stucco-and-timber Town Hall is matched by its nearby firehouse.

East Orange Veterans Administration Hospital (Tremont St., off S. Central Ave. [Rte. 508]). Built in 1952, this fifteen-story H-shaped building, surrounded by wings of staggered heights, is a modern version of a style popular in the prewar period. Modernistic decorative elements in shining steel are a stunning touch.

Orange Public Library (Main [Rte. 508] and S. Essex sts.). The Orange Public Library owes its intellectual origins to the Orange Lyceum, one of many such centers which flourished in the 1830's and 1840's. Dedicated in 1901, the library was designed by McKim, Mead & White, who, harking back to Classical forms for their inspiration, gave the town a distinguished landmark.

Llewelyn Park

Main St., end of Park Ave.,
West Orange
OPEN: Private, but open to holders of
tickets for Glenmont (see next
entry)

Under the influence of European Romantics and American landscape painters, particularly of the Hudson River School, idealists of the mid-nineteenth century sought a refuge from burgeoning industrialism in the picturesque countryside. If the idealists were also wealthy, they had an opportunity to create their own version of paradise in the suburbs.

Llewelyn Haskell was one such man— head of a large chemical company and a follower of intellectual pursuits. In 1853, with his friend and partner, the architect Alexander Jackson Davis, he built the first Romantic suburb in the United States, on Eagle Ridge in the then-undeveloped Orange Mountains. The site plan itself was drawn by Eugene A. Baumann, following the principles of A. J. Downing. Haskell wanted his development, called Llewelyn Park, to be a "retreat for businessmen and intellectuals . . . a place for a man to exercise his rights and privileges."

In the 400-acre park, a 50-acre strip called The Ramble was set aside as a common park. The Ramble today exists much as it did in the 1850's, graced with bridges, lookouts, arbors, and statuary.

Davis designed many houses in the original development, including Haskell's, called Eyrie Eagle Park, another for himself, and the gatehouse. Of the original structures, only the gatehouse (which resembles Haskell's demolished residence), topped with a conical roof, and one Davis cottage (corner of Park Way and Oak Bend) still stand. Davis built this cottage with a large studio for a landscape painter, Edward W. Nicholls. Later, Charles McKim, the noted architect, lived in it as a boy.

The residents of Llewelyn Park in the early days had to agree to certain restrictions. No house could be built on less than an acre of land, and there were to be no fences or commercial enterprises. However, the Llewelyn Park group tended to be unconventional. The staid community of Orange was shocked by the presence of atheists in its midst and by a marriage held at sunrise under the trees.

Most of the richly varied dwellings in Llewelyn Park date from later periods, but among picturesque vistas and curving roads, they seem as Romantic as the original conception.

Glenmont

Glen Ave., Llewelyn Park, West Orange
*OPEN: Mon.–Sat., 10 a.m.–4 p.m.
  Closed holidays. Tickets must be purchased at Edison Headquarters, Main St. and Lakeside Ave.
PHONE: (201) 736–0550

Thomas Edison was one of Llewelyn Park's most famous residents. He bought a house here at the time of his second marriage in 1886 and lived in it until his death in 1931. The Edison home, Glenmont, is a rambling twenty-three room mansion designed by the office of Henry Hudson Holly in 1880.

Holly was among the first to praise early-eighteenth-century American ver-nacular architecture. These houses "really have nothing by which to fix their date," he wrote in his immensely popular book, *Modern Dwellings in Town and Country*, published in 1878 in the wake of the self-conscious search for a truly American style that followed the Centennial. For his own day Holly advocated the style known variously as Queen Anne, "cottage," or "free Classic," which made creative use of historic American forms and materials —scalloped shingles, exposed timbers, spacious chimneys; but for the successful execution of this inventive style, wrote Holly, the architect was as important as "the physician to his patient."

Two floors of the home are open to the public, furnished with many of the Edison family's furniture and mementoes. Seated at his desk, which he called his "thought bench," Edison looked past the spacious lawns of Llewelyn Park and devised the technology of the future. Glenmont is maintained by the National Park Service.

Thomas A. Edison Laboratory

Main St. and Lakeside Ave.,
West Orange
*OPEN: Daily, 10 a.m.–4 p.m.
  Closed major holidays
PHONE: (201) 736–0550

Edison worked for forty-four years in this complex of red-brick laboratories, developing and improving the phonograph, the motion picture, and others of his 1,093 patented inventions. At his death he was working on a natural substitute for rubber, and the chemical laboratory remains as it was set up for those experiments.

Glenmont

Henry Hudson Holly designed the original laboratory buildings in 1886. Among other structures on the grounds is a reproduction of the "Black Maria," an early motion-picture studio that was rotated on a platform to catch the sunlight. Edison's library contains a fascinating collection of materials on the inventor and his times.

Force House

366 S. Livingston Ave. (Rte. 527),
Livingston
OPEN: 2d and 4th Sun. of the month,
    Sept.–Nov., April–June;
    and by appointment

Samuel Force, of French Huguenot descent, purchased a farm and small house in 1763; his son Thomas came home from service in the Revolutionary War and became a prosperous farmer and a sawmill operator here. Successive owners have made additions, with the result that the Force dwelling is the picturesque accretion of two centuries of family life.

The Condit Williams Cook House, a small building dating from 1700, was moved to the grounds of the Force House. Its single room and loft have been used for many purposes. Originally a dwelling, it has served as an outside kitchen and washhouse, a playhouse, a storage shed, and possibly a slaughterhouse. It presently houses a collection of hand tools.

Both houses are owned and maintained by the Livingston Historical Society.

Bloomfield Green (Broad St. [Rte. 509]). Despite the dense construction that surrounds it, the expansive Bloomfield Green still conveys a flavor of the eighteenth century. It is dominated by the First Presbyterian Church, a brownstone structure with a brown wooden octagonal belfry and bell-shaped cupola, which was built in the 1790's. The campus of Bloomfield College is at the eastern end of the Green.

Montclair Railroad Station (Historical Society Antiques Market) (Bloomfield Ave. [Rte. 506] and Elm St.). Montclair's city fathers were indeed grateful to the Delaware, Lackawanna & Western Railroad for building this fine station in 1912. They commended the president of the line for building a station "distinguished for its architectural beauty and commanding proportions." Classical detailing is used on rough concrete and a tapestry brick veneer.

View of the Presbyterian Church at Bloomfield.

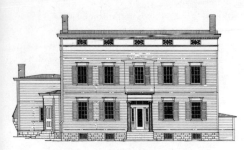

Israel Crane House

Israel Crane House

110 Orange Rd., Montclair
OPEN: Sun., 2–5 p.m., except July and
Aug., and by appointment
PHONE: (201) 744–1796

Israel Crane, a businessman whose acumen earned him the title of "King" Crane, built this house in 1796. Crane owned a general store and cider mill, and leased a mill site in Paterson in 1801. Aided by New York financing, he built the Newark and Pompton Tnpk., a toll road, and later owned several brownstone quarries in Newark.

Crane's son James took over the two-and-a-half-story house in 1838 and gave it a fashionable Greek Revival facelifting. A flat roof above a Classical cornice with cast-iron grills was added, as well as a portico with two Ionic columns. No doubt for symmetry, windowless frames were added on the second story to each side of the house.

After serving as a YWCA, the Crane House was saved from demolition in 1965 and moved to its present site by the Montclair Historical Society. It has been restored to its 1830's appearance. Inside, rooms are furnished in various periods.

Unitarian Church (67 Church St., Montclair). This highly original shingle-and-stucco church recalls the Craftsman movement of the early twentieth century when it was built.

Montclair Art Museum

Bloomfield and S. Mountain aves.
OPEN: Tues.–Sat., 10 a.m.–5 p.m.;
Sun., 2–5:30 p.m.
Closed July and Aug.
PHONE: (201) 746–5555

An outstanding collection of American art is housed in the Montclair Art Museum, a formal two-and-a-half-story brick building with four marble Ionic columns in front. The building was presented to the Montclair Art Association in 1914 by Florence Rand Lang. The museum's goal of collecting American art was initiated by William T. Evans' gift of thirty American paintings.

After 1875, George Inness, the noted American impressionist painter, spent much of his time in Montclair. The quiet mood of his glowing landscapes have recorded the rural peace of Montclair

Unitarian Church, Montclair

during that period. The museum has a fine collection of Inness' work and much reference material on him.

North, Upper, and South Mountain roads, Montclair. On these and surrounding streets are both palatial and picturesque homes of the late nineteenth and early twentieth centuries, the period of Montclair's prominence as a resort and exclusive suburban community.

Bond House (848 Valley Rd., Montclair). Originally the Van Reyper House, this white frame structure adds a dignified nineteenth-century touch to the campus of Montclair State College. It has a four-story tower and cupola, and was built in 1876 and moved to the campus in recent years. It is now part of the Department of Adult and Continuing Education.

Grover Cleveland Birthplace

207 Bloomfield Ave. (Rte. 506), Caldwell
*OPEN: Tues.–Sat., 10 a.m.–noon, 1–5 p.m.; Sun., 2–5 p.m. Closed Thanksgiving, Christmas, and New Year's Day
PHONE: (201) 226–1810

It's hard to imagine Presidents as babies, particularly one as austere as Grover Cleveland. Nevertheless, the cradle in which the 22d and 24th President slept is on display in this house, formerly the parsonage of the First Presbyterian Church where his father was minister in 1837.

Cleveland lived in this three-story clapboard house only until he was three, and then his family moved to Buffalo, New York, from where he was elected to the presidency in 1885. The Cleveland house was presented to the State of New Jersey in 1934 and contains many of his belongings.

First Presbyterian Church (Bloomfield Ave., Caldwell). This fine Victorian Gothic church of rusticated brownstone has delicate pierced-iron cresting and molded-wood mullions. Fine foliate details decorate the columns. Grover Cleveland's father preached in the earlier church on this site.

Nutley Historical Society Museum

65 Church St.
OPEN: Sun., 2–5 p.m., and by appointment
PHONE: (201) NO7–7892

This prim 1875 schoolhouse stands tall and narrow; its gabled façade is organized into three bays, each set between projecting brick piers. A fanciful wooden cupola throws severity to the winds. The museum contains mementoes of Annie Oakley (who lived for a time in Nutley) and changing exhibits of Jerseyana and antiques. Across the street is the Franklin Reformed Church, a vigorously decorated structure built in 1860.

Town Hall (Chestnut St., near Franklin Ave., Nutley). Built in 1852 as a woolen mill, this three-story red-brick structure also served the town as a school before it became the municipal office building in 1894. It has been remodeled extensively.

Nutley Woman's Club (Chestnut St. and Vincent Place). In 1912 a group of determined women saved this low brownstone Dutch house from destruction, and formed the Woman's Club to maintain it. The house had been built in 1702 by Jacob Vreeland, a mason, for Abraham Van Giesen and his family. The Van Geisens were Loyalists in the Revolution, and their house was confiscated and sold to a Continental officer, Capt. Speer. In 1783 Speer sold it to John Vreeland, a descendant of the builder, and that family occupied it until the early 1900's.

Kingsland Manor

3 Kingsland Rd., at Lakeside Dr., Nutley
OPEN: 3d Sun. afternoon of the month,
and by appointment
PHONE: (201) 661–3410

Kingsland Manor is a typical brownstone house built in the Dutch Colonial style, but it has had a livelier history than many. The original section was built by Nathaniel Kingsland in the early 1700's, and the house was a meeting place for Continental soldiers in the Revolution. It is believed to have been a station on the Underground Railroad, which seems only just, for the house had been built by slave labor. In 1910 Kingsland Manor was purchased by Daniel McGinnity, manager of the prizefighter Bob Fitzsimmons. As Fitzsimmons' training camp, the house

was a popular spot with New York celebrities and politicos. During Prohibition McGinnity's widow and son ran a flourishing speakeasy and, later, a licensed tavern. The house was purchased by the Town of Nutley and is being restored to face a perhaps less eventful but more stable future.

Fairleigh Dickinson University (W. Passaic and Montross aves., Rutherford). When Peter Sammartino and his wife, Sally, were looking for a place to establish a new junior college in New Jersey in 1942, they found the perfect place right across the street from Sally's parents' home. It was Iviswold, a masterful Richardsonian creation of cut brownstone, built in the 1880's for David Ivison, founder of the firm that became the American Book Company; the house had stood vacant for many years. With funds from Sally's father and Col. Fairleigh Dickinson, the junior college bought the castle and set up a school. With its turrets, towers, and great arched porte cochere, the house still dominates the campus, now the main branch of a university.

Dr. Sammartino continued his preservation efforts by buying the Kingsland House (245 Union Ave., corner of Prospect St.) in 1955 and restoring it as a classroom building. The original part of the tiny salt-box was built in the 1670's. In that same year the college was given the Outwater House, a red sandstone dwelling whose earliest walls were built about 1720. It was moved from East Rutherford to a site adjoining the Kingsland House, to which it was connected. It was restored to serve as the headquarters of the School of Education. The Outwater House is a curious amalgam of Dutch Colonial and Federal styles.

The Castle, Fairleigh Dickinson University

First Presbyterian Church (1 Passaic Ave., at Ridge Rd., Rutherford). This handsome brownstone structure, built in 1888, has a deep arched porte cochere and a squat crenellated tower. Its windows display rich tracery mullions.

William Carlos Williams House (9 Ridge Rd., across from First Presbyterian Church, Rutherford). The poet and physician William Carlos Williams lived in this restrained Queen Anne house with scalloped shingles from 1912, shortly after his marriage, until his death in 1963. The house is still the family residence. Williams loved Rutherford, describing it as "a town lying in the narrow sun-baked strip of good soil, land which the Dutch farmers cultivated so well in the old days, between the low Watchung Range and the swamp land of the Hackensack Meadows."

St. Paul's Church (18th St. and Broadway [Rte. 4], Paterson). The picturesque and irregular masses of the battlemented, rough-hewn stone church add up to a delightful whimsey. Romanesque inspiration—low arches and squat columns—is lightened by adroit details such as the narrow cylindrical tower tucked in against the weightier square one. W. Halsey Wood was the architect of the church, completed in 1892.

Danforth Library (Broadway and Auburn St., Paterson). Henry Bacon designed this library in the neo-Classical style in 1903. Four Ionic columns in front of the recessed portico complement the dignified gray limestone façade.

New Jersey Bank (129 Market St., Paterson). Monumentally scaled and extremely simplified, this Art Deco bank building, completed in 1927, has a high, marble-faced, arched door opening.

City Hall (Market St., between Washington and Colt sts., Paterson). John M. Carrère of Carrère & Hastings designed this three-story gray limestone building in 1894 and embellished it with all the "City Beautiful" touches of the period—eagles, urns, cartouches, wreaths, arches, balustrades, and heavy cornices. It is capped by a cupola and weathered copper dome.

Passaic County Courthouse and Annex (Ward and Hamilton sts., Paterson). The Courthouse, in imposing neo-Classic style, makes a stunning contrast to the Annex, which was built in 1908 and modeled after the Haarlem Market in Holland.

Great Falls of Paterson and Society for Useful Manufactures Historic District, Paterson

Bounded by W. Broadway and Ryle Ave.; Grand St.; Morris, Barbour, Spruce, and River sts.; and west bank of Passaic River, crossing at Wayne and McBride aves., then south to Grand St.

When George Washington was inaugurated, newspapers pointed out with some satisfaction that he was wearing a suit made of American-woven broadcloth. The new nation was understandably sensitive about its industrial backwardness, a condition imposed on it by the British imperialists.

To remedy this situation, Alexander Hamilton, first secretary of the Treasury,

197

View of part of Paterson.

envisioned a great manufacturing center at the 70-foot Great Falls of the Passaic River. Hamilton and a group of energetic businessmen formed a stock company in 1791 called the "Society for the Establishment of Useful Manufactures" (SUM) and named the site of the new "Federal City" Paterson in honor of the governor of New Jersey, an enthusiastic supporter of the plan.

However, the scheme failed. Pierre L'Enfant's design for the "National Manufactory" proved as impractical and grandiose for the times as his plans for the capital city, and the SUM had to call in Peter Colt, treasurer of the State of Connecticut and owner of the only clothing factory in the country, to succeed him. Although Colt built two mills, by 1796 the SUM was bankrupt.

Beginning in the early 1800's, however, under the leadership of the Colt family, Paterson did become a great industrial center, manufacturing cloth (first cotton and later silk), guns, and locomotives. The relocation of the textile industry to the South in the early 1920's started Paterson, along with other industrial centers in the northeast, on a slow decline.

The dozens of dignified, rationally planned brick and masonry structures which remain from the nineteenth and early twentieth centuries, pressing against the narrow pavements bordering the Passaic River, form a virtual museum of factory architecture.

Next to the 1860 pumping station on the far side of the river are the offices of the Great Falls Development Corporation, housed in the Conduit Gatehouse built in 1906 for the Passaic Water Company. The office has produced brochures describing walking tours, and will organize tours for groups. Cross the river for a view of the spectacular Great Falls and the SUM Dam, built during 1838–40. Along Spruce St. are the Rogers Locomotive and Machine Works. The Rogers Administration Building, erected in 1881, later housed a silk mill. Behind the complex are the middle race, the canal begun by Maj. L'Enfant in 1793 to extend the available supply of water power into the city; the upper race, whose brownstone retaining walls were built in the 1820's; and the remains of the old stone road that was built in 1797 as a passage to the raceway.

The earliest parts of the Dolphin Jute Mills complex (corner of Spruce and Barbour sts.) date from 1844. An addition (corner of Grand and Morris sts.), which cost nearly $500,000 when completed in the 1880's, is one of the most lavish factories in the district.

Someday, in addition to industrial production, the wonderful variety of flexible space contained within the thick masonry walls of these old factories may well house a spectrum of contemporary urban activities—theaters, craft and education centers, and museums. Such is the goal of a dedicated group of Patersonians. Assisted by Urban Deadline, a group of action-oriented urbanists, they have developed ingenious schemes to revitalize Paterson, but progress has been slow. Like the SUM, they face innumerable problems.

Lambert Castle

Garret Mountain Reservation, Valley Rd., at the Lackawanna Railroad bridge, Paterson
OPEN: Wed., Thurs., Fri. 1–4:45 p.m.;
       Sat., Sun., 11 a.m.–4:45 p.m.
PHONE: (201) 523–9883

For Catholina Lambert, an English immigrant who came to America in 1844, the road to riches was not paved with gold but

lined with silk. The Boston company he joined at the age of seventeen and in which he later became a partner moved to Paterson, the "Silk City." In 1890 Lambert built a massive brownstone castle on a mountain overlooking Paterson. In Belle Vista Lambert displayed his collection of paintings and objets d'art. The silk strike of 1913, however, wiped out his holdings, and he was forced to sell at auction and at a loss most of his valuable collections.

The castle is now owned by Passaic County and houses the collections of the Passaic County Historical Society.

Dey Mansion

199 Totowa Rd., in Preakness Valley Park, Wayne Township
OPEN: Tues., Wed., Fri., 1–5 p.m.;
       Sat., Sun., 10 a.m.–5 p.m.
PHONE: (201) OX6–1776

In October 1780 George Washington made this "handsome farm" his headquarters, and his hideout, too, for Sir Henry Clinton, angered over the recent execution of Maj. John André, made plans to have Washington kidnapped. When Washington heard the news of his pursuers, he set out for the 600-acre Dey estate, called Bloomsbury Manor, with a guard of 150 men.

Rogers Administration Building   **199**

The mansion, begun in the 1740's by Dirck Dey and completed by his son Theunis, is forthright and unaffected. The main elevation clearly reflects the interior plan, in which four spacious rooms on each of the two main floors are arranged in pairs on both sides of a broad center hall. A tripartite window which lights the wide hall is a simplified version of the high-style Palladian motif. Other Georgian elements are the string course at the second story, the splayed lintels on the main-floor window openings, and the stepped brownstone quoins. The use of brick laid in Flemish bond also followed English practice; the more easily obtainable brownstone, cut and rubble, was used on the side and rear walls.

Serious interest in preserving the house, so closely associated with Washington, dated from the 1876 Centennial; but funds were not found until 1930, when it was purchased by the Passaic County Park Commission. The federal Civil Works Agency supplied artisans to restore the mansion in 1933.

Van Riper–Hopper House (Wayne Museum)

533 Berdan Ave., off Franklin Lakes Tnpk. (Rte. 502), Wayne
OPEN: Fri.–Tues., 1–5 p.m.
Closed Christmas and New Year's Day
PHONE: (201) 694–7192

In its pleasant setting, facing the Point View Reservoir and surrounded by grassy lawns and a Colonial herb garden, the Van Riper–Hopper House presents a particularly attractive view of the Dutch style in New Jersey. The eaves overhang the one-and-a-half-story rubble brownstone structure, forming a wide veranda; a frame wing adjoins it.

The house was built in 1786 by Uriah Richard Van Riper, a prosperous farmer, when he married Maria Berdan. One of his descendants married into the Hopper family in 1872, and the house acquired its second name. The property was acquired by Wayne Township in 1964, and is now the headquarters of the Wayne Historical Commission.

American Cyanamid Executive and Administrative Center (Cyanamid Dr., off Hamburg Tnpk. [Rte. 23], Wayne). American Cyanamid opened its headquarters here in 1962. Vincent Kling designed the serpentine building, influenced by the natural contours of the 180-acre site. Fieldstone retaining walls and brick-paved terraces provide a transition from the woods to the immense yet unassuming structure.

Boonton. Boonton's former status as an iron-mining and manufacturing center is marked by its once-proud railroad station on Division St. and by the fine buildings on Main St. (Rte. 202) and nearby streets. The Boonton Public Library (619 Main St.) was once the home of James Holmes, superintendent of a nail factory who invested his earnings in real estate and became a philanthropist. Two octagon houses stand on Cornelia St., near the board-and-batten St. John's Episcopal Church, designed by Richard Upjohn in 1863.

Montville Historical Museum (Taylorstown Rd.). This prim 1864 red-brick schoolhouse is now a museum designed

Montville Historical Museum

to instruct visitors in the history of Montville. Open Sat., 2–4 p.m.

Waterloo Village

West of Rte. 206, near Stanhope
*OPEN: Daily, 10 a.m.–6 p.m.,
April–June; Tues.–Sun.,
10 a.m.–6 p.m., July–Dec.
PHONE: (201) 347–0900

First an iron-producing center and then a busy port on the Morris Canal, with mules braying on its towpaths, Waterloo Village declined when the canal, an engineering marvel, proved to be a financial debacle. The canal, which was the work of George P. Macculloch, stretched from Newark Bay to the Delaware River at Philipsburg. Because of the mountainous terrain it covered, it was built on a series of inclined planes. A boat was floated onto a "cradle" that ran under the water on tracks and was transported by water power over the mountains through a series of locks. Mrs. Francis Trollope, an English visitor, commented in 1832, the year after the canal opened, on the ingenious arrangement.

She found it "one among a thousand which prove the people of America to be the most enterprising in the world."

Although the canal proved of some benefit to the iron companies of Morris County, giving them easier access to the Pennsylvania coalfields, the company succumbed to competition from railroads, mismanagement, and high operating costs.

Waterloo Village was almost deserted until a few years ago when two interior designers, Percival Leach and Louis Gualandi, saw restoration possibilities in the existing buildings. Seventeen have now been restored, and eleven of them open to the public, including the yellow stone gristmill; the General Store; an elegant early-nineteenth-century Old Stage Coach Inn; the Canal House, originally workmen's living quarters; Wellington House, an elaborate Victorian residence dating from 1859; and the Methodist Church. Several clapboard and stuccoed-stone dwellings complete the picturesque scene.

Main Street, Hackettstown

Hackettstown today seems to be prospering, surely an enviable state for any community. However, in the rush to "fix up" Main St., aluminum siding and plastic permastone seem to be the favored building materials. They threaten to conceal not only the blemishes but the intrinsic quality of the architecture in the Main St. Historic District.

Hackettstown was named, so it is said, after Samuel Hackett, who endeared himself to the community in the 1750's by setting up free drinks for everyone when a

Madison Street, Hackettstown

new hotel was opened. Most of the buildings along Main St. date from later periods—the First Presbyterian Church School (1819), the Warren Hotel (1840), the Gothic Revival First Presbyterian Church (1861), and the Central House (mid-nineteenth century). The Hackettstown Community House is a cut-stone mansion with delicate lead tracery in the transom light.

On nearby Washington St. there is a superb display of nineteenth-century architecture. Number 50 is a brick octagon with stone lintels and a central chimney. St. James Episcopal Church (corner of Washington and Moore sts.) was built in 1859 but prospered most when nearby Schooley's Mountain became a popular spa in the 1890's.

Centenary College for Women
(Moore, Jefferson, and Plane sts., Hacketts-

202

town). Ten communities, from Newark to Bernardsville, competed for the honor of being the home of the Centenary Collegiate Institute, a Methodist Episcopal school for girls founded in 1869. Hackettstown won out, because ten citizens donated ten acres, $10,000 in cash, and a sidewalk to the center of town.

The campus now includes buildings from various periods. The Edward Seay Administration Building and the adjoining semicircular North and South Halls were designed in 1901 by Oscar S. Teale. The Seay Building, with its tall clock tower, presents a gracious entrance to the campus. The Taylor Library and the Reeves Building, an octagonally shaped student center, are fine modern additions, both designed in 1954 by Jan Hird Pokorny. Du Bois Hall, an 1880's mansarded mansion, was acquired by the college and moved to the campus in 1965.

Hope Historic District

Hickory St., Cider Lane, and High (Rte. 519), Union, and Walnut sts.

Work and worship were the tenets of the Moravians who moved from Bethlehem, Pennsylvania, and settled Hope, New Jersey, in 1774. Evidence of their pious labor can still be seen in the communal structures which were the start of their society, in the massive stone mill, which was intended to give them economic self-sufficiency, and in the rugged stone houses and barns lining the pleasant streets.

Moravian life was wholly devoted to the service of God, and a strict regimen organized work among clearly defined groups. Property was held communally,

and a rational scheme was the basis for the village plan, drawn in 1774 by Bishop Ettwein of the Mother Church in Europe. Remarkably, the plan remains essentially intact today. The vast three-and-a-half-story stone gristmill at the foot of High St. was one of the first structures in Hope; a 1,000-foot race, cut in places as deep as 22 feet into the slate bedrock, provided abundant energy. The cut-limestone *Gemeinhaus* (corner of High and Union sts.), built about a decade later, at first served as a community center and place of worship, though the long two-and-a-half-story building has since seen use as a courthouse and, more recently, a bank.

Following Germanic vernacular tradition, several typical Moravian dwellings on High St. are built of roughly cut ashlar,

with smooth blocks for corner quoins, and stone or brick arches to support door and window openings. An unusual feature of the Moravian dwelling is its two-story attic, permitting an additional story while it maintains the balanced proportions that distinguish the design. Several of these dwellings are located on Union St. as well. The Single Sisters Choir (Union St.), a seven-bay stone structure with a later addition, housed the colony's unmarried women. It was later known as the American House Hotel.

The Moravians refused to fight in the Revolutionary War, but earned their neighbors' admiration for their care of the wounded. The Moravian experiment failed in 1808, because the settlers were cut off from the parent body and weakened by their losses in a smallpox epidemic. The survivors moved back to Bethlehem.

Only a few structures were built by later settlers; one is the traceried St. Luke's Church (High St.). But the Moravian way of life determined for future generations the special character of the town.

American House Hotel
(Single Sisters Choir)

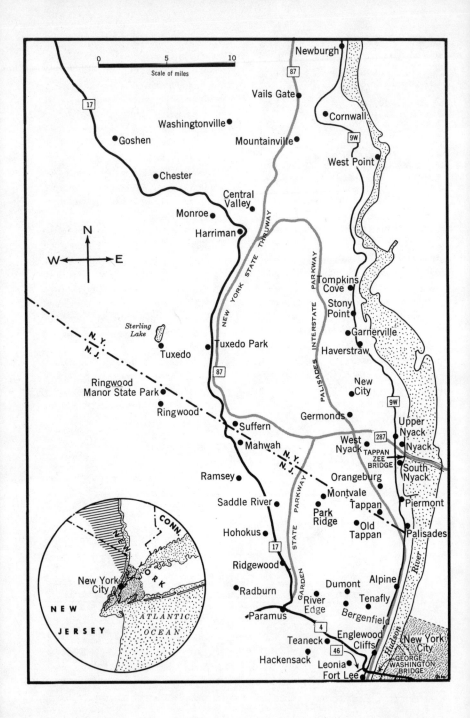

7 | Northern New Jersey and Southern New York

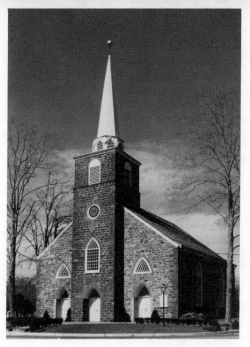

Saddle River Reformed Church

The Dutch settlers were the first to venture west across the Hudson River in the seventeenth century; their descendants have left a tangible heritage in the numerous sturdy stone houses that are a distinctive feature in Bergen and Rockland counties. The Revolutionary War is still a vivid memory, too. Associations with events of that turbulent period have no doubt been responsible for the preservation of many structures.

But the area's predominant flavor is of the nineteenth and twentieth centuries. At first railroads brought industry, commerce, and prosperity to the small towns and villages that nestle in the Ramapo Valley and dot the west banks of the Hudson. In modern times rapid suburban growth has engulfed the remaining farmland in the areas close to New York. However, large tracts have been reserved for parkland; and farther from New York, the rural ambience is still strong.

The sites described in this section follow two main routes, both starting at the George Washington Bridge. The first route follows, in a general way, Rtes. 4 and 17 through New Jersey and the New York State Thruway as far as Goshen, where rural simplicity and urban sophistication mingle comfortably. The second follows Rte. 9W north along the scenic Palisades to Newburgh, a Hudson River town whose architectural riches are still impressive.

George Washington Bridge

For efficiency, economy, and sheer scale, the George Washington Bridge, completed in 1931, was a high point in the development of the suspension bridge. With a main span of 3,500 feet, it was nearly double the length of any bridge previously constructed. Steel truss towers, soaring more than 600 feet above supporting piers, are actually immense space frames able to sustain an unprecedented load of 100,000 tons. Swiss-born engineer Othmar H. Ammann was the designer.

The bridge was immediately acclaimed for its functional appearance, created by the exposed steelwork in the suspension towers. However, economic rather than aesthetic considerations were the source. The Port of New York Authority rejected architect Cass Gilbert's plan to sheath the towers with Gothic-styled granite because steelwork could be protected more cheaply by paint than by masonry.

Church of the Madonna (2070 Hoefley's Lane, Fort Lee; off Rte. 46, Main St. Leonia–Bogota exit). One of the few Roman Catholics who settled in northern New Jersey in the early nineteenth century was Joseph Riley. He purchased several hundred acres of land above the Palisades and in 1830–35 built this simple Gothic-style fieldstone chapel.

Vreeland House

125 Lakeview Ave., east of Grand Ave.
(Rte. 93), Leonia

The English conquest of New Netherland in 1664 encouraged settlers to move northward to the verdant lands that one Englishman later called "the garden of America." The lands owned by English proprietors were sold as patents to speculators, who then resold much of the land to farmers.

Although the Dutch predominated in northern New Jersey, many Englishmen and French Huguenots joined them. The English were the majority in the so-called "English Neighborhood" (present-day Leonia, Englewood, and Ridgefield). Derrick Vreeland, descendant of a patroon's farm servant, settled on a large farm in the neighborhood in 1737; as his family prospered, they built successively more comfortable and solid dwellings. This pattern, repeated again and again, created a distinctively American form of dwelling, which evolved from the link between Old World taste and experience and the restless ingenuity of American craftsmen–builders.

In the case of Vreeland House, the smaller section, probably dating to the mid-eighteenth century, is characteristically built of sandstone; side walls are laid in coursed rubble, and the main façade in dressed blocks. The two-and-a-half-story frame addition, much larger than the original wing, has a lofty gambrel roof and elaborately leaded fanlights and side lights.

Civil War Armory and Drill Hall (130 Grand Ave., at Oakdene Ave., Leonia).

The Jersey Blues Company of the English Neighborhood Troops trained for the Civil War in this white clapboard armory built in 1859. The building was used as an armory until 1910, and then as a workplace for finishing raw lumber to build suburban Leonia. The English Neighborhood Historical Society plans to restore it as a museum. Open by appointment. Phone: (201) 944–0690.

First Presbyterian Church (E. Palisade and Hillside aves., Englewood). The English Gothic country church has been translated into the American vernacular in this red sandstone structure with tan limestone trim, built in 1870. Adjacent to the church is a robust stone-and-shingle rectory.

Brinckerhoff–Demarest House (493 Teaneck Rd. [Rte. 129], opposite Copley Ave., Teaneck). Like many of the Dutch houses in the area, the Brinckerhoff-Demarest House faces south, to gain the benefit of maximum sunlight. Throughout its 200-year history, this stone house has rarely changed family ownership. A squat and comfortable farmhouse, it seems to embody the constancy of its owners to the land.

Guido's Restaurant (John Hopper House) (249 Polifly Rd., Hackensack). In the late eighteenth century, when times were hard, John Hopper built a modest farmstead for his family on the east side of Polifly Rd. After the Revolution, his son felt that the little brown sandstone house did not reflect the affluence of the times. So it was torn down and in 1816–18 he built a new twenty-room mansion. Although he clung to tradition in the broad gambrel roof and the flaring

eaves at the rear, he also added some fashionable Federal details, such as the splayed stone window lintels, half-round windows in the gabled end, and an elliptical fanlight over the front door.

First Reformed Church on the Green (northeast corner of the Hackensack Green). The churches known today as Dutch Colonial, of which this is an early example, were built in the 1790's and early 1800's, in a style related to that of the Anglican churches in New York. This red sandstone church was built in 1791 and enlarged several times in the nineteenth century. The adjacent graveyard has many old stones.

In the early 1800's, when religious revivalism was sweeping the area, French Huguenots joined the Dutch church and doctrinal controversy disrupted the congregation. During one stormy meeting, a bolt of lightning split the keystone over the doorway, and the awestruck disputants settled their differences amicably. More often, lightning struck the spires of these churches; as a result, the spires seen today are seldom original and have often been replaced unsympathetically.

Bergen County Courthouse (Court St., between Main and River sts., on the Hackensack Green). This courthouse was de-

John Hopper House 207

Bergen County Courthouse

North Reformed Church of Schraalenburgh (corner of Washington and Madison aves., Dumont). The present structure, whose tall tower is topped by an elegant belfry and lofty spire, was built in 1800. The wooden porch, decorated with scrollwork, is especially charming. The Parsonage (191 Washington Ave.) was added in 1834.

North Reformed Church of Schraalenburgh, Dumont

signed in 1912 in the current version of the Classical style by J. R. Gordon. Colossal columns embellish the façade, and the structure is crowned by a tall dome.

From the courthouse to the Bergen County Jail is but a few easy steps. This functionally simplified five-story brick building is oddly decorated with medieval battlements.

Old South Church (W. Church St., Bergenfield). This typical Dutch Reformed church, built in 1799 and now occupied by a Presbyterian congregation, is enhanced by its placid lakeside setting. John Goethius, one of its early pastors, was a leader of the liberal wing of the church that sought independence from the clergy in Holland. Goethius, like many others, believed that the Dutch language was particularly well suited for sermons. When an English clergyman commented on his severe preaching manner by saying, "It always seems to me, when I hear you preach, that the law must have been given in the Dutch language," Goethius replied, "And I have always thought that English must have been the language in which the serpent spoke to Eve in Paradise."

208

County Trust Bank (Washington and Madison aves., Dumont). Now sharing the center of town with the church is the bank built in 1920, a forthright example of modernism. The curved façade, which turns the corner, is fronted by massive fluted Doric columns.

Von Steuben House

1209 Main St., off New Bridge Rd.,
River Edge
*OPEN: Tues.–Sat., 10 a.m.–noon,
       1–5 p.m.; Sun., 1–5 p.m.
PHONE: (201) 487–1739

The Von Steuben House has many architectural features associated with the style known as Dutch Colonial, although, strictly speaking, these distinctive houses are neither Dutch nor Colonial. Though built generally by Dutch settlers and their descendants, they have no direct antecedents in Dutch architecture; and, though some of the early wings were built in the Colonial period, much of the construction postdates the Revolution. Possibly because these houses are so adaptable and comfortable, a great many have survived. (In addition to those listed here, many others can be discovered in the area; their

presence usually indicates an early road.)

The special character of these houses has been recognized for a long time. A mid-eighteenth-century traveler in New Jersey remarked "the peculiar neatness in the appearance of these dwellings," with "an airy piazza supported by pillars in front, and their kitchens connected at the ends in the form of wings." An enthusiastic observer surmised, nearly a century later, that these houses "must all have been designed by one architect," because of the common use of "trimly cut freestone in front and sides, rough dressed in the rear, curb roofs, large porches, made by the continuation of the roof projecting over the front of the house and immense chimneys."

The long, low buildings were commonly built of brown or red sandstone, the same stone used to face New York City "brownstones." In the Von Steuben House, the brownstone is enhanced by the contrasting color, texture, and size of the bricks under the gabled end. The house appears unusually long because the continuous gambrel roof unites the several sections, which were built at different times.

The house was confiscated from its Loyalist owner, John Zabriskie, in 1777,

Von Steuben House

and presented in 1783 to Gen. Friedrich von Steuben by the New Jersey legislature in response to his request for a suitable reward for services rendered in the Revolution. But Von Steuben never lived in it, and the original owner eventually bought it back from the state.

The building is now the headquarters of the Bergen County Historical Society. It is one of the few Dutch Colonial houses open to the public and offers a rare chance to see the craftsmen's techniques and materials.

Demarest House (Main St., adjacent to the Von Steuben House, River Edge). David des Marest, a French Huguenot fleeing from religious persecution, arrived in New Netherland just before its surrender to the English in 1664. An aggressive, ambitious man, he had no intention of returning to the Old World and quickly set about making his mark in the New. He built this house near the French burial ground in New Milford, and the Demarest family figured prominently in the development of the area.

The simplicity of the plan of this rubblestone dwelling is characteristic of the early eighteenth century. Each of the two rooms on the first floor has an outside door. Practical settlers found that the steeply pitched roof and the elimination of hallways achieved the most efficient use of space.

Unoccupied in modern times, it was moved from its original site to a more protected one on the property of the Bergen County Historical Society in 1956. It is owned by the Blauvelt–Demarest Foundation.

Bergen Community Museum (Ridgewood and Fairview aves., Paramus). Displays of local history are presented in this imposing brick building, formerly the County Home for the Aged. Open Wed.–Sat., 1–5 p.m.; Sun., 2–6 p.m. Phone: (201) 265-1248.

Paramus Park (Midland Ave., off Rte. 17). On the flat fields of Paramus enormous shopping centers have replaced celery as the big-ticket item. The latest and most spectacular is Paramus Park, a mall lined with nearly a hundred small shops linking two giant stores. Potted trees landscape pedestrian streets, whose intersections are marked by cleverly terraced plazas. In the central areas, the glass-covered, steel-framed, ridge-and-furrow roof rises to a two-story height. Escalators flank a giant cascade and lead to an upper level where vendors sell a staggering variety of foods, to be consumed at "picnic" areas on terraces overlooking the waterfall. Is anything missing from this modern-day "downtown"? Only the church, school, and town hall.

Paramus Public Library–Midland Avenue Branch. This gable-fronted frame structure with simple carpenter trim has served Midland Township since 1876—as a schoolhouse, borough hall, and now as a branch library.

Paramus Park

Radburn (streets on both sides of Howard Ave., between Plaza Rd. N. and Radburn Rd., off Fairlawn Ave., Fairlawn Borough). "How to live with the auto," or "How to live in spite of it," was the rationale of the "Radburn idea," according to architect–planner Clarence Stein. In 1928, working with Henry Wright, Stein developed the plan for this model suburban community, which relegated the automobile to an inconspicuous role through the provision of a variety of pedestrian pathways. Only a fragment of the scheme was built, but the essential quality of "the first major innovation in town-planning since [towns] were built" can still be grasped.

Automobiles can enter each of two "superblocks" (residential parks with streets bearing "A"-lettered names on one side and "B"-lettered ones on the other) only by short service roads leading to a series of cul-de-sacs. Closely spaced brick-and-frame dwellings, some connected by their garages, line the cul-de-sacs. Pedestrians can follow paths to the large open commons at the core of each superblock, the unifying principle of the Wright–Stein plan. A pedestrian underpass near the elementary school connects the "A" Park and the "B" Park.

The Radburn idea has been extremely influential in the development of planning philosophy here and abroad. A walk through Radburn inspires a wish that there had been more actual imitators.

Old Paramus Reformed Church (E. Glen Ave. and Franklin Tnpk. [Rte. 17], Ridgewood). This church, a fine example of the Americanization of the Dutch church, is built of native sandstone, with brick openings and window trim. In the 1872 renovation some Victorian features enhanced the spartan simplicity of the original structure. Richly detailed woodwork adorns the doors, eaves, and porch; and an exceptionally beautiful iron lancet fence with cast-iron posts encloses the adjacent old graveyard.

Paramus Historical Museum (650 E. Glen Ave., west of Reformed Church, Ridgewood). Post–Civil War prosperity, which made possible the renovation of the Old Paramus Reformed Church, also was responsible for the construction of this frame structure which originally served as a schoolhouse. The "stick" portico is a charming period note. The building now serves another educational purpose—displaying artifacts of earlier periods. Open Wed., 2:30–4:30 p.m., and Sun., 3–5 p.m., April–Oct. Phone: (201) 445–1778; 447–3242.

Paramus Historical Museum   211

David A. Ackerman House (Ackerman–Naugle House) (415 E. Saddle River Rd., Ridgewood). Like many other Dutch houses, this roadside dwelling is the result of several building periods. The one-story rear wing gives the structure its unusual salt-box appearance, while the graceful flare of the overhanging eaves on the façade is a more common embellishment of Dutch Colonial architecture. The origin of this feature has been the object of much speculation. Was it intended to protect the soft clay mortar between the stones? Was it a re-creation of a feature found in seventeenth-century Flemish cottages? Or was it simply intended to protect the residents from the sun? The last explanation is most likely the more important one, since the overhang was commonly on the long southern façade, and in many examples extends even farther to form a covered porch.

The rich variety of forms found within the Dutch style is revealed by a comparison of this house with the larger Ackerman–Van Emburgh House, around the corner at 789 E. Glen Ave.

The Hermitage

335 N. Franklin Tnpk. (Rte. 507), south of Prospect St., Hohokus

As The Hermitage, this eighteenth-century house served as a stopping place for Washington during the war and as the residence of Theodosia Prevost, later the wife of Aaron Burr. Renamed Waldwic Cottage, it survives as a fine Gothic Revival remodeling, one of the few remaining works of architect William Ranlett.

Ranlett opened his first architect's office in New York City in 1840, at a time when the trend toward professional architectural education was transforming building practice and popular taste. One of his major contributions was publication of the monthly trade journal *The Architect*, a "scientific and practical guide for the erection of country and suburban dwellings of all grades."

Commissioned by Dr. Elijah Rosencrantz, Ranlett in 1845 transformed The Hermitage, an ordinary albeit "substantial

first-class country house," into an elaborately executed Gothic villa. Its picturesque façade gave no hint of the sophisticated technology inside, which included such features as central heating serviced by a Walker furnace and a system of running water which daily drew as much as 500 gallons from the Hohokus River to an attic tank. Owned by the State of New Jersey.

Saddle River. In the early days, industrious farmers carved prosperous farms out of the lands surrounding the Saddle River, named, so it is said, by the original land speculators after a stream in Scotland. The rural ambience, combined with a studied air of suburban chic, survives today, embodied in buildings from the eighteenth century to the present day.

The open space in front of the modern neo-Georgian Municipal Hall recalls the flavor of a historic Green. Facing the Green are the Zion Evangelical Lutheran Church (Allandale Ave.), a simple church with long pointed-arch windows, built in 1820; an early clapboard barn; and a Victorian schoolhouse, still in use.

Creative Gardens (409 E. Saddle River Rd. [Rte. 75], Upper Saddle River). An elegant Italianate house with a wide front porch and porte cochere has been effectively converted into a garden center. The barn serves as the sales area.

Saddle River Reformed Church and Cemetery (E. Saddle River and Old Stone Church rds., Upper Saddle River). "The Old Stone Church" was built of coursed and random-laid stone in 1819 and was renovated in 1972. The old cemetery behind has gravestones predating the Revolution.

Wortendyke Barn (13 Pascack Rd., Park Ridge). Many travelers have noted the distinctive appearance and construction methods of the New World Dutch barn. This one, a rare survival, is typical. Four massive wooden H-frames, interlocked by mortise and tenon, support a steeply pitched roof which comes down to low side walls. The vast interior space, cathedrallike, is thus divided into aisles and bays. The eighteenth-century Swedish naturalist Peter Kalm, much impressed by these lofty structures, noted that the openings at each of the gable ends were so great that "one could come in with a cart and horses through one of them and go out the other." The original homestead, a brownstone dwelling, is across the street at 12 Pascack Rd.

Terrace Realty (13 Grand Ave., Montvale). Orson Fowler, the phrenologist who popularized octagon houses in the 1850's, designed this octagonal structure for his friend John Blauvelt. It was home to three of Montvale's mayors, served as a flag stop for the railroad, survived a serious fire in 1955, was remodeled as a restaurant, and, finally, has been converted to a real-estate office.

Old Stone House (536 Island Rd., Ramsey; south of Rte. 17, Spring Street Exit). Tracing the history of old houses is often a matter of interpreting scarce clues. Rosalie Fellows Bailey, whose painstaking compilation of pre-Revolutionary Dutch houses existing in the 1930's was originally published in a limited edition of 334 copies for members of The Holland Society (Publication Chairman: Franklin D. Roosevelt), believed that this house was originally a tavern. The evidence? A 1778 map of the area shows a house in the

Railroad Station Museum

general vicinity named Brickman's, the apostrophe suggesting its use as a tavern; and a family named Brueckman worshiped in the Lutheran Church.

Even if it is not Brickman's, and later evidence suggests the Westervelts as the original owners, the house is undoubtedly of an early date—about 1740—since it is built of undressed and very irregular stone. The ceilings are low with very large exposed beams. Maintained by the Ramsey Historical Association. Open Sun., 2–4:30 p.m., May–Oct., and by appointment. Phone: (201) 825–1126.

Ramapo College of New Jersey (Ramapo Valley Rd. [Rte. 202], 1 mile south of intersection with Rte. 17, Mahwah). Past and present have joined together on Ramapo Valley Rd., and the union appears, at least for now, to be harmonious. A gambrel-roofed fieldstone-and-frame structure at No. 398 has had associations with several old New Jersey families—Van Alens, Hoppers, Van Horns—and now serves as the residence of the president of Ramapo College.

The fences, fields, and barns of the nineteenth-century gentleman farmer still characterize the landscape. Since 1877 much of the area had been the estate of the wealthy sugar-refining Havemeyer family. An elegant French Renaissance

Ramapo College

villa and elaborate landscaping remain from that period and have been sensitively woven into the plan of Ramapo College. Designed by the firm of Mahoney–Zvosec/DeMay, discreet two-story steel–and–reflecting-glass classroom buildings encircle the gardens of the former estate. The carved brownstone arch, which was brought to the Ramapo Valley when the Havemeyers' New York townhouse was razed in the 1900's, strikes a nostalgic note.

Railroad Station Museum (Old Station Rd., Mahwah). The first station in Mahwah was built in 1871 and served until 1902, when it was moved from its original site to make way for new tracks. For the next fifty years it served as a storehouse. To save it from destruction, the Mahwah Historical Society purchased it and moved it to its present site. In 1968 it reopened as a small railroad museum. Behind the station, with its wide, bracketed eaves, is a cheerful red caboose. The museum is open Sun., 2–4 p.m.

Motel on the Mountain (Suffern). Perched high above heavily traveled Rte. 17 and the New York State Thruway, this motel complex consists of angular, low redwood units ingeniously sited on terraces in the steeply sloping, rocky hillside. California architect Harwell Hamilton Harris, a noted modernist, used traditional Japanese devices—exposed timbers and wide overhanging eaves. The major part of the complex was completed in 1956.

Ringwood Manor

Ringwood Manor State Park, Sloatsburg Rd., Ringwood; off Rte. 17, near New York State border
*OPEN: Tues.–Fri., 10 a.m.–4 p.m.;
      Sat.–Sun., 10 a.m.–5 p.m.;
      May–Oct.
PHONE: (201) 962–7031

When Peter Hasenclever, a German with British financial backing, answered an advertisement in 1764 for the sale of various mining properties in New Jersey, including "a well-built furnace, good iron mines near the same, two forges . . . a saw mill . . . several dwelling houses and several tracts of land," Ringwood Mines were already some twenty years old. Hasenclever bought the mines from David Ogden and began the operation of the American Company, the largest industrial enterprise in the Colonies.

When the Revolution broke out, Robert Erskine, then manager of the ironworks, sided with the Americans, despite the loss of credit from his British employers. He borrowed money on his own and put the mines on a solid financial footing. Ringwood provided ammunition and cannon for the Continental Army and some of the iron for the Great Chain (see p. 229) installed in the Hudson between West Point and Constitution Island. Ringwood was of strategic importance and its defense was one of Washington's prime goals after the fall of New York.

Martin Ryerson, another prominent ironmaster, dominated Ringwood in the early 1800's; during his tenure the original part of Ringwood Manor was constructed. In 1853 the forges were taken over by Peter Cooper, who had already established successful ironworks in New York City and Trenton and Philipsburg, New Jersey.

For Cooper, Ringwood was a country home, comfortable if old-fashioned. His successor at Ringwood, who was also his

Ringwood Manor

partner and son-in-law, Abram Hewitt, raised the dwelling to mid-Victorian standards. One-time mayor of New York, Hewitt used Ringwood Manor as a summer home, and the additions and renovations of his family greatly changed its appearance. The fine Gothic hall at the entrance, part of this renovation, typifies the grand concepts of the post–Civil War period.

The rambling house is a melange of architectural styles, with late Victorian dominating. The interior is furnished in styles of both the early nineteenth century—the Ryerson period—and the Hewitt period.

The Hewitt family inherited the Ringwood interests and operated the mines until 1931. The estate was bequeathed to the State of New Jersey in 1936. On the spacious landscaped grounds are also other buildings of the Hewitt period—a large barn, icehouse, and other reminders of Ringwood's intriguing past.

Skylands Manor

Ringwood Manor State Park (1½ miles
east of Ringwood Manor)
*OPEN: Tues.–Sat., 10 a.m.–4 p.m.;
Sun., noon–5 p.m.;
May–Oct.
PHONE: (201) 962–7031

Skylands, Ringwood Manor's near neighbor, was built in 1924 as a lavish showplace for millionaire Clarence M. Lewis. A stone-and-timbered forty-four-room mansion in the Jacobean style, it was designed by architect John Russell Pope, who cannily built in the appearance of great age through the use of weathered stone and sagging tiles on the roof. Although Pope

was an eclectic architect, borrowing from the Romans for his design for the Jefferson Memorial in Washington, D.C., and from English country houses for the dwellings of private clients, his designs were sure and sensitive.

Inside, the rooms are not furnished. However, the lavish use of wood paneling and rare stained glass in the windows are evidence of the original decor. Formal gardens surround the hilltop house. Owned by the State of New Jersey.

Tuxedo Park

Rte. 17

"Some people have called Tuxedo a social half-way house to Newport," commented Emily Post in 1911. But, she continued, "This is a great mistake. The social climber would, I think, make much better headway in Newport than in Tuxedo. Old Tuxedoites are very conservative . . . not living from excitement to excitement. . . . Newport loves to be entertained; Tuxedo does not care a bit."

Mrs. Post wrote with authority; though she had not yet written the first edition of *Etiquette*, she was a keen observer of the niceties of society. Furthermore, she lived in Tuxedo Park and was in fact the daughter of its architect, Bruce Price.

Tuxedo Park was established in 1885 by Pierre Lorillard, a descendant of a millionaire in the snuff and tobacco industry who bought the Tuxedo property in 1814. Lorillard decided to found a hunting and fishing club and game preserve on the undeveloped property, known only as the Erie Railroad's "Wood Pile," because its lumber fueled the wood-burning engines. A man accustomed to having his desires

Tuxedo Park in 1911

police headquarters), and highly original workers' dwellings with distinctive two-story attics along Rte. 17. Other notable structures around the enclave are three churches, including St. Mary's, designed in 1885 by William Appleton Potter.

Construction within Tuxedo Park has continued to the present day. However, changing tastes and high maintenance costs have gradually diluted its distinctive quality.

Although Tuxedo Park remains private, the Tuxedo police may, on special request from architecture buffs, permit entry onto the grounds.

Gate Lodge, Tuxedo Park

carried out immediately, Lorillard imported 1,800 workmen from Italy, built housing for them, and directed his architect and chief engineer to fulfill his plans. Mrs. Post recalled, "Mr. Lorillard ordered houses in the same way other people might order boots."

Life at Tuxedo Park in its heyday was exceedingly formal; the only concession to country living was the gentlemen's use of English dinner jackets instead of tails, introduced by Pierre's son Griswold. Even so, many Tuxedo residents thought this a decided breach of manners, and were horrified that the word "tuxedo" came to describe the new style.

Price's work at Tuxedo shows the strong influence of H. H. Richardson, whose expressive use of stone and shingle in suburban locations set the pace during the 1870's and 1880's. The gate lodge and gatekeeper's cottage at the entrance are examples of the style at its finest; though the buildings are sophisticated in conception, chunky rocks are laid with primitive vigor.

Other designs by Price include the post office, the former railroad station (now

Sterling Forest Conference Center (Tuxedo, near Sterling Lake). Once the site of rich iron mines and an early manufacturing center, Sterling Forest has become the site of a modern corporate, recreational, and housing development since City Investing Company purchased the 22,000-acre tract in 1959.

Among the twenty or so buildings on the grounds of the Conference Center, the most striking is the IBM building, a compact, steel-framed structure sheathed in reflecting blue-tinted glass and metal, with double tiers of circular ventilating open-

217

IBM Building, Sterling Forest Conference Center

ings defined in intense orange aluminum. Architect Gunnar Birkerts conceived this building, completed in 1971, as an "abstract container for computer technology." It was meant to appear as a "foreign object in the landscape—like the slab in the film *Space Odyssey*. To this end it has no base—the metal comes right to the stone and is scribed to the rock."

Arden House (Meadow Rd., east of New York State Thruway Exit 16, Harriman). In 1885 Edward Harriman, whose genius at rebuilding bankrupt railroads was a combination of his superb talent for railroad administration and his iron will, wanted to find a peaceful retreat from the machinations of industry. He purchased 20,000 acres of land near Tuxedo and called it "Arden." Part of his plan was to preserve the wild forest area from the invasions of the lumbering industry.

Here in 1905 he began to build Arden House, a formal cut-stone villa, completed in 1909, a few months before he died. Peabody, Wilson & Brown were the architects. The house and adjoining property were donated to Columbia University in 1950 by Harriman's sons, one of whom is former Governor Averell Harriman. Arden House is now used as a conference

center for educational and charitable groups.

From the thruway exit, stone silos, large stables, and substantial farm buildings belonging to the former Harriman estate are visible.

Gasho Steak House (Rte. 32, off Rte. 17, Central Valley). A fifteenth-century Samurai farmhouse called Gasho was brought over to the hills of Orange County and rebuilt in the traditional Japanese manner, in which interlocking members are fitted together without nails. A Japanese waterwheel, rock garden, and teahouse complete the restaurant's attractions.

Museum Village

Smith's Clove, Monroe (Rte. 17, Exit 129; Thruway Exit 16)
*OPEN: Daily, 10 a.m.–5 p.m., May 15–Nov. 15
PHONE: (914) 782–8247

A collection of forty-one buildings, mainly from the mid-nineteenth century, has been reassembled to show "Smith's Clove," a simulated village bearing the early name given to the area. Although the setting is clearly artificial, the endeavor has accomplished the preservation of many simple buildings—farmhouses, stores, workshops—which are frequently overlooked. The displays and demonstrations emphasize the development of American crafts and industry.

Monroe. More popularly known for the summer resort and bungalow colonies that have grown up on the outskirts, the

center of Monroe (Stage Rd. and Rte. 17M) retains the appearance of a mid-nineteenth-century village street. The First Presbyterian Church has an inspired portico with fantastic carpenter detailing. Many of the late-nineteenth-century dwellings have been adapted for business or professional use. The piano and organ store is especially notable.

Nearby towns have a similar flavor. Among the handsome buildings on well-scaled Main St. in Chester is the distin-

House in Washingtonville

guished Greek Revival First Presbyterian Church. In Washingtonville, fine mid-nineteenth-century dwellings are abundant. The Moffat Library (Main St.), built in 1887, has a Richardsonian flavor with its red-brick and -shingle exterior and its extraordinary flaring tower.

Historic Track

Main St., Goshen

Prosperous farmers in Goshen (whose rich lands indeed proved as fertile as its biblical namesake) liked to challenge each other to horse races or "brushes" near the site of Messenger's big oak tree, now in the center of Historic Track. The informal sport was modified, codified, and institutionalized by the middle of the nineteenth century and gave rise to the modern sport of harness racing.

Good Time Track, near Rte. 207, is older than Historic Track, but none of the original buildings are left. It was the home of the Hambletonian Stakes from 1930 to 1956 and is now used as a training track for Yonkers Raceway.

The sense of the sport in its early days can still be felt at Historic Track. The small grandstands face the two judges' stands and the tote board. The betting windows are behind the grandstands. In July the track is still used for daytime Grand Circuit Racing, and horses work out at various times during the summer months.

Hall of Fame of the Trotter

240 Main St., Goshen
OPEN: Daily, 10 a.m.–5 p.m.; Sun. and holidays, 1:30–5 p.m.
PHONE: (914) 294–6330

The elegant Tudor Revival stables of Stony Ford Farm, a stud farm that developed some of the great harness racing horses,

has been converted into a museum devoted to the sport. Lively exhibits portray the horses, their riders, and equipment; a special gallery contains a fine collection of nineteenth-century art depicting harness racing.

Orange County Courthouse (Main and Court sts., Goshen). Goshen's sophistication is a result not only of the prominence of its horse breeders and racing patrons; the town has been, since the 1700's, the county seat of Orange County, which until 1798 included present Rockland County as well. Travelers on legal business came to Goshen, stayed at the Orange Inn (Main St.) and took care of their affairs in the civic buildings on Main St.

In 1840 Goshen and Newburgh were "half-shire" towns, alternating as county seats. Both towns needed new courthouses, and after the idea of setting up a separate county was defeated, the legislature voted money to build in both places. The same architect, Thornton M. Niven, designed the two structures. The Goshen Courthouse, built in 1842, has six imposing Doric columns across the matchboarded façade. Criminal and civil county court sessions were held here until 1970.

The Old County Building across the street, built in 1851 and remodeled in 1887, housed all county offices until 1970. Its assertive forms are now muted by inappropriate pastel paint.

Main Street, Goshen. A sophisticated row of townhouses, built in the 1830's and succeeding decades, and converted in modern times to professional office use, adds urbane polish to Goshen. Number 210, now the offices of a law firm, has floridly shaped brackets at the eaves and brownstone lintels. In 1873, U. S. Grant, a

racing devotee, stayed here as a guest and watched horses racing at Historic Track from a barn in the rear. Number 212, the Clothes Horse Building, has a gambrel roof at one end and a gable at the other.

Orange County Community of Museums and Galleries (101 Main St., Goshen). This information center in the old County Courthouse Building coordinates news about fourteen participating museums in Orange County. Open Mon.–Fri., except holidays, 9 a.m.–5 p.m. Phone: (914) 294–5657.

Orange County Courthouse and government buildings (Main St., at Erie St., Goshen). A striking complex of poured-concrete buildings around a central terraced plaza now serves Orange County's official business. Architect Paul Rudolph used projecting and receding bays to fragment the massive bulk, and the rich texture of the deeply striated concrete is relieved by the smooth concrete of the door and window surrounds. The complex, completed in 1970, is carefully scaled to its three-acre site and respects the scale established by the distinguished nineteenth-century houses on the surrounding streets.

St. James Episcopal Church (Church St., Goshen). This gabled church with a square tower has a Norman flavor; it shares Church St. with many elegant nineteenth-century homes.

First Presbyterian Church (Harriman Sq., Goshen). The Village Green is dominated by this Gothic-style church, built of a distinctive blue-hued local fieldstone. The Town Clock in the tall spire was provided by public subscription in 1953.

Orange County Courthouse

George Washington Bridge to Newburgh

Prentice-Hall (Rte. 9W, Englewood Cliffs). The spare silhouette of the long, low, aluminum-sheathed publishing headquarters was designed in 1957 by Kahn & Jacobs. This is a fine early example of a form that is now devouring open spaces in the suburbs of every city.

One Byrne Road (off Inness Rd., Tenafly). The impressive stone gateposts at Inness Rd. leading off Engle St. are the only clue that beyond the suburban housing development lies a richly detailed, slate-roofed Tudor house. Herbert Coppell imported architectural elements from England to build his residence in the 1920's, but when he lost his money in the Crash, the house was turned into an elegant apartment building and the land sold off to developers.

Roelof Westervelt House (81 Westervelt Ave., east of Tenafly Rd., Tenafly). Roelof Westervelt's family lived, ate, and slept in the single first-floor room of the original wing of this Dutch house, built in 1745. The upstairs garret, reached by a ladder, was used for slave quarters. In 1737 about 10 per cent of the population of Bergen County was slave; much of the construction of stone houses was possible only because of the extensive use of slave labor.

Westervelt's thrifty grandson Daniel retained the one-room section and added a much finer wing in the early 1800's.

Country Station (1 Piermont Rd., Tenafly). Passenger trains no longer travel the Erie–Lackawanna line, but the picturesque railroad stations that used to serve commuters and summer residents are still standing. They have been put to a variety of uses; this one is a dress shop. Attributed to architect J. Cleveland Cady, the stone station is a fine example of Venetian Gothic design.

Country Station, Tenafly

221

Grindelwald (corner of Park St. and Highwood Ave., Tenafly). This enormous, imaginatively massed clapboard structure, with impressive posts guarding its entrance, appears the very model of Victorian gentility. But for the years 1869–97 it was the home of a rebel against those standards—Elizabeth Cady Stanton, the advocate of women's rights. During this period she wrote, lectured around the country, and campaigned vigorously (she tried unsuccessfully to vote in Tenafly). But she was also a devoted mother of seven, and in her reminiscences she recalled, "I laugh, as I write, at the memory of all the frolics we had on the blue hills of Jersey."

Cornwallis Headquarters (north end of Alpine Boat Basin, Palisades Interstate Park, Alpine). Originally this two-story fieldstone-and-clapboard building, built about 1750 at the river edge, was used as a tavern for the ferrymen who plied the Hudson. Traditionally it is designated as the headquarters of British Maj. Gen. Cornwallis in November 1776 when his troops were being ferried from New York to attack Fort Lee on the Jersey Palisades. Tradition in this case is an inaccurate historical source, but it saved this building, which is maintained by the New Jersey Federation of Women's Clubs. It is generally open on Sundays during the summer.

The tavern was the first headquarters of Palisades Interstate Park, founded in 1900 as a result of conservationists' concern that rock quarrying along the Palisades would completely destroy its natural beauty.

Huyler Homestead and Outbuildings (50 County Rd., just past Crest Dr. N.,

Cresskill). The passions aroused by the conflict between Loyalists and patriots during the Revolution were particularly strong in northern New Jersey. One of the milder forms of retribution was confiscation of property. Although many Loyalists remained in the area and often rebought their lands and houses, John Eckerson, the Tory owner of this house, did not. It became the property of Capt. John Huyler. A major addition to the homestead was built about 1836, with some earlier portions surviving. The stone fence formed by wickets and lancet shapes is particularly attractive.

Benjamin B. Westervelt House (235 County Rd., corner of Westervelt Place, Cresskill). This house was probably built in the late eighteenth century, although a house marked "Westerfells" (probably a wing) was marked on ironmaster and surveyor Robert Erskine's Revolutionary map. A fine example of the Dutch style, this house was used as background when Fort Lee was a center of the infant movie industry in the early 1900's.

Haring House (95 De Wolfe [Pearl River] Rd., Old Tappan, N.J.). The substantial home of Cosyn Haring, one of the original patentees in the area, still stands. The first-story level had only two rooms, while the attic was used as a sleeping garret.

Gerrit Haring House (244 Old Tappan Rd., across from Borough Hall, Old Tappan, N.J.). This building, with several wings, nestles beneath the hillside. It was built in the mid-1800's by Gerrit Haring, grandson of Cosyn Haring.

Dutch Reformed Church, Tappan

Dutch Reformed Church (Rte. 110, Tappan, N.Y.). Until 1798, Tappan was the county seat for "Orange County South of the Mountains," now Rockland County. As early as 1740 it was a well-developed village, with a courthouse and jail, duplicating similar facilities for "Orange County North of the Mountains" at Goshen. However, its most famous trial took place under military auspices, in the original church on this site. This was the espionage trial of Maj. John André in 1780 before the Board of Enquiry appointed by Gen. Washington.

The present brick structure was built in 1835; its proportions are particularly pleasing, and details are treated with sen-

sitive restraint. The Manse was the original parsonage for the church, a Dutch house built in the 1720's for the pastor, who, in addition to the rent-free house, received an annual salary of £70, free firewood, and burial in the churchyard. When the present church was built, some bricks were left over; they were used to construct a dignified townhouse standing on the corner of Main St. and Old Tappan Rd.

The Old '76 House (Main and Washington sts., Tappan, N.Y.). In 1776 this low sandstone building, now a restaurant, was Mabie's Tavern, a stagecoach stop on the Albany–New York run. It served as Maj. André's prison during his trial, and from here he was led to his execution.

Giulio's Restaurant (154 Washington St., Tappan, N.Y.). "Recycling" this shingled mansion into a restaurant has preserved its late-nineteenth-century flavor. White outbuildings at its rear now serve an antiques shop.

De Wint House (Washington's Headquarters)

Livingston Ave. and Oak Tree Rd., Tappan, N.Y.
OPEN: Daily, 10 a.m.–4 p.m.
Closed Christmas
PHONE: (914) 359–1359

Several times during the Revolution, Washington occupied this house, built by Daniel De Clark and owned in the Revolutionary period by John De Wint, a wealthy retired sugar-grower from St.

Gerrit Haring House

WASHINGTON'S HEAD-QUARTERS AT TAPPAN.[4]

Thomas. Washington stayed here during the trial and execution of Maj. André.

In 1850 Benson Lossing, the historian who revisited the sites of the Revolution and described them in his *Field Book of the Revolution*, sketched the house. "The view," he said, "is from the yard, near the well. The date of its erection (1700) is made by a peculiar arrangement of the bricks on the front wall." The house was built of brick and local sandstone. The steep gabled roof with flared overhanging eaves and irregular window placement are evidence of its early date.

The De Wint House is maintained by the Masons of New York State. George Washington, like many American generals of the time, was a prominent Mason.

Sneden's Landing (off Rte. 9W, Palisades). When Mollie Sneden and her husband, Robert, ran a ferry across the Hudson in the late eighteenth century, in partnership with Jeremiah Dobbs, their landing was first known as Dobbs Ferry on the West Bank. During the Revolution, Mollie and all but one of her sons were staunch Loyalists and were forbidden to operate the ferry. Nevertheless, they are believed to have transported many British

soldiers across the river and even to have protected one from pursuing patriots by hiding him in a large chest covered by pans of cream.

Apparently the patriots bore no ill will toward Mollie after the war, for she lived on in the town until the age of 101, and the spot has continued to be known as Sneden's Landing.

Today it is a picturesque enclave combining sophisticated elegance with rural charm, qualities carefully nurtured by its residents, who have included many notable theatrical, literary, and musical personalities. The seventy or so houses tucked in and around the roads that wind around to the river range from riverside Cheer Hall (Washington Spring Rd.), one of the original Sneden houses, to great mansions of the post–Civil War period, such as Cliffside, the house with five chimneys at the Landing built in 1877 for the parents of sculptor Mary Lawrence Tonetti and designed by architect J. Cleveland Cady.

Crescent Ribbon Factory (corner of Rockland Rd. and Ferdon Ave., Piermont). Located on the Sparkill Creek, this two-story factory was originally a silk mill. Its façade is decorated with inventive brick patterning, which was often a special feature of late-Victorian industrial architecture. Across the street are an impressively scaled Greek Revival mansion and a delightful Victorian cottage.

Paradise Avenue, Piermont. The genteel homes along Paradise Ave., ending in a cul-de-sac called Paradise Alley, are reminders of the time when Piermont, originally called Tappan Landing, was an active port, the western terminus of the Erie Railroad. At Piermont passengers from the west boarded a steamboat for New York City. The railroad changed its routes in the 1870's and Piermont was left a backwater.

Piermont Avenue, Piermont. The nineteenth century predominates in this street's rich mix of styles. The downtown section has several fine commercial structures. The northern end of Piermont Ave. continues as a charming residential street, never forgetting its relationship to the river.

Piermont Avenue, Piermont

Onderdonk House (756–758 Piermont Ave., corner of Ritie St., Piermont). In 1736 Abraham and Garret Onderdonk opened a red-sandstone quarry on the Hudson River near the mouth of the Sparkill River. Here they established a thriving business and built a house a year later on the banks of the Hudson from the rock they had dug from its bluffs. The sturdy house later passed to a branch of the family named Haring. The later, larger wing has splayed lintels and a deeply recessed door.

Piermont Public Library (153 Hudson Terrace, near First St.). This two-story

Greek Revival building was originally the home of an Erie Railroad executive. The tracks have been taken up but the nearby railroad station is now used as a dwelling. The house became a library in 1896. Neighboring rowhouses are a civilized embellishment to the lane.

Broadway, South Nyack to Upper Nyack. Along this road the feeling of the Hudson and of the nineteenth century is strong—in the stately homes with wide porches set back on ample sloping lawns, built to take advantage of the river view, and in the commercial structures of the period, many adapted vivaciously to modern use. Occasionally an enclave of small, early-nineteenth-century dwellings creates a gentle contrast that sets off both periods to good advantage. From Broadway many streets worth exploring wind down to the river. Nyack has become a marketplace for antiques and handicrafts.

Edward Hopper Birthplace (82 N. Broadway, near Second Ave., Nyack). "What I wanted to do," said Edward Hopper, "was to paint sunlight on the side of a house." Hopper was influenced to some extent by the Rockland County homes he saw throughout his boyhood;

North Broadway, Nyack   225

"The House by the Railroad," painted in 1925 and showing a mansarded Victorian structure standing deserted by the railroad tracks, is believed to be a local house. Hopper's birthplace in Nyack, a two-story frame dwelling built in 1858, is now being restored by the Edward Hopper Landmark Preservation Foundation.

Village Hall (330 N. Broadway, Upper (Nyack). The municipal offices and firehouse for Upper Nyack are located in this red-brick building decorated with inlaid bricks. The bell tower is frame. The building was designed in 1887 by R. G. Knapp, an architect from New York.

Old Stone Church (Broadway, near Birchwood Ave., Upper Nyack). Built in 1813 and marked as the oldest existing church in Rockland County, this simple, rubble brownstone, gable-fronted structure has splayed brownstone lintels over the single door and the three side windows.

Clarksville Corner

Strawtown Rd., West Nyack
PHONE: (914) 358–8899

The Clarksville Inn, in the 1850's and 1860's a busy stopping point on the Nyack Tnpk. and a center for the social life of Rockland County as well, is the focal point of a group of buildings restored by Stephen Leeman, an active preservationist. At the inn, now a restaurant, gala balls were held, including one in 1860 to honor the local boys leaving to serve in the Civil War.

Earlier, President Van Buren visited here, accompanied by Washington Irving; they were overcharged for a carriage repair by a local blacksmith, to the chagrin of local residents. The blacksmith shop itself is located at 11 Strawtown Rd. The other buildings in the area used to be local tradesmen's shops; they now house an art gallery, a craft shop, and a clockmaker's shop.

Clarkstown Reformed Church (107 Strawtown Rd., West Nyack). This church was formed by a congregation that broke away from the Reformed Church at Tappan in 1769; however, until 1830 the same minister conducted services, in the Dutch language, at both places. The present structure was built in 1871 and modeled after the Swiss Reformed churches. It has fish-scale shingles on the roof and an elaborate open belfry in the square tower.

John Hill House (628 W. Nyack Rd., West Nyack). In 1843 John Hill, the English-born engraver, built this white frame house as a summer home. In his sixties at the time, and a successful artist in New York, he soon retired here but continued to work. Hill raised the medium of aquatint to an exceptional level in the series, completed in the 1820's, called *Hudson River Portfolio*. The aquatints, after William Guy Wall's paintings and watercolors, not only were a superb artistic achievement on their own but also spurred the development of the Hudson River School of painting.

Hill's son, John William, and his grandson, John Henry, were both prominent artists whose works depict many Rockland County sites. John William's house, built in 1847, is at 597 W. Nyack Rd.

West Nyack Historic Zone. In the area, which includes Strawtown, Sicketown,

House in West Nyack Historic Zone

and Germonds rds., are many structures that lend a strong eighteenth- and nineteenth-century flavor to the region.

Germonds Barn (Germonds Rd., off old Rte. 304). The only remaining barn in New York State with stone walls, the gambrel-roofed barn was part of Maj. John Smith's homestead, built about 1735. The barn is almost hidden from sight, but the homestead itself, which hugs the road, is clearly visible.

Rockland County Courthouse (Main St., at Congers Rd., New City). Considered a gross extravagance in 1928, this massive Art Moderne building was designed by Dennison & Hirons. Abstract motifs embellish the façade.

Germonds Barn

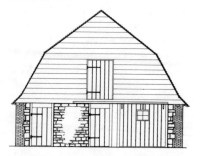

Jacob Blauvelt Homestead

20 Zukor Rd., end of N. Main St., New City
OPEN: Sun., 2–5 p.m.
PHONE: (914) NE4–9629

The Blauvelt family purchased land in the Kakiak Patent here in the 1760's, and as they prospered, they tore down the original sandstone dwelling and used the stone for the foundation of a new, more substantial house built of brick in 1834. The three-section house, with a high gambrel roof and flaring eaves, remained in the family until 1970. Four acres of land and a barn built in 1790, as well as some outbuildings of a later date, surround the house. Many of the furnishings in the restored rooms belonged to the Blauvelts. Maintained by the Historical Society of Rockland County, whose museum building is being constructed next door.

Haverstraw (off Rte. 9W). James Wood, an Englishman, started making bricks in Haverstraw in 1815; the vast deposits of clay, the rich supply of wood, and the cheap transportation afforded by the Hudson River made the industry thrive. Although no brickyards remain, the architectural configuration of the mid-nineteenth century, the height of Haverstraw's prosperity, still distinguishes Main St. and the tight grid of streets east and west of it. The richly decorated mansions on Allison Ave. (north of Main St.) are fine examples from its wealthy days; and structures on First St. illustrate a continuity with the preindustrial past.

Garnerville (Railroad Ave., west of Rte. 9W, and nearby streets). In the mid-nineteenth century Garnerville was a company town, dominated by the Garner family and their thriving Rockland Print Works, a textile printing and dyeing company. The gabled red-brick factories (Railroad Ave., near Bridge St.) with Gothic arched windows and tall, stout smokestacks were guarded by the ornate brick factory office. A neat grid of semi-detached workers' dwellings, frame structures with brick foundations and eyebrow windows beneath the eaves, surround the factories. Proud, free-standing dwellings belonging to managers and supervisors were at some distance from the center of town, and most remote of all was the Garner family mansion (Brush Court, off Andrews Ave., off Railroad Ave.), an enormous columned red-brick mansion with an Italianate cupola and Gothic windows.

All of these are to be found today, bearing the marks of age but with the pattern of a Victorian industrial community intact. The Garnerville Holding Company, formed to lease the industrial space to a variety of manufacturers when the print works moved south in the 1930's, occupies the factories. And, symbolic of the change in Rockland County in the postwar years, the Garner mansion, now vacant, stands in the middle of a development of brick-veneered and asphalt-sheathed "split levels."

Stony Point Battlefield Reservation and Lighthouse

Off Rte. 9W
OPEN: Daily, 8 a.m.–sunset; museum
open 9 a.m.–5 p.m.; May–Oct.
PHONE: (914) ST6-2701

In a daring move, "Mad Anthony" Wayne led an attack on British-held Stony Point in July 1779. The assault succeeded, and after everything of value was removed, the fort was demolished. Although the British soon took possession again, the patriots' purpose had been accomplished.

The battle is commemorated in this park area, with a small museum containing artifacts and displays of the Revolution and a series of paintings about Maj. André.

On the point is Stony Point Lighthouse, a 30-foot fieldstone structure built in 1826. Only once in its 100 years of service did the light fail to warn upriver craft of the narrow margin of safety between Stony Point and Verplank's Point on the opposite shore. Maintained by the Palisades Interstate Park Commission.

Boulderberg Manor (east of Rte. 9W, Tomkins Cove). "Boulderberg"—now a restaurant—was mid-nineteenth-century industrialist Calvin Tomkins' dream for a mansion overlooking the Hudson. It was also a concrete symbol of his material success, for Tomkins was a major force in exploiting the materials used in "natural cement" and in their manufacture and transportation. By 1838 Tomkins had acquired lime quarries in Rockland County and extended his business along the east

Boulderberg Manor

coast as far north as New Brunswick, Canada.

Considering the source of his income, it is not surprising that he built his villa of poured concrete, although in 1858 stone or brick masonry was the favored building material in this country. "Natural cement" concrete had been used for bridges, sewers, aqueducts, and other utilitarian structures but generally not for dwellings. Tomkins' innovation did not set a trend; poured concrete as a building material slowly came into use later.

Nevertheless, his vision remains in nearly its original form. Gloriously irregular in silhouette, the Gothic forms are embellished by curved and carved bargeboards, diamond panes, and rich moldings. The interior as well is profusely decorated. A central hot-air heating system, employing sheetmetal-lined ducts embedded in the concrete walls, is hidden behind the ornate wall surfaces, another example of Tomkins' astute planning.

Constitution Island

East bank of the Hudson, opposite
West Point. Boat transportation
provided from West Point South
Dock or Garrison Marina
*OPEN: Tues. and Wed. afternoon,
June–Sept. Reservations re-
quired from Constitution Island
Association, Box 41, West
Point, N.Y. 10966, or by phone
PHONE: (914) 446–8676
Mon.–Fri., 10–11:30 a.m.

The history of Constitution Island is linked to that of West Point. In 1778–82 that link was literal, as a great iron chain—500 yards long with links weighing 300 pounds—was stretched across the Hudson at this point to prevent the British from dividing New England from New York and the other Colonies. No British ship challenged the Great Chain in the five summers it was used, although an earlier chain had been breached.

In 1836, Henry Warner, whose brother Thomas was chaplain and a professor at the Military Academy, purchased the island. He added a wing to the small cottage then standing, called it Wood Crag, and moved in with his sister and two daughters, Susan and Anna.

The Warner sisters lived on Constitution Island for most of their lives, conducting Bible classes and befriending homesick young cadets. Miss Anna wrote books on gardening and children's stories. Miss Susan's first novel, *Wide, Wide World*, was second in sales only to *Uncle Tom's Cabin*.

Constitution Island was presented to the U.S. Government by Anna Warner and her friend Mrs. Russell Sage. It became part of the USMA Reservation in 1908. Both sisters were given military funerals and were buried in West Point Cemetery. The site is maintained by the Constitution Island Association.

West Point
(United States
Military Academy)

Rte. 9W, near village of Highland Falls
OPEN: Daily. Visitor's Information
Center open April 15–Nov. 15;
West Point Museum open daily,
10:30 a.m.–4:15 p.m., except
Christmas and New Year's Day
PHONE: (914) 938–3507

229

In 1842 a foreign visitor wrote of West Point: "In this beautiful place, the fairest among the fair and lovely Highlands of the North River, shut in by deep green heights and ruined forts, and looking down upon the distant town of Newburgh . . . hemmed in besides, all around with memories of Washington, and events of the revolutionary war, is the Military School of America." The visitor was Charles Dickens, and though he was perhaps more eloquent than most, his response to the grandeur of West Point is not uncommon.

The splendid location and the unmistakable power of tradition are awesome. West Point was one of four fortifications in the Hudson Highlands in the Revolutionary War, and it was authorized as the site of a military academy in 1802. Since then it has undergone successive stages of growth. The present predominating Gothic style was established about 1900.

The reorganization of the Academy involved reconstruction of not only the main buildings but also the roads, power, light and sewage systems, and service installations into one integrated plan. The win-

ners of a public competition to undertake this enormous job was the firm of Cram, Goodhue & Ferguson of Boston. The choice was a surprise, for although the firm was well known, it had never attempted a project of this scope. The architects, however, proposed to "preserve the natural features which give to West Point an extreme distinction of landscape, and make the architectural style harmonize with the majority of the existing buildings."

The Gothic plan provided two main axes—a north–south route along Thayer Rd. and an east–west one along Jefferson Rd.—to facilitate the visits of thousands of tourists as well as to provide a convenient plan for the Academy's program.

Construction continued from 1903 to 1914. The Administration Building (Thayer Rd.), completed in 1904, was mainly Cram's work. A 160-foot tower keep on the southeast corner dominates the solid masonry structure with its battlements and buttresses. Its somber gray granite is trimmed with limestone. Gothic ornamentation is seen in the ribbed vaulting of the ceilings, the traceried windows, and the shields located in the inner courts and outer walls.

The chapel towers loftily above the rest of the Academy and is perhaps its most imposing structure. Completed in 1910, it is reached by several flights of stone steps. Bertram Goodhue designed this tall gray granite structure, which has pointed-arch

Cullum Hall, West Point

construction and a high buttressed tower. Throughout he added symbolic details uniting themes of conquest and religion.

Thayer Hall (originally called Riding Hall) rises from the Hudson's edge and is also built of rugged granite. The building's original use is suggested in the Gothic equestrian grotesques over the main entrance.

Several buildings from earlier periods also remain. The Superintendent's Quarters (Jefferson Rd.) were built in 1820, and next to them stand the Commandant's Quarters, built the next year.

The first chapel, built in 1836 in the Greek Revival style, has survived several moves. It now stands in the cemetery and is used for funerals. Its use of locally quarried stone set a precedent for construction.

Two imaginative Gothic Revival cottages are located near the Superintendent's Quarters, one used as a residence and the other currently empty.

Cullum Hall (Cullum Rd.), a hipped-roof, neo-Classic building built by McKim, Mead & White in 1896, is two stories high and adorned with Ionic columns. Stanford White, who designed this building, developed a great affection for West Point and also designed Battle Monument on Trophy Point.

Storm King Art Center

Old Pleasant Hill Rd., off Orrs Mills Rd., between Rtes. 32 and 94, Mountainville
OPEN: Tues.–Sun., 2–5:30 p.m.,
April–Nov.
PHONE: (914) 534–3115

More than sixty sculptures, large and small, are artfully placed about the spa-cious hills and meadows of this outdoor museum. Among the most outstanding works are thirteen pieces by David Smith. A Tudor Revival mansion, the former country home of Vernon Hatch, serves as a gallery for changing exhibitions of paintings and other art works.

Sands–Ring Homestead (Academy Ave. and Main St , Cornwall). This eighteenth-century clapboard farmhouse, used as a general store and for Friends' meetings during the Revolutionary War, has been restored and is open by appointment. Phone: (914) 534–8422. The Friends Meeting House, built in 1790, with a wide front porch and a separate door leading upstairs, is nearby (Rte. 307).

New Windsor Cantonment

Temple Hill Rd., between Rtes. 207 and 32; south of New York State Thruway, Exit 17, Vails Gate
*OPEN: Wed.–Sun., 10:30 a.m.–5 p.m., May–Oct.
PHONE: (914) 561–1765

While Gen. George Washington was headquartered nearby in Newburgh in 1782—the final year of the war—his army of 6,000 to 8,000 men was camped at New Windsor. In the Temple, or Publick Building, Washington put down a conspiracy among his officers, establishing the principle of the supremacy of the civilian over the military. Here he also awarded the first military recognition for the courageous acts of enlisted men, the "Purple Heart."

The Old Officer's Hut, built in 1782, is the only structure built by the Continental

Army known to have survived. The Masonic Museum presents materials on freemasonry in the eighteenth century, and special events include craft demonstrations and military musters. Administered by the New York State Division for Historic Preservation.

Knox Headquarters

Junction of Forge Hill Rd. and Rte. 94, Vails Gate
OPEN: Tues.–Sat., 9 a.m.–4:30 p.m.;
     Sun., 1–5 p.m.
PHONE: (914) 561–5498

John Ellison's house—solid, comfortable, with two-foot-thick fieldstone walls—was a desirable quarters for Washington's officers. Gen. Henry Knox occupied it on four occasions, from 1779 to 1782, and so it has been known as Knox Headquarters, but other Continental Army officers also stayed here. The Ellisons ran a gristmill nearby and supplied wheat and large amounts of wood to the Continental troops.

The house was built in 1754; the one-story clapboard wing was added at a later date. The long sloping back roof limited the upstairs space, but the downstairs has a gracious wide hall, high-ceilinged rooms, and tall 12-over-12 pane windows. Administered by the New York State Division for Historic Preservation.

Edmonston House (Rte. 94, Vails Gate). Not far from Knox Headquarters is the stone Edmonston House, where Maj. Gen. Arthur St. Clair spent the final winter of the war. All the leading officers were nearby—Washington in Newburgh, Gates

in the Ellison House, Knox at West Point, and Von Steuben across the river at Fishkill.

The earliest section of the house was built about 1755. The house is now being restored by the National Temple Hill Association. Open on Sun. afternoon, in July and August.

Washington's Headquarters and Museum (Hasbrouck House)

Liberty and Washington sts., Newburgh
OPEN: Wed.–Sat., 9 a.m.–5 p.m.;
     Sun., 1–5 p.m.
PHONE: (914) 562–1195

From January 17 to March 27, 1782, twenty-one carpenters and a director worked feverishly at Jonathan Hasbrouck's fieldstone house in Newburgh, "erecting buildings and fitting [it] up . . . for recreation of his Excellency the Commander in Chief, Repairing a Store for a Magazine and fitting a Room for Taylors to make Soldiers Clothing." Despite all their efforts, the house was too small for the many visitors, and Gen. Washington described his quarters as "confined." Nevertheless, he stayed here until August 1783, through the long last winter of the war. Martha Washington spent much time here too, acting as hostess to the many officers quartered in the area. Mrs. Hasbrouck, then a widow, had moved out, claiming, according to a friend's recollection, that "General Washington and her could not both live in the House."

Here Washington wrote the "Crown" letter in which he rejected an officer's

Hasbrouck House in 1875

proposal that would have made the new nation a monarchy. Here too he composed his reply to the anonymous "Newburgh" letters circulating among the officers at the New Windsor Cantonment. And here as well he wrote to the state governors setting out the framework for what was to become the federal form of government.

The Hasbrouck House had by 1770 reached its present size. The original one-room house built in 1724 had been enlarged in 1750–53 when the Hasbroucks bought it, and a further addition was made in 1770. The additions made the roof line unusually long and sloping. Datestones are visible over the east and west doorways.

In 1850 New York State took over Washington's Headquarters from the Hasbrouck family, the first historic preservation effort by any state or federal agency. A museum was erected on the grounds in 1910. Maintained by the New York State Division for Historic Preservation.

Crawford House

189 Montgomery St., Newburgh
OPEN: Tues.–Thurs., 2–4 p.m.
PHONE: (914) 561–2585

In 1838 James Buckingham, a British journalist and member of Parliament, traveled up the Hudson and wrote enthusiastically of Newburgh: "The buildings have all that newness and freshness of appearance which is so characteristic of American settlements; and being built chiefly of wood (though there are many

233

Hodges Funeral Home

fine stone houses in Newburgh) . . . they seem as if they were hardly a month old."

One of the "mass of well-built houses, symmetrically arranged, and sloping down the steep bank of the Hudson on the west" (the present historic district north of Broadway in the Montgomery–Grand–Liberty sts. area), was the Crawford House. David Crawford, a prosperous steamboat owner who had served as a naval officer in the War of 1812, signed a glebe lease for "Life, 900 years" on a lot on Montgomery St. in 1830; here he built a dramatic mansion, a fine example of the Greek Revival style, worthy of his standing in Newburgh's mercantile community. The attic story projects over the portico, supported by four 40-foot Ionic columns. The intricately carved door is especially handsome. Now

the headquarters of the Historical Society of Newburgh Bay and the Highlands.

In 1849 Frederika Bremer, the Swedish novelist, was the guest of the Andrew Jackson Downings in their Newburgh home and attended the wedding of Anna Crawford, David Crawford's only surviving child. The wedding was held at 9 a.m. because the newlyweds "were to commence their journey through life immediately after the marriage ceremony, sailing for Niagara and must therefore hasten away to the steam-boat." Bremer found the marriage ceremony "characteristic of that haste and precipitation for which I have heard Americans reproached."

Hodges Funeral Home (196 Montgomery St., across from Crawford House, Newburgh). In 1850, in *The Architecture of Country Houses*, Andrew Jackson

Downing wrote of his native Newburgh: "It is in such picturesque scenery as this . . . that the high tower, the steep roof, and the boldly varied outline, seem wholly in keeping with the landscape." Downing established a studio here and brought Calvert Vaux, a young British architect, to work with him. After Downing's accidental death in 1852, Vaux continued to work in the Hudson River valley and designed several homes in the Newburgh area.

This house, described in Vaux's *Villas and Cottages* (1857) as "A Picturesque Symmetrical House," is now a funeral parlor. Like many other buildings converted to this use, it is well preserved. Vaux designed it, he said, "cunningly," to "maximize the height of the street elevation, with steeply pitched roof and gables." In the rear, where the ground slopes away, a flat roof deck minimizes the height.

"Quality Row," Newburgh (112–120 First St., at Liberty St.). The five two-story wooden rowhouses, designed in 1836 by local architect Thornton M. Niven, were built on land owned by Rev. John Brown, pastor of St. George's Episcopal Church. Brown's own house was No. 114. The simple masses of the Greek Revival dwellings are relieved by carved columns and rich geometric detailing.

Brown and his neighbors planted shade trees along the sidewalks. By 1866 the trees were well developed, but the new city government decided that they were in the way and cut them down. Those who failed to share Dr. Brown's outrage at the removal of the trees derisively called the street "Quality Row."

Newburgh City Library (Grand St., south of Second St.). Sophisticated urban structures line many of Newburgh's streets. The expressive Victorian styling of the library, built in 1876, includes a full range of decorative motifs which add richness to the imposing brick building. An elaborate cornice is surmounted by carved finials. The portico too is heavily carved. The schoolhouse across the street is an earlier and slightly simpler version of mid-Victorian public architecture.

Newburgh City Club (120 Grand St.). Calvert Vaux described Grand St., the location for his design of this "suburban house with a curved roof," as "the handsomest throughfare that passes through the town. . . . The often-recurring glimpses of the Hudson, with its gleaming and ever-shifting freight of sails that one catches at intervals framed in the foliage of the trees

Newburgh City Library

on the side streets give it a charming pictorial quality that is rarely obtainable.''

Courthouse Square, Newburgh (Grand St. and First and Second sts.). The Orange County Courthouse, designed in Greek Revival style by Thornton M. Niven in 1841, took its place in an already well-developed section of a prosperous river village. St. George's Episcopal Church, a rectangular stone structure, was built in 1819 and its steeple added in 1834. The First Associate Reformed Church, a small wooden structure, was built in 1799 and altered in 1821. A new congregation formed in 1835 constructed an imposing new building, the Dutch Reformed Church (Grand and Third sts). The young A. J. Davis, then practicing in the Greek Revival mode, modeled this Church on the design for the Eglise du Saint Esprit in New York City, which he and Ithiel Town had built four years earlier. Four tall Ionic columns carry a deep entablature and a gabled pediment across the façade of the building.

Twentieth-century Newburgh, no longer the trading center of the mid-1800's or the manufacturing and rail center of the late 1800's, has lost much of the "commanding air and pleasing aspect" that enchanted Buckingham on his travels in 1838.

Coming too late to save many of the smaller elements which were the warp and woof of central Newburgh, current redevelopment at least promises to respect the essential character of Courthouse Sq. The courthouse itself will be restored and expanded, and the Dutch Reformed Church will be renovated for use as a municipal center. Adjacent to it, a four-story glass-and-masonry library and administrative facility is being built on terraces sloping down the hillside toward the Hudson River. Hugh Stubbins & Associates of Cambridge and the local firm of Flemming & Silverman are the architects.

A visit to Newburgh inspires respect for the past, concern for the present, and cautious hope for the future.

Architecture Field Guide
and Illustrated Glossary

1. Colonial Georgian 1680–1820
FORM: High-style examples are formal and symmetrical (1A). Vernacular types are blunt and robust, low to the ground, and often built in several stages, with rear or side sheds or wings. Window openings often small and irregularly spaced. These types survived for more than a generation past the Colonial period (1B).
MATERIALS: Shingle, clapboard, local fieldstone.
DETAILS: High-style examples have quoins, modillions, and other popular English motifs (1A). Vernacular examples have few embellishments (1B).

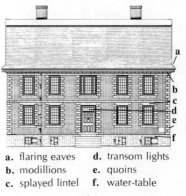

a. flaring eaves	d. transom lights
b. modillions	e. quoins
c. splayed lintel	f. water-table

1A

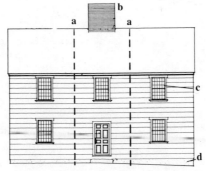

1B
   a. three-bay elevation
   b. central chimney
   c. 12-over-12 paned windows
   d. low stone foundation

237

2. Federal (early Classic Revival) 1780–1820

FORM: Simple, contained forms. Smooth surfaces. Regular placement of windows. Chimneys symmetrically placed at sides of buildings.

DETAILS: High-style examples have refined ornaments—ovals, carved urns and festoons, leaded fanlight over doors.

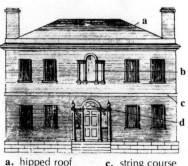

a. hipped roof   **c.** string course
b. Palladian window **d.** leaded fanlight

2A

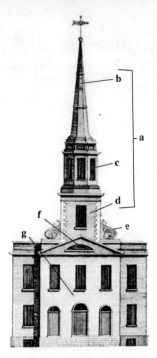

2B **a.** steeple
     b. spire
     c. belfry
     d. tower
     e. scroll pediment
     f. fanlight
     g. projecting pavilion

3. Greek Revival 1830–50

FORM: Emphasis on bold cubic volumes; horizontal quality.

MATERIALS: Matchboarding and cut stone.

DETAILS: Geometric detailing. Contrast of ornamented and smooth surfaces. Window openings are ample; 6-over-6 panes common. Doors have side lights. Columns, entablatures, pediments, and other Classical details.

238

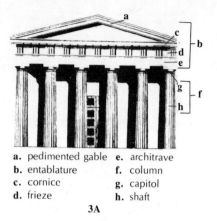

a. pedimented gable   e. architrave
b. entablature   f. column
c. cornice   g. capitol
d. frieze   h. shaft

3A

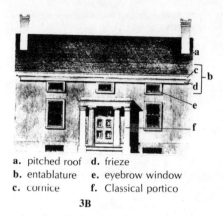

a. pitched roof   d. frieze
b. entablature   e. eyebrow window
c. cornice   f. Classical portico

3B

4A
a. spire
b. finial
c. gable
d. louvered belfrey
e. pointed-arch window openings
f. hood molding
g. board and batten
h. canopy

4. Picturesque Revival (early Victorian) 1840–60

FORM: Irregular massing. Wings and bays break away from square plan. Vertical and thrusting forms. Relatively small in scale. Architecture conceived as part of landscape. Architectural styles "borrowed" for picturesque effect—Swiss cottage, Tuscan villa, especially Gothic cottage and church.

MATERIALS: Vertical board-and-batten siding; local cut stone.

DETAILS: Round and pointed arches, steeply pitched roofs, towers.

4B

5. Italianate and French Second Empire (mid-Victorian) 1850–80

FORM: Heavy and complex masses. Architectural elements (columns, round arches, brackets, mansard roof) "borrowed" for formal effect on both vernacular (5A, 5B) and high-style (5C) examples. Windows often paired and symmetrically placed. Doors have double leaves.

MATERIALS: Dark-hued cut stone, or wood in imitation of stone.

DETAILS: Curved wooden moldings often applied to surfaces; decorative ironwork.

5A **a.** iron finial
      b. arched gable
      c. shaped lintels
      d. incised ornament

5B **a.** flat eaves
      b. paired brackets
      c. applied molding

5C **a.** mansard roof
      b. pedimented dormers
      c. flaring eaves
      d. brackets
      e. cast-iron portico
      f. projecting bay

6. Stick-style Picturesque (mid-Victorian) 1870–90

FORM: Complex massing—cross gables, bays, chimneys, and exposed framing create an irregular and lively silhouette.

MATERIALS: Wood shingles and boards, masonry, stucco, and slate often combined for surface richness.

DETAILS: Wooden members are "stick"-like. Stone is often incised or carved and used for variety and color contrast (Venetian Gothic).

7. Shingle-style Romanesque (late Victorian) 1875–90

FORM: Heavy masses. Intersecting volumes act against voids. Window openings grouped in bands. Later versions add variety of "early American" decorative motifs, more rigid composition (7B).

MATERIALS: Shingles wrap around surfaces with skinlike quality, often in combination with rough-hewn stone.

DETAILS: Low, round-arched doors and window openings (inspired by H. H. Richardson).

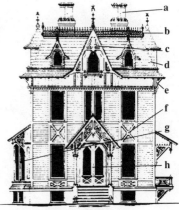

7A
a. gambrel roof
b. scalloped shingles
c. cross gable
d. overhanging gable
e. Richardsonian arch
f. rough-hewn masonry
g. small panes ("Queen Anne")

6 a. grouped chimneys
b. iron cresting
c. scroll-decorated bargeboards
d. mansard roof
e. bracket
f. exposed diagonal bracing
g. projecting bay
h. portico

a. eyebrow dormer   c. turret
b. carved festoons   d. shaped posts

7B

241

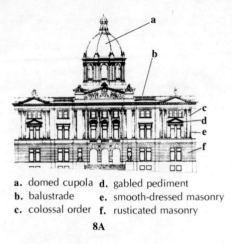

a. domed cupola   **d.** gabled pediment
b. balustrade   **e.** smooth-dressed masonry
c. colossal order   **f.** rusticated masonry

8A

8. Period Revivals (late Victorian and Victorian Revival) 1880–1930

FORM: Reproduction of variety of historical styles, especially Tudor, Renaissance, Baroque, Georgian. Public architecture is grand in scale, with formal, Classical details (8A). Domestic architecture mixes historical details with modern plan (8B and 8C).

8B

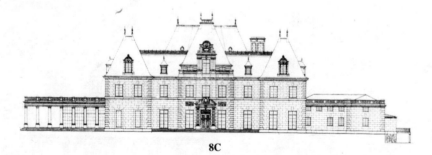

8C

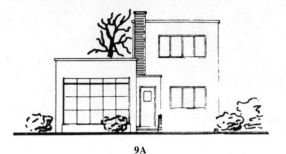

9A

9. Modern 1900–1950

FORM: Emphasizes geometrical volumes. Smooth surfaces. Highly organized composition (International style) (9A).

MATERIALS: Concrete, glass, steel, stucco.

DETAILS: Chunky, angular, modernistic detailing (Art Deco and Art Moderne) (9B). A second trend favors craftsmanlike quality and rustic effects. Structural expressiveness, close integration with landscape. Often associated with Frank Lloyd Wright (9C).

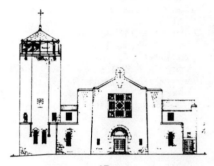

9B

9C

243

Index

Acorn Hall, 186
Aldrich Museum of Contemporary Art,
  61–62
Allaire, N.J., 147–48
Allen Homestead, 143
Alpine, N.J., 222
Amityville, N.Y., 125
Architects Collaborative, The, 51, 89, 98
Armonk, N.Y., 47
Asbury Park, N.J., 146

Babylon, N.Y., 126–27
Bainbridge House, 156
Banksville, N.Y., 47
Barnum, P. T., Museum, 93–94
Basking Ridge, N.J., 189
Bates–Scofield Homestead, 85
Bay Head, N.J., 148
Bay Shore, N.Y., 127
Bayard Cutting Arboretum, 128–29
Beacon, N.Y., 31–33
Bedford Village, N.Y., 51–52
Belcher–Ogden Mansion, 137
Bergenfield, N.J., 208
Bernardsville, N.J., 188–89
Blauvelt, Jacob, Homestead, 227
Bloomfield, N.J., 193
Boonton, N.J., 200
Boscobel, 29–30
Boxwood Hall, 137–38
Branch, The, N.Y., 114–15
Brentwood, N.Y., 128
Brett, Madam, Homestead, 32
Bridgeport, Conn., 93–94
Bronxville, N.Y., 38–39
Buccleuch Mansion, 165
Bush Homestead, 78
Bush–Holley House, 81–82

Caldwell, N.J., 195
Caldwell Parsonage, 180
Cannonball House, 181
Caramoor, 54
Carrère & Hastings, 144, 197
Cartoon Art, Museum of, 81
Centennial Cottage, 147
Centerport, N.Y., 113
Central Valley, N.Y., 218
Chappaqua, N.Y., 48–50
Chatham, N.J., 182
Chester, N J., 198
"Church of the Presidents," 144–45
Civil War Armory and Drill Hall, 206–7
Cleveland, Grover, Birthplace, 195
Clinton, N.J., 179–80
Clinton's Headquarters, 149
Cobb House, 150
Cold Spring, N.Y., 30–31
Cold Spring Harbor, N.Y., 108
Conklin, David, Farmhouse, 111
Constitution Island, N.Y., 229
Cornwall, N.Y., 231
Cos Cob, Conn., 81–82
Cram, Goodhue & Ferguson, 50, 158,
  230
Cranbury, N.J., 152
Crane, Israel, House, 194
Cranford, N.J., 174–75
Crawford House, 233–34
Cresskill, N.J., 222
Croton Falls, N.Y., 58
Croton-on-Hudson, N.Y., 26–27

Darien, Conn., 85–86
Davis, A. J., 8, 16, 74, 76, 169, 191–92,
  236
Deal, N.J., 145
Delano & Aldrich, 40, 105, 153

Deserted Village of Allaire, 147–48
De Wint House, 223–24
Dey Mansion, 199–200
Dobbs Ferry, N.Y., 8–10
Doric House, 162–63
Drake House, 177
Dumont, N.J., 208–9

Early Trades and Crafts, Museum of, 182
East Meadow, N.Y., 124
East Willison, N.Y., 100–101
Eastchester, N.Y., 37
Eastview, N.Y., 21–22
Eaton's Neck, N.Y., 113–14
Edison, Thomas A., Laboratory, 192–93
Edwards Homestead, 130
Elberon, N.J., 144–45
Elephant Hotel, 56–57
Elizabeth, N.J., 136–38
Englewood, N.J., 207
Englewood Cliffs, N.J., 221
Englishtown, N.J., 150

Fairfield, Conn., 91–92
Falaise, 99–100
Fire Island, N.Y., 127–28
Fleming Castle, 163
Flemington, N.J., 162–63
Force House, 193
Fort Lee, N.J., 206
Foundry School Museum, 30–31
Freehold, N.J., 148–50
Freeport, N.Y., 121
Frelinghuysen House, 178–79

Garden City, N.Y., 121–23
Garnerville, N.Y., 228
Garrison, N.Y., 28–30
Geddes, Brecher, Qualls & Cunningham,
  159–60
Germonds, N.Y., 227
Gilbert, Cass, 62, 171, 172, 206
Gillette & Walker, 44, 75, 106
Glen Cove, N.Y., 103–4
Glenmont, 192–93
Goodhue, Bertram, 10, 50, 185, 230–31
Goshen, N.Y., 219–21
Great Neck, N.Y., 98
Great River, N.Y., 128–29
Greenburgh, N.Y., 43–44
Greenfield Hill, Conn., 92–93
Greenvale, N.Y., 104
Greenwich, Conn., 79–81

Gregory Museum, 105
Groveville, N.Y., 33
Guest House, 165

Hackensack, N.J., 207–8
Hackettstown, N.J., 201–2
Hall of Fame of the Trotter, 219–20
Hammond House, 21–22
Hammond Museum and Oriental Stroll
  Garden, 60
Hanford–Silliman House, 65–66
Harrison & Abramovitz, 84
Hartsdale, N.Y., 43
Hasbrouck House, 232–33
Hastings-on-Hudson, N.Y., 7–8
Haverstraw, N.Y., 227
Head of the Harbor, N.Y., 115
Heckscher Museum, 110
Hempstead, N.Y., 121
Heritage Museum, 64
Hewlett, N.Y., 120
Hicksville, N.Y., 105
Highlands, N.J., 140–41
Hightstown, N.J., 151
Hoboken, N.J., 168–70
Hohokus, N.J., 212–13
Holmdel, N.J., 142–43
Holmes–Hendrickson House, 142–43
Hope, N.J., 202–3
Hopewell, N.J., 161–62
Hoyt–Barnum House, 83–84
Hudson River Museum, 6–7
Hunt, Richard Morris, 31–32, 33, 128,
  130, 134
Hunterdon Art Center, 179
Huntington, N.Y., 110–12

Irvington, N.Y., 10–14
Islip, N.Y., 128

Jay, John, Homestead, 53
Jersey City, N.J., 134–46
Johnson, Philip, 66, 68, 78
Judson, Capt. David, House, 95

Kahn, Louis, 49–50, 151
Katonah, N.Y., 53–55
Kearney Cottage, 139
Keeler Tavern, 62
Kings Park, N.Y., 114
Kingsland Manor, 196
Kingston, N.J., 160
Knox Headquarters, 232

Lakewood, N.J., 148
Lamb & Rich, 101, 107
Lambert Castle, 199
Lambert House, 64
Larchmont, N.Y., 74
Latrobe, Benjamin, 157
Lauder Museum, 125
Lawrence, N.Y., 119–20
Lawrenceville, N.J., 152–53
Leonia, N.J., 206–7
Lienau, Detlef, 87, 135, 164–65
Lindenhurst, N.Y., 126
Little Red Schoolhouse, 65
Livingston, N.J., 193
Lloyd Harbor, N.Y., 108–9
Lloyd Neck, N.Y., 109–10
Lockwood–Mathews Mansion, 87–88
Long Beach, N.Y., 120
Long Branch, N.J., 143–44
Lyndhurst, 16–17

Macculloch Hall, 185
McComb, John, Jr., 113–14, 159, 164
McKim, Mead & White, 23, 101, 102,
   157, 170, 180–81, 184, 185, 191, 231
Madison, N.J., 182–84
Mahwah, N.J., 214
Mamaroneck, N.Y., 74–75
Manhasset, N.Y., 98–99
Marlpit Hall, 141–42
Matawan, N.J., 139–40
Mather, John R., House, 118
Melville, N.Y., 112–13
Mendham, N.J., 189
Merchants' and Drovers' Tavern, 138
Middletown, N.J., 141–42
Mies van der Rohe, Ludwig, 173
Mill Hill Historical Site, 88–89
Millburn, N.J., 180
Miller, Elijah, House, 46–47
Miller–Cory House, 175
Millstone, N.J., 163
Mineola, N.Y., 123
Monmouth Beach, N.J., 143
Monmouth County Historical
   Association, 149
Monroe, N.Y., 218–19
Montclair, N.J., 193–95
Montvale, N.J., 213
Montville, N.J., 200–201
Moore, Charles, 111–12
Morley, Christopher, Knothole, 100
Morris Museum of Arts and Sciences, 185
Morristown, N.J., 184–88

Morristown National Historic Park,
   186–87
Morven, 154
Mountainville, N.Y., 231
Mount Kisco, N.Y., 50–51
Mount Vernon, N.Y., 36, 71–72
Museum Village of Smith's Clove, 218

Nassau County Historical Museum, 124
Newark, N.J., 170–74
New Brunswick, N.J., 164–65
Newburgh, N.Y., 232–36
New Canaan, Conn., 65–66
New City, N.Y., 227
New Jersey Historical Society, 174
New Providence, N.J., 181–82
New Rochelle, N.Y., 37–38, 73–74
New Windsor Cantonment, 231–32
Niven, Thornton M., 220, 235, 236
Noroton, Conn., 86–87
North Greenwich, Conn., 47
North Salem, N.Y. 58–60
North Tarrytown, N.Y., 20–21, 22
Northport, N.Y., 113
Norwalk, Conn., 87–89
Notman, John, 157, 158
Nutley, N.J., 195–96
Nyack, N.Y., 225–27

Oakdale, N.Y., 129–30
Ocean Grove, N.J., 146–47
Oceanside, N.Y., 120
Ogden, David, House, 92
Old Bethpage Village, 125–26
Old Dutch Parsonage, 177–78
Old Greenwich, Conn., 83
Old Marble School, 37
Old Red Mill, 179
Old Stone House, 213–14
Old Tappan, N.J., 222
Old Village Hall Museum, 126
Old Westbury, N.Y., 104–5
Old Westbury Gardens, 105
Olmsted, Frederick Law, 102, 129, 153
Oranges, The, N.J., 190–93
Ossining, N.Y., 24–26
Oyster Bay, N.Y., 106–8

Paine, Thomas, Cottage, 37–38
Paramus, N.J., 210–11
Park Ridge, N.J., 213
Paterson, N.J., 197–99
Peabody & Stearns, 153
Peach Lake, N.Y., 61

Peekskill, N.Y., 27–28
Pelham Manor, N.Y., 73
Perth Amboy, N.J., 139
Philipsburg Manor, 19–21
Philipse Manor Hall, 3, 26
Piermont, N.Y., 224–25
Plainfield, N.J., 176–77
Planting Fields Arboretum, 106
Pleasantville, N.Y., 48, 50
Pluckemin, N.J., 179
Pocantico Hills, N.Y., 22–23
Pope, John Russell, 73, 216
Port Chester, N.Y., 78–79
Port Jefferson, N.Y., 118
Port Monmouth, N.J., 140
Port Washington, N.Y., 99–100
Post, George B., 174, 188
Potter, William Appleton, 157, 159, 217
Pound Ridge, N.Y., 63
Powell–Jarvis House, 110
Princeton, N.J., 153–60
Purchase, N.Y., 67–68
Purdy, Jacob, House, 44–45
Purdy's, N.Y., 58
Putnam Cottage, 81

Queenston, N.J., 160

Radburn, N.J., 211
Rahway, N.J., 138
Railroad Station Museum, 214
Ralston's, John, General Store, 190
Ramsey, N.J., 213–14
Raritan, N.J., 178–79
Raynham Hall, 106–7
Reader's Digest, 50
Ridgefield, Conn., 61–62
Ridgewood, N.J., 211–12
Ringwood Manor, 215–16
River Edge, N.J., 209–10
Rock Hall, 119
Rockingham, 161
Rocky Hill, N.J., 161
Roosevelt, N.J., 150–51
Roslyn, N.Y. 100–103
Rudolph, Paul, 68, 123–24, 220
Rutherford, N.J., 196–97
Rye, N.Y., 75–78

Saarinen, Eero, 55, 142
Saddle River, N.J., 212
Saddle Rock Grist Mill, 98
Sagamore Hill, 107–8
Sagtikos Manor, 127

St. James, N.Y., 115
Salem Center, N.Y., 59
"Salt Box" Historical Society Museum, 181–82
Sayville, N.Y., 130–31
Scarborough, N.Y., 23
Scarsdale, N.Y., 41–42
Schuyler–Hamilton House, 185
Scotch Plains, N.J., 175–76
Sea Bright, N.J., 143
Sea Cliff, N.Y., 103
Setauket, N.Y., 117–18
Sherwood House, 5
Sherwood Mills Smith Partnership, 6, 80, 85
Sherwood–Jayne House, 118
Shoal Harbor Marine Museum, 140
Short Hills, N.J., 180–81
Shrewsbury, N.J., 143
Skidmore, Owings & Merrill, 8, 47, 79, 123, 181
Skylands Manor, 216
Smith, Caleb, House, 115
Smith, Epenetus, Tavern, 114
Smith, Obadiah, House, 114
Smithtown, N.Y., 114–15
Sneden's Landing, N.Y., 224
Somers, N.Y., 56–58
Somerville, N.J., 177–78
South Salem, N.Y., 62
Southport, Conn., 90–91
Sparta, N.Y., 23–24
Speedwell Village, 187–88
Springfield, N.J., 181
Square House, 77–78
Stamford, Conn., 66–67, 83–84
Statue of Liberty, 134
Steadman, Charles, 152, 155, 156
Stein, Clarence, 211
Stony Brook, N.Y., 115–16
Stony Point Battlefield Reservation, 228
Storm King Art Center, 231
Stratford, Conn., 94–95
Suffern, N.Y., 214–15
Summit, N.J., 181
Sunnyside, 13, 14–16
Syosset, N.Y., 105

Tappan, N.Y., 223
Tarrytown, N.Y., 14–20
Teaneck, N.J., 207
Tenafly, N.J., 221–22
Thompson House, 117
Tomkins Cove, N.Y., 228–29

Tuckahoe, N.Y., 41
Tuxedo Park, N.Y., 216–17

Union, N.J, 180
Upjohn, Richard, 29, 73, 115, 138, 141,
 169, 171, 200

Vails Gate, N.Y., 231–32
Valhalla, N.Y., 46–47
Van Cortlandt Manor, 26
Van Cortlandtville, N.Y., 28, 29
Van Riper–Hopper House, 200
Vanderbilt Museum and Planetarium,
 113
Vaux, Calvert, 103, 234, 235
Von Steuben House, 209–10

Wallace House, 178
Wantagh, N.Y., 124
Washington's Headquarters, 44–45,
 46–47, 161, 178, 186–87, 223–24,
 232–33

Waterloo Village, 201
Wayne, N.J., 199–200
Wayside Cottage, 41
West Point, 229–31
Westchester Historical Society, 41
Westfield, N.J., 175
Westport, Conn., 89
Whaling Museum, 108
White, Stanford, 12, 74, 183 (see also
 McKim, Mead & White)
White Plains, N.Y., 44–46
Whitman, Walt, Birthplace, 112
Wildcliff Natural Science Center, 74
Willets House, 99
Wilton, Conn., 63–64
Woodbury, N.Y., 105–6
Wright, Frank Lloyd, 48, 98, 163

Yonkers, N.Y., 3–7
Yorktown, N.Y., 55–56

Sources of Illustrations (figures in italics refer to Glossary illustrations):

American Architect (1928), 76 bottom, 109; (1932), *8B*, *9B*; American Architect and Building News (1880), 128; (1884), 180 bottom; (1887), 184, *7A*; (1897), *8A*. Argosy Gallery, 91 center left. Avery Library, Columbia University, 87, 135 bottom. J. Barber, *Historical Collections of the State of New Jersey* (1844), 193 bottom. J. Barber, *Past and Present of the United States* (1861), 198. Baskin and Burr, *Orange County Atlas* (1875), 233. Asher Benjamin, *The American Builder's Companion* (1806), *2B*. Asher Benjamin, *The Country Builder's Assistant* (1797), *2A*. A. J. Bicknell, *Wood and Brick Buildings* (1875), *6A*. R. Bolton, *A History of the County of Westchester* (1848), 52, 53. Century Magazine (1911), 217 top. W. Comstock, *Modern Architectural Designs* (1890), *7B*. Fox Connor (1889 advertisement), 25 top. A. J. Downing, *Architecture of Country Houses* (1850), *4B*. A. J. Downing, *Theory and Practice of Landscape Gardening* (1841), 15. A. J. Downing and C. Vaux, *Villas and Cottages* (1857), 234, *5C*.

Horace Greeley, *Autobiography of Horace Greeley* (1872), 49 bottom. Historic American Buildings Survey, 16, 21, 32, 49 top, 57 bottom left, 72, 91 top left, 92, 107, 119, 172, 186 bottom, 194 top, 203 bottom, 207, 208 bottom, 212, 227 bottom, *1A*, *1B*. The House Beautiful (1909), *9C*. J. Kelly, *Early Domestic Architecture of Connecticut* (1924) (Courtesy, Yale Library), 95. Minard Lafever, *The Young Builder's General Instructor* (1829), *3A*, *3B*. B. Lossing, *The Pictorial Field-Book of the Revolution* (1850), 161 top, 224. Metropolitan Museum of Art, 9 bottom. The Modern Home (1931), *9A*. Monograph of the Work of McKim, Mead & White (1915), 157 top, 230 bottom, *8C*. New York State Division for Historic Preservation, 3. T. Scharf, *History of Westchester County, New York* (1886), 12 bottom. D. W. Teller, *History of Ridgefield* (1878), 61. R. Upjohn, *Rural Church Architecture* (1876), *4A*.

Some of the photographs of sites in Westchester County, New York, were taken by Carole Rifkind for the Archive of Architecture in Westchester at the Hudson River Museum. Permission to use them here is gratefully acknowledged.